I0824809

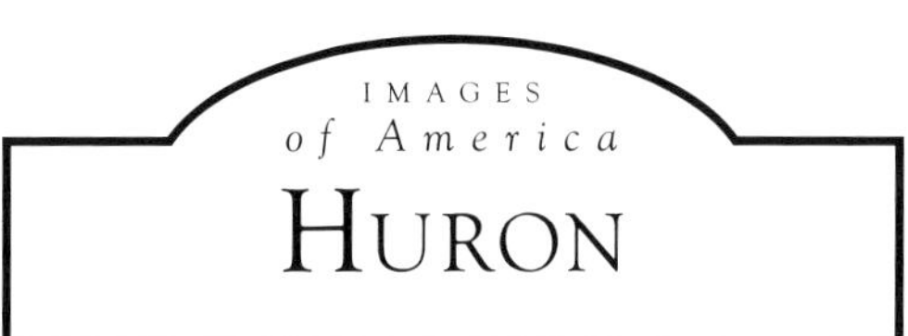
IMAGES
of America
HURON

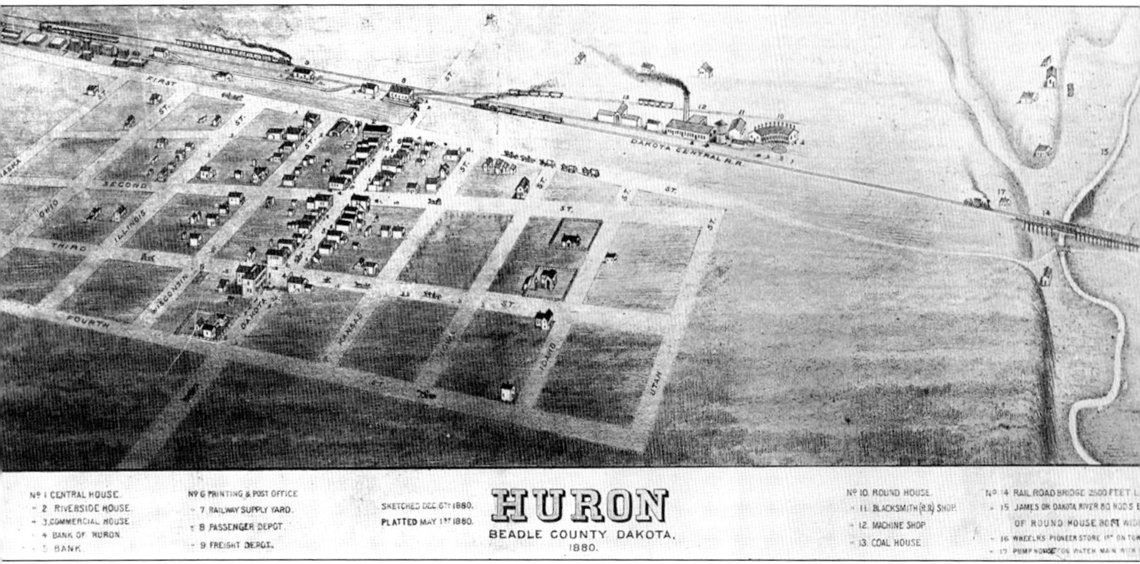

The original townsite was platted on May 1, 1880. The town was 11 blocks from First Street to Third Street and Iowa Avenue Southeast to Ohio Avenue Southwest. Local historians do not know who chose the name "Huron" but believe the townsite was named after the Huron Indians. By 1882, the town had grown to 70 blocks and boasted a population of 1,500. (Courtesy of Huron Public Library.)

On the Cover: Fire Chief William Herman, far right, and two unidentified men pose in the city's fire trucks outside the city hall building constructed in 1921. Located on the corner of Iowa Avenue and Third Street Southeast, the building brought all the city's departments under one roof including the jail and the garage for the fire trucks. (Courtesy of Huron Fire Department.)

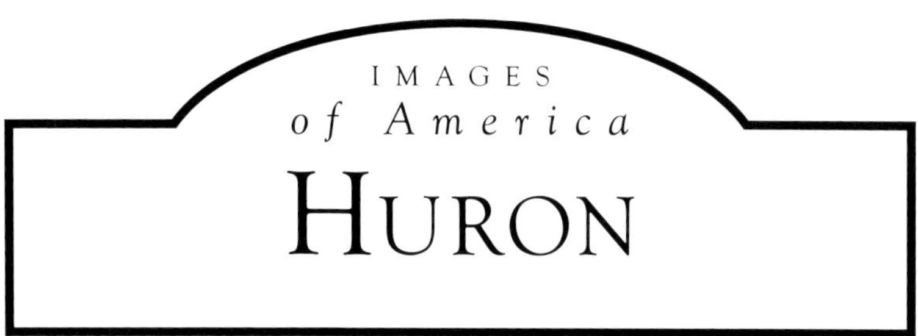

Jennifer Littlefield, Huron Public Library, and
Louise Van Poll, The Dakotaland Museum

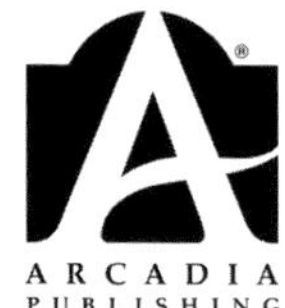

ISBN 9781-4671-6173-2

Published by Arcadia Publishing
Charleston, South Carolina

Printed in the United States of America

Library of Congress Control Number: 2024934667

For all general information, please contact Arcadia Publishing:
Telephone 843-853-2070
Fax 843-853-0044
E-mail sales@arcadiapublishing.com

Visit us on the Internet at www.arcadiapublishing.com

This book is dedicated to the pioneers of Huron, past, present, and future.

Contents

Acknowledgments

We would like to extend heartfelt gratitude to the following individuals and organizations whose invaluable contributions made this project possible:

The Dakotaland Museum Archives research assistant Anna Gednalske, whose meticulous efforts in searching through the Dakotaland Museum photo archive greatly contributed to the richness of this book; the Dakotaland Museum, for generously granting access to its extensive photo archives, and the members of the Dakotaland Museum Inc. Board of Directors for their support and cooperation; the Beadle County Commission, for its support and generous monetary contribution to this project; Angela Bailey, Huron Public Library director, and the esteemed members of the Huron Public Library Board, for their support and facilitation throughout the research process; the Huron City Commission, for its approval and support of this project; the community of Huron, whose participation and generous provision of photographs enriched the content of this project; the Huron Chamber of Commerce, for its efforts in publicizing and promoting this project to the wider community; Marilyn Hoyt, for use of the Huron College Archive photo collection; Craig Pfannkuche, Chicago & Northwestern (C&NW) Historical Society archivist, for reading and providing additional information on the railroad chapter; and the dedicated individuals who served as advanced readers, for offering insightful feedback and constructive criticism. These contributions have not only enhanced the quality of this book but have also made it a more comprehensive and enriching resource for all who read it.

Unless otherwise noted, all images appear courtesy of the Dakotaland Museum.

Introduction

This book aims to capture the history of Huron, a town currently in the process of growth, to prevent its valuable photographic past from fading into obscurity. The task, however, proved challenging, as early original photographs of Huron were hard to come by. Many collections have fallen victim to floods and fires or have been misplaced or discarded by family members who failed to see the significance of holding onto old photographs. Searching for these historical photographs took us into basements and sheds, some infested with mice, some covered with dirt and mold, to uncover remnants of the past that have been hidden away. Today, as we transition into a digital age, the mindset of keeping photographs and information in a digital format means fewer tangible items remain. Preserving historical photographs and documents now becomes even more pressing.

This book is a practical effort to safeguard the visual history of Huron before it is lost forever. It is not just about pictures; it is about recognizing the contributions of those who have come before us and ensuring that their legacy lives on in the town's collective memory. It is important to note that we strived to include as many significant establishments, businesses, organizations, and people as possible. The lack of photographs, the constraints of time, and the physical size of this publication made it necessary to be selective.

The photographs and history assembled here create a compelling narrative of the development of Huron during the first half of the 20th century. The story unfolds throughout eight chapters that delve into various aspects of Huron's history, each providing an exploration of a significant topic. Our goal is to pay tribute to the individuals who shaped Huron's history and inspire others to appreciate, explore, and preserve their history. Join us on this journey to retain the tangible remnants of Huron's past before they vanish completely.

Chapter One, "First of the Pioneers," depicts the construction and story of how the railroad left a permanent mark on the history of Huron. At a time when Huron was but a fragment of the broader Dakota Territory, settlers embarked on a westward migration that would shape the town's destiny.

Chapter Two, "From the Ground Up," describes how early Huron was transformed into a modern community, implementing major infrastructure projects such as water and sewer lines, electric and telephone wires, and paved streets. Despite facing financial challenges during campaigns to become the state capital, Huron continued to grow, providing essential services including public transportation, a secure water source, hospitals, and a federal agency headquarters.

Chapter Three, "Building a Community," outlines the early development of Huron with the construction of downtown businesses linked to the Chicago & Northwestern Railroad. Huron's strategic location as a railroad hub attracted major industries, leading to economic prosperity and substantial retail growth in the first half of the 20th century.

Chapter Four, "Reading, Writing, and 'Rithmetic," illustrates the development of schools in Huron and the importance of education to new settlers. Due to the growing population, the Huron School District was established in 1883 and then the Dakota Educational Society in 1884. Huron soon became known as an educational center in the Dakota Territory.

Chapter Five, "Huron Was a College Town," provides a captivating window into the early student life at Huron College and its profound influence on the town. The college no longer exists, but the photographs and historical information provide a glimpse of the impact the college made on the community. For those who experienced Huron College in its prime, the chapter becomes a nostalgic journey with fond reminiscences.

Chapter Six, "Founded in Faith," describes the religious roots of Huron, presenting a concise history of the town's earliest churches. The enduring influence of religion is evident in the many churches and religious groups present in Huron today.

Chapter Seven, "The Fair City," outlines the evolution of the South Dakota State Fair, which began as a promotional tool for the Dakota Territory in 1885. Over the years, the fairgrounds have expanded to encompass 190 acres, featuring buildings for livestock, displays, trade shows, and events.

Chapter Eight, "Community Involvement," highlights the formation of a variety of civic, fraternal, and community organizations. Organizations ranging from fraternal orders to church groups provided personal connections, business relationships, and community development. These groups engaged in charitable projects, organized events, and provided platforms for shared interests, contributing to a sense of community and mutual support.

The endeavors of the early pioneers were instrumental in the construction of churches, schools, businesses, and homes—a testament to their commitment to building a new life in Huron. The challenges were formidable, especially during harsh winters and unforeseen disasters, yet life persisted and flourished. Through the lens of the photographs collected here, we glimpse the resilience and determination that has characterized Huron throughout its early history. What began as a modest settlement within the Dakota Territory has evolved into a thriving community, and the echoes of those early days still resonate in the fabric of Huron's present. This collection invites you to witness this transformative journey from the struggles and triumphs of the past to the vibrancy of today—a testament to the enduring spirit that defines Huron.

HURON

Where the buffalos roam was a prairie dog home
In 1880 in June.
Where his rails crossed the Jim seemed a good place to him
For the town Marvin Hughitt had soon.

As the rails bridged the stream a dam filled the dream
And a lake of fresh water was saved,
For the homes that were raised as the antelope gaze—
For a city whose streets are all paved.

So this century date we should all celebrate—
I'm thankful to beat it a year.
Let us do our full best with a will and a zest
And fill both with hope and good cheer.
We are proud of our businesses, churches and schools,
As aid from the Father above
The FAIR CITY, THE FRIENDLY CITY,
The beautiful homes that we love.

—George Costain, age 101
Written for Huron's Centennial, May 8, 1980

Costain was an early settler in Huron, arriving in 1900. He was one of the first students of Huron College, co-owner of Costain Brothers Music Store, and one of the founders of the Huron Chamber of Commerce. Costain was a great supporter of Huron, the college, and preserving Huron's history.

One

First of the Pioneers

On June 29, 1880, crowds lined the banks of the James River to watch the first Chicago & Northwestern train cross the river and arrive at the new town of Huron. It was a momentous occasion that brought with it the first wave of settlers to this part of the Dakota Territory.

The location of the town on the west bank of the river was selected by Marvin Hughitt, general manager of the Chicago & Northwestern Railroad. Huron was designated a divisional headquarters for the railroad, which meant more traffic, larger storage facilities, and a larger roundhouse to service locomotives. Huron travelers and businessmen now had access to larger cities such as Chicago and Omaha.

The Great Northern Railroad soon followed. In the late 1880s, the company completed a railway line that provided a north and south route with connections to the Twin Cities and Duluth, Minnesota. The Great Northern Railroad built a small roundhouse and depot at Fifth Street and Nevada Avenue Southwest.

Being a railroad hub for two major railroads accelerated the growth of Huron. Settlers and homesteaders came to acquire their piece of the Midwest. Business owners received train carloads of supplies to sell to the new settlers. During the summer, trains brought visitors to the South Dakota State Fair, and throughout the winter, they brought much-needed food and supplies. The depot was a gathering place where the community welcomed home members of the armed forces and listened to campaign speeches by dignitaries such as Pres. William McKinley and Pres. William Howard Taft.

The railroad enterprise and the services it provided were central to the growth and development of Huron for more than 80 years. The number of trains decreased in the 1950s with the accessibility of alternative modes of transportation. Today, the Rapid City, Pierre & Eastern Railroad continues to use the railroad facilities and services locomotives in the same roundhouse that was built 140 years ago.

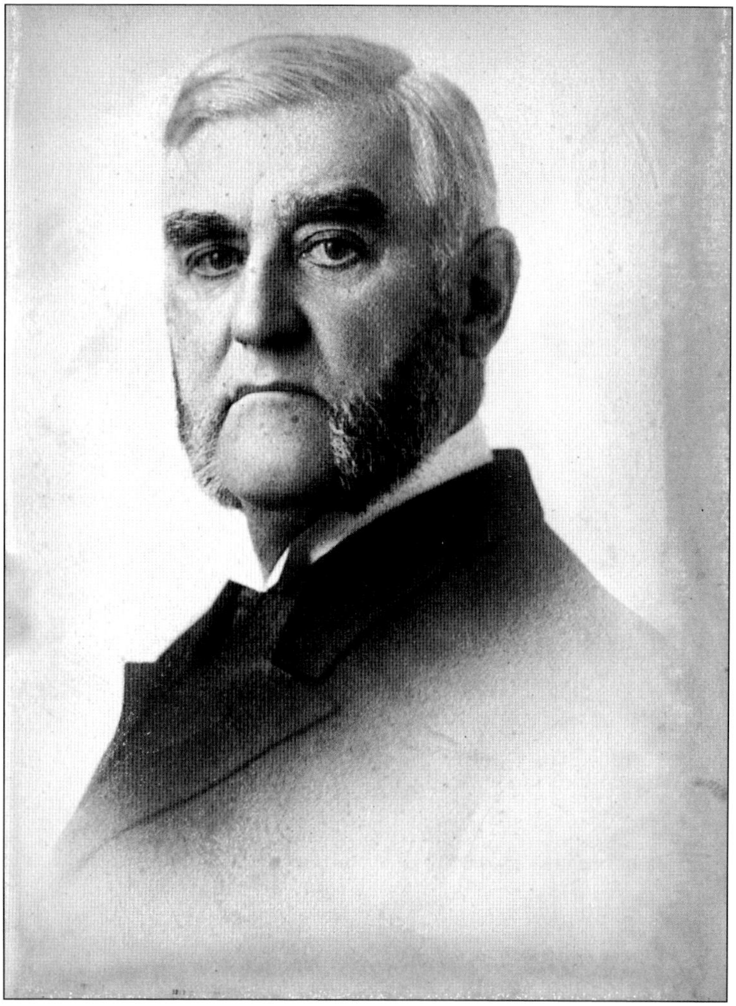

Marvin Hughitt, general manager of the Chicago & Northwestern Railroad, looked across to the west bank of the James River and determined that spot would be the location of the company's new division headquarters. In August 1879, the townsite location was finalized and given the name Huron. (Courtesy of Library of Congress, LC-B2-121-14 [P&P].)

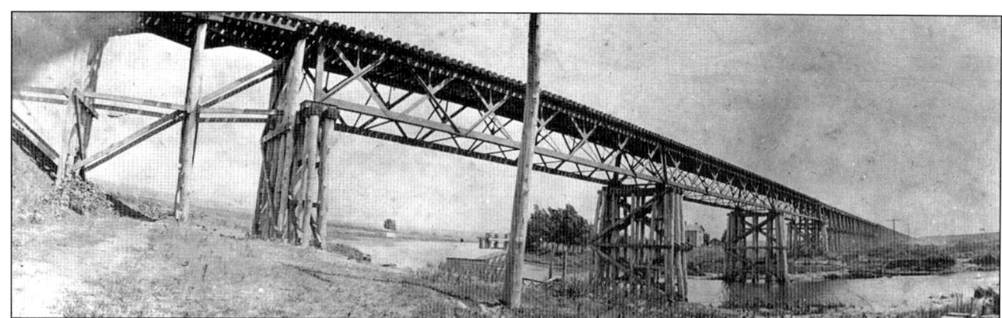

The first railroad bridge to span the James River was completed in 1880. It was a trestle bridge built of large timber posts with a wood bridge deck supported by many timber pilings sunk into the stream bed. Wooden trestles were cheaper and easier to build but cost more to maintain than structures made from more durable materials like concrete or steel. (Courtesy of Huron Public Library.)

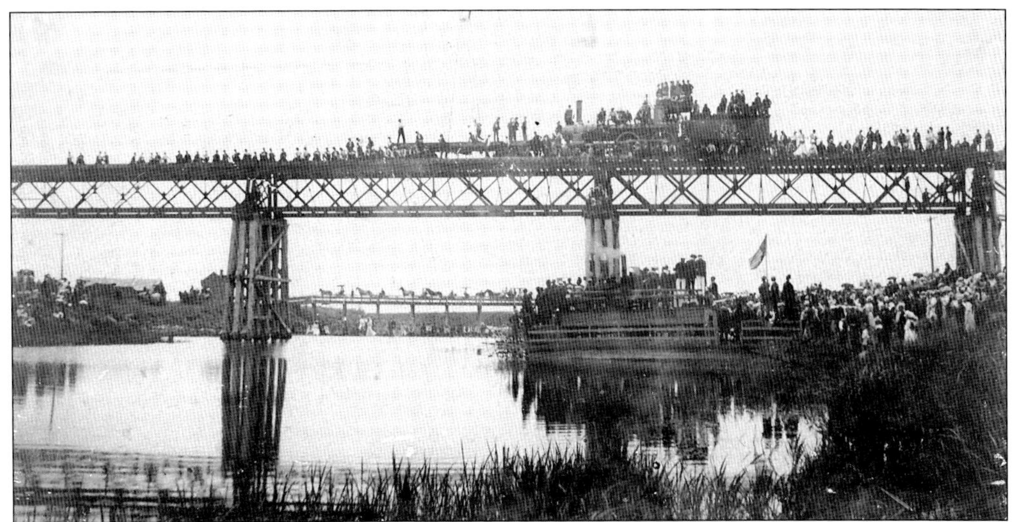

The first Chicago & Northwestern locomotive crossed the James River on June 29, 1880. Onlookers crowded the river bank to celebrate the arrival of the *Pioneer* and the future it promised of a growing, vibrant city. Settlers soon flocked to Huron in hopes of finding land, new opportunities, and a chance for a better life.

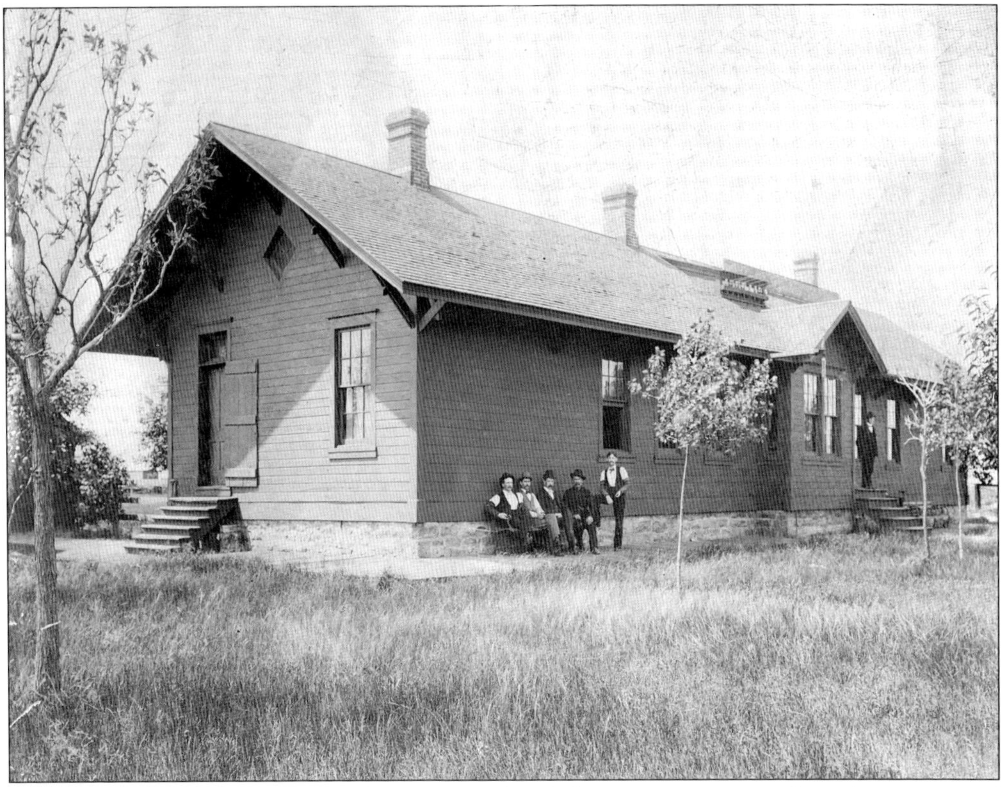

In 1880, the first Chicago & Northwestern Railroad depot was constructed on the west side of Dakota Avenue. The depot was the location for many church services and business meetings until a larger depot with a hotel was completed on the opposite side of Dakota Avenue. (Courtesy of Huron Public Library.)

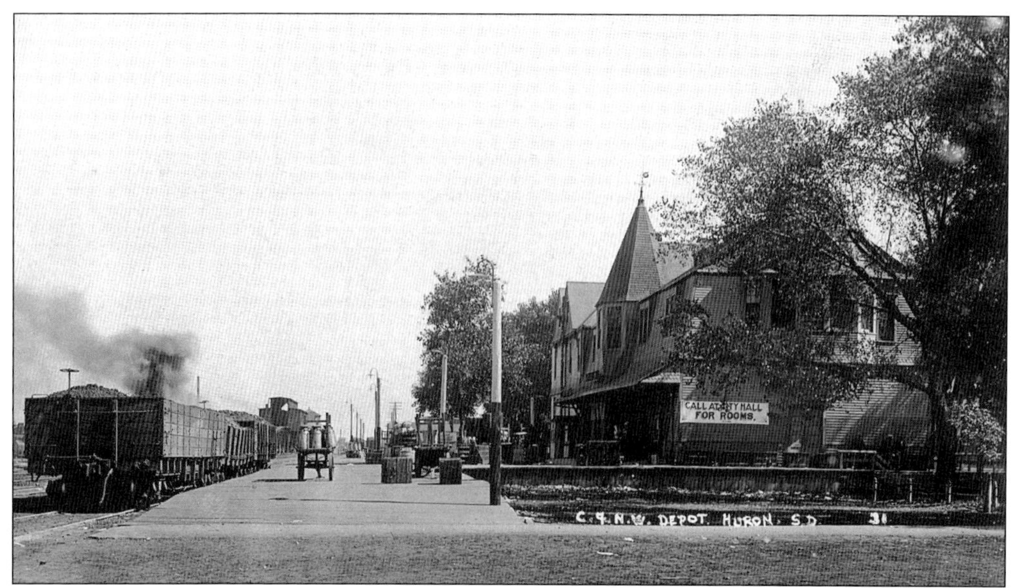

The Depot Hotel was constructed in 1883 for $16,000. It was a two-and-a-half-story Queen Anne–style building. The first floor contained a dining room, offices, waiting rooms, and a baggage area. Twenty-four guest rooms were located on the second floor. The hotel became known as the Kent House, named after Frederick Kent, who managed the hotel and dining room for 30 years.

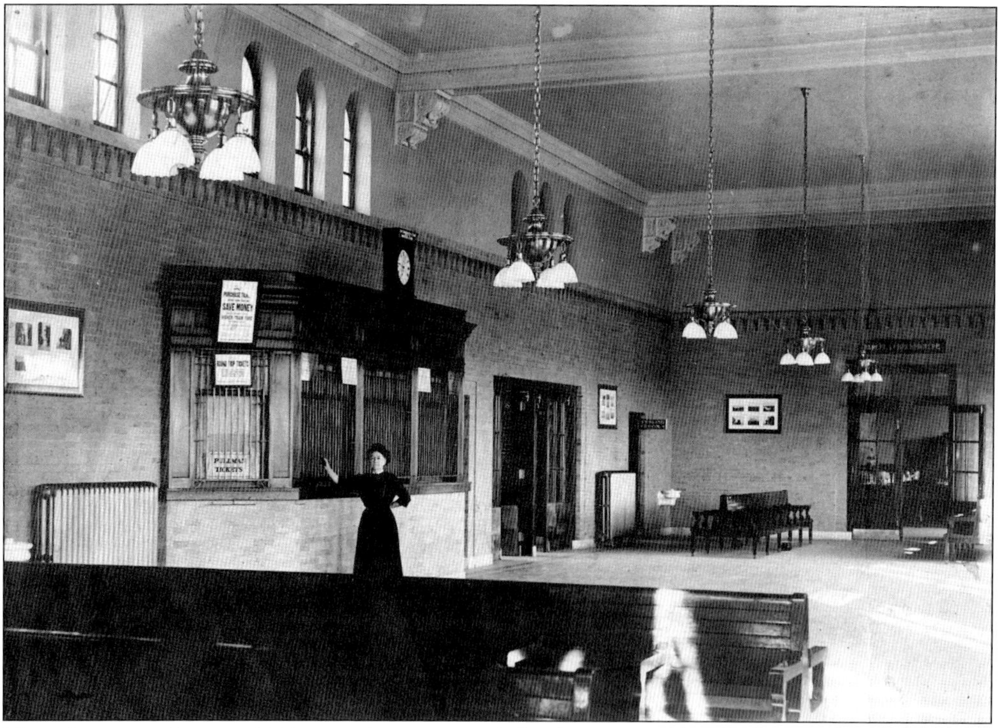

Eliza Cass, seen here in 1914, was the matron of the depot for eight years. Passengers called her "Mother" because she took care of all the weary travelers. Cass met every train that arrived, answered travelers' questions, gave directions, took care of the women and children, and made travelers feel welcome. (Courtesy of Huron Public Library.)

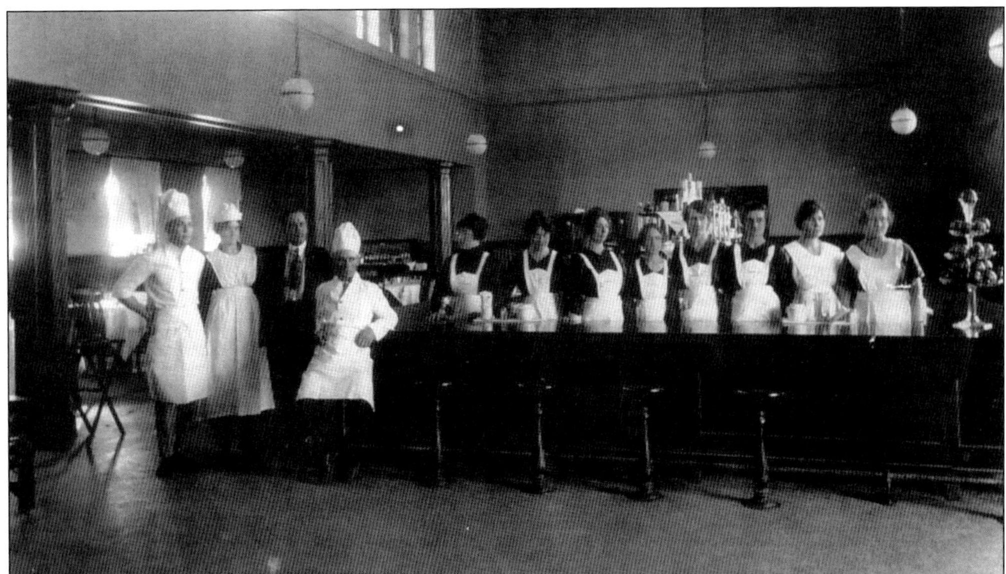

Originally from Indiana, Frederick Kent moved his family to Huron in 1883 to manage the Depot Hotel. The expensive furnishings and delicacies served in the dining room reflected Kent's upper-class Eastern lifestyle, making the hotel one of the finest establishments along the Chicago & Northwestern railways. The hotel had a reputation for elaborate banquets and grand parties where guests wore formal attire and ate multiple-course meals. The photograph above shows the chef and waitstaff. The Christmas dinner menu below is from 1904. Entrees included delicacies such as frog legs, roast pig, and buffalo ribs delivered directly to the hotel by train.

BLUE POINT COCKTAIL
STUFFED OLIVES

—

BOUILLON IN CUPS
CELERY

—

BOILED FRESH COD, SHRIMP SAUCE
PARISIENNE POTATOES
SLICED TOMATOES SALTED ALMONDS

—

FROGS LEGS, TARTAR SAUCE
FRENCH PEAS

—

ROAST SUCKING PIG
CANDIED SWEET POTATOES
YOUNG TURKEY, CHESTNUT DRESSING
CRANBERRY SAUCE
RIBS OF PRIME BUFFALO
BROWNED POTATOES

—

MARASCHINO PUNCH

—

SWEETBREAD MAYONNAISE

—

ENGLISH PLUM PUDDING,
BRANDY AND HARD SAUCE
MINCE PIE APPLE PIE
WALNUT ICE CREAM
MACAROONS KISSES CIDER
NUTS AND RAISINS
EDAM AND CAMEMBERT CHEESE
WATER CRACKERS
COFFEE

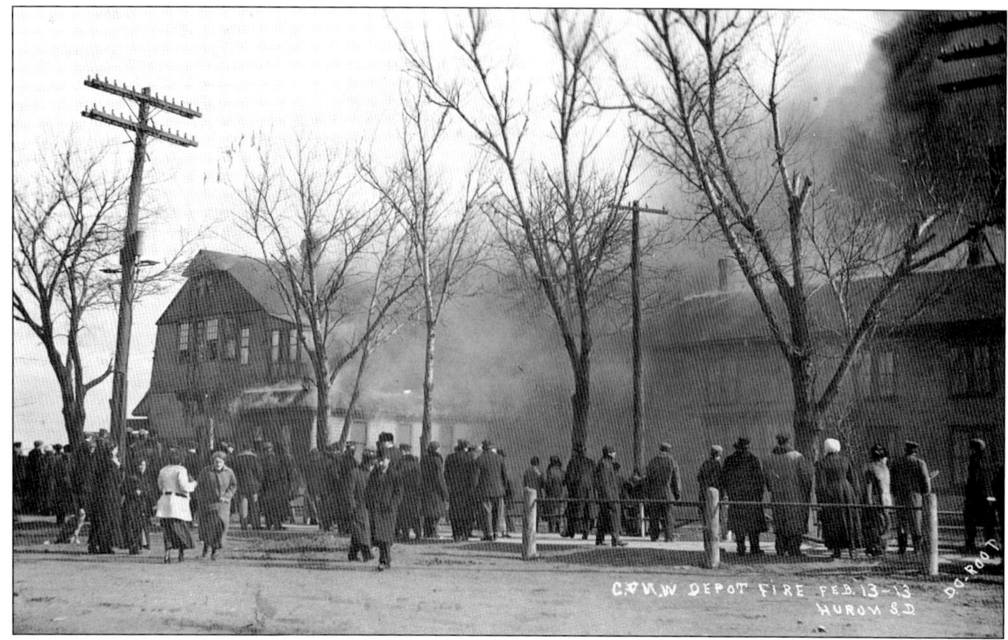

On February 13, 1913, a large fire engulfed the building that housed the Kent House Hotel, the Chicago & Northwestern Railroad depot, and the American Express office. The fire started in the basement and spread rapidly through the wood building. The railroad and city fire departments were able to contain the blaze before it spread to other buildings in the rail yard.

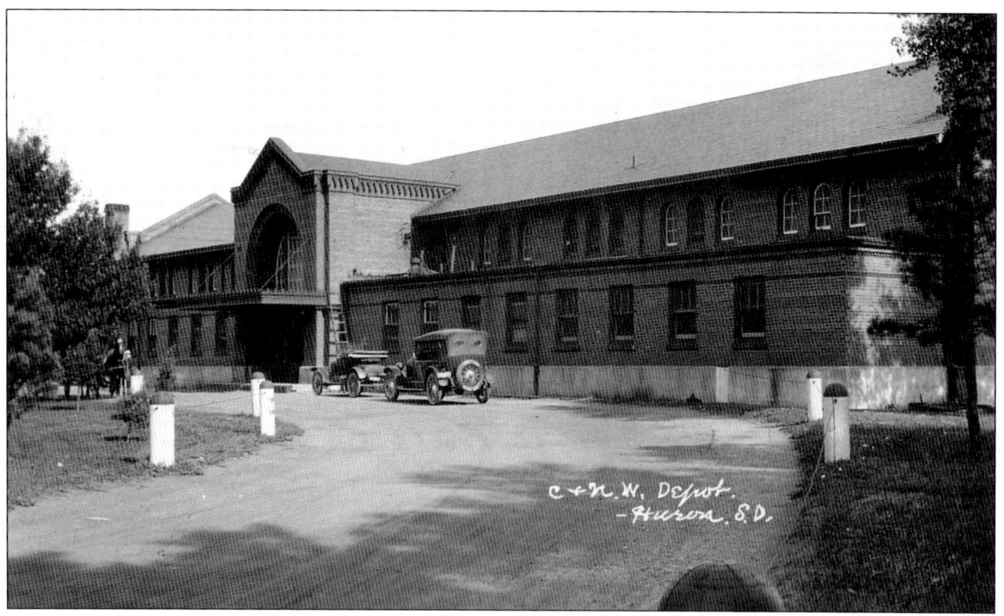

After the depot fire, a new brick passenger depot was constructed on the west side of Dakota Avenue. The building contained a long waiting room, dining room, kitchen, offices, and restrooms. Baggage was stored at the west end of the building along with space for the Railway Express Company. A park with flower beds on the east end of the building welcomed arriving passengers.

The locomotive in this photograph from 1895 is being repaired at a facility in Huron. The stern of the locomotive was lifted so the rear drive wheels could be removed. The axle could then be replaced, and a steel band was fitted to the metal wheels to protect them.

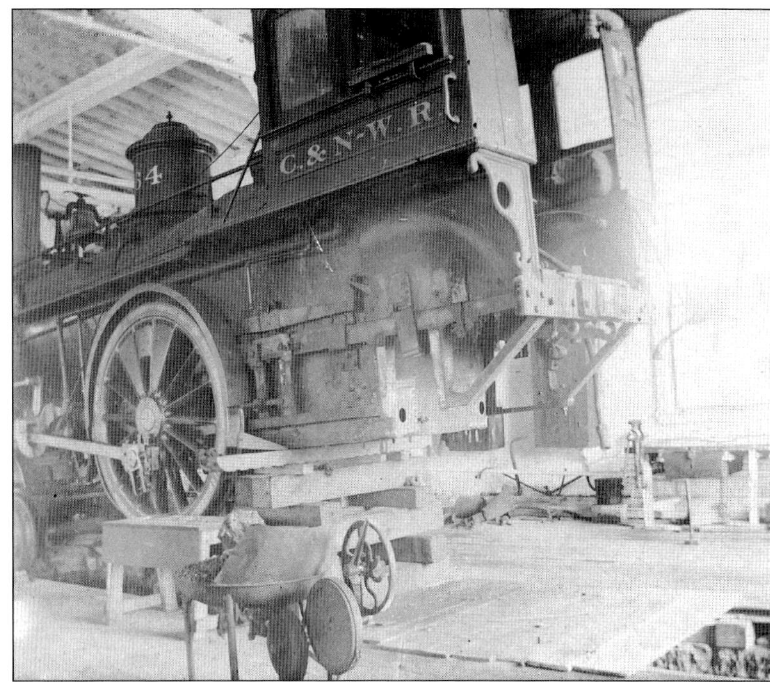

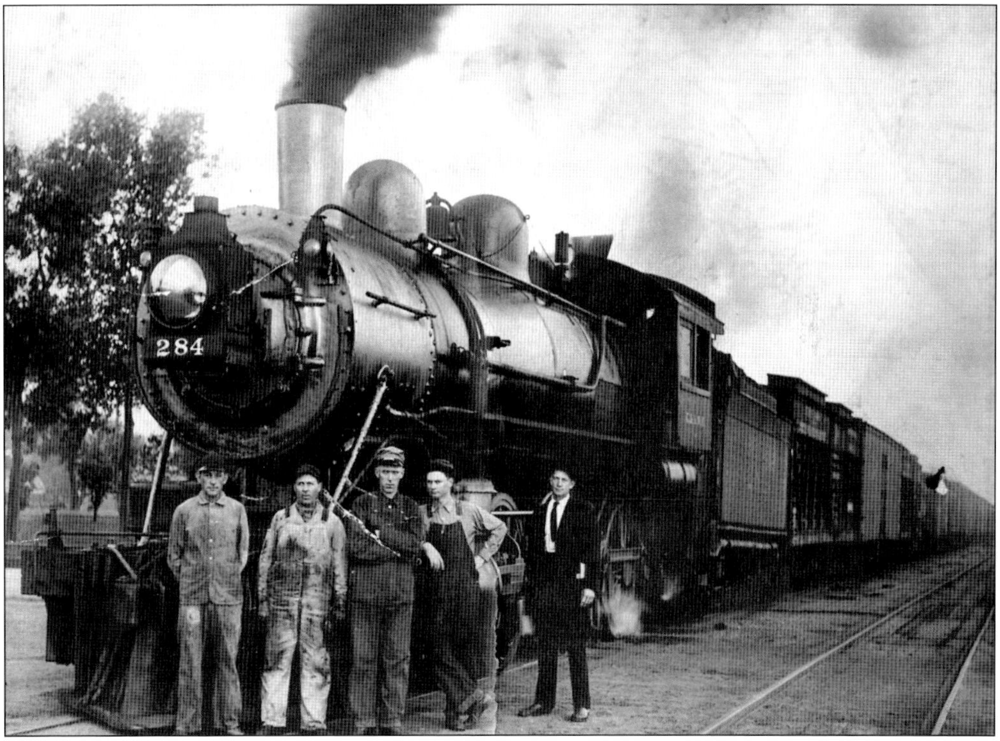

Engine No. 284 was a steam locomotive owned by the Chicago & Northwestern Railroad. A five-man crew operated this engine as it traveled between Huron and Centerville. Crew members from 1911 are pictured here; from left to right are R.A. Hyde, John Gascoigne, J.G. Jackson, Frank Lillebridge, and conductor Robert Lockwood.

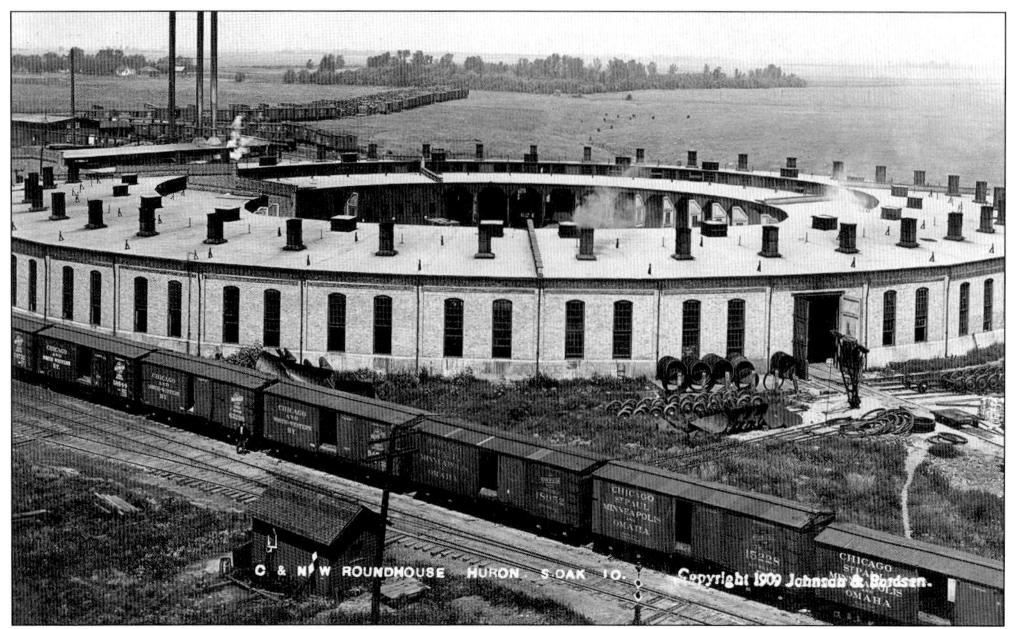

As a divisional headquarters for the Chicago & Northwestern Railroad, the Huron rail yards were busy 24 hours a day. The photograph above shows the 45-stall roundhouse built in 1907 to accommodate the dozens of locomotives coming for maintenance and repairs. There were only two roundhouses of this size built in South Dakota. One was in Huron, and the second was built by the Chicago, Milwaukee, St. Paul & Pacific Railroad in Aberdeen. The photograph below shows the turntable in the center of the roundhouse. The engines were driven onto the turntable and then turned toward an open stall for maintenance or completely around so they could leave the roundhouse.

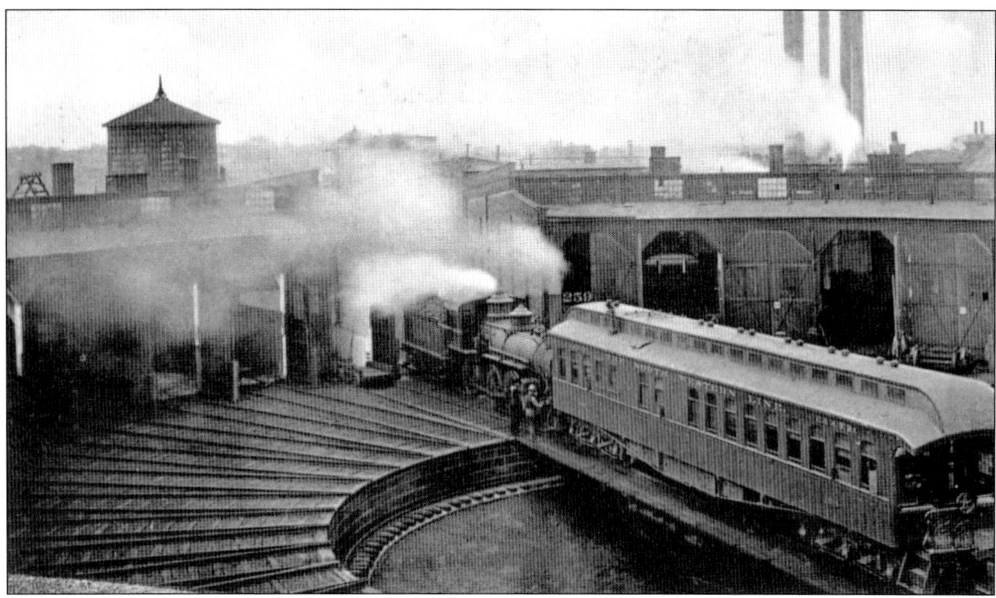

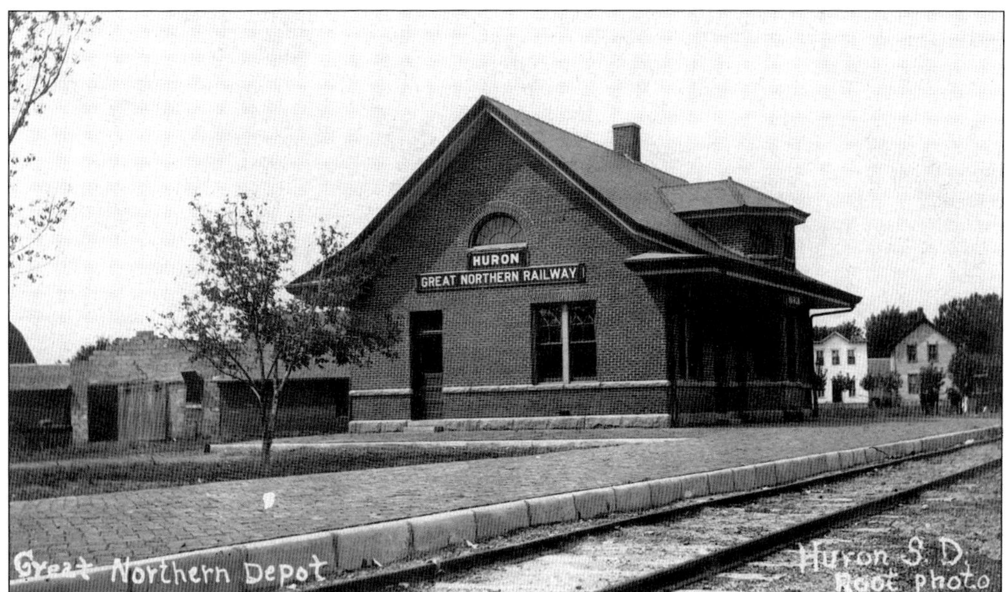

The Great Northern Railroad constructed a railway line from Watertown to Huron in the late 1880s. The first depot was constructed of wood and located on the west side of town at Fifth Street and Nevada Avenue. Later, a brick depot, seen here, was constructed closer to downtown on Dakota Avenue. The original wood structure was moved to this location for storing freight. (Courtesy of Andy Gross.)

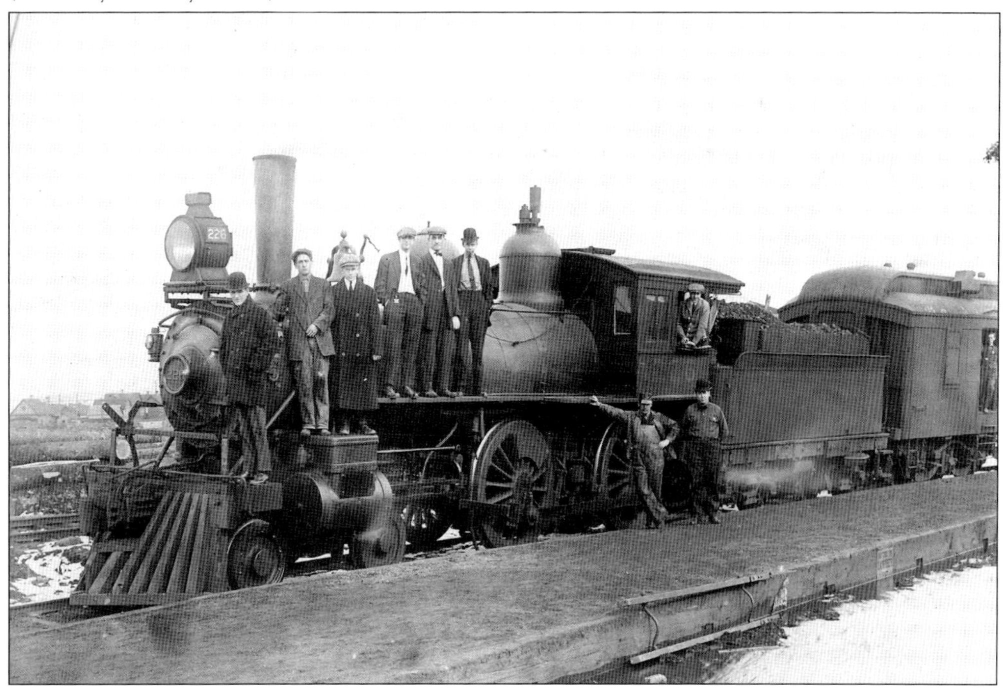

The men seen here were crew members on the Great Northern Railroad's engine No. 226. The photograph was taken outside the city limits. This type of steam engine was the most common type of locomotive in the United States. It was classified as a 4-4-0, which referred to the number and arrangement of the wheels.

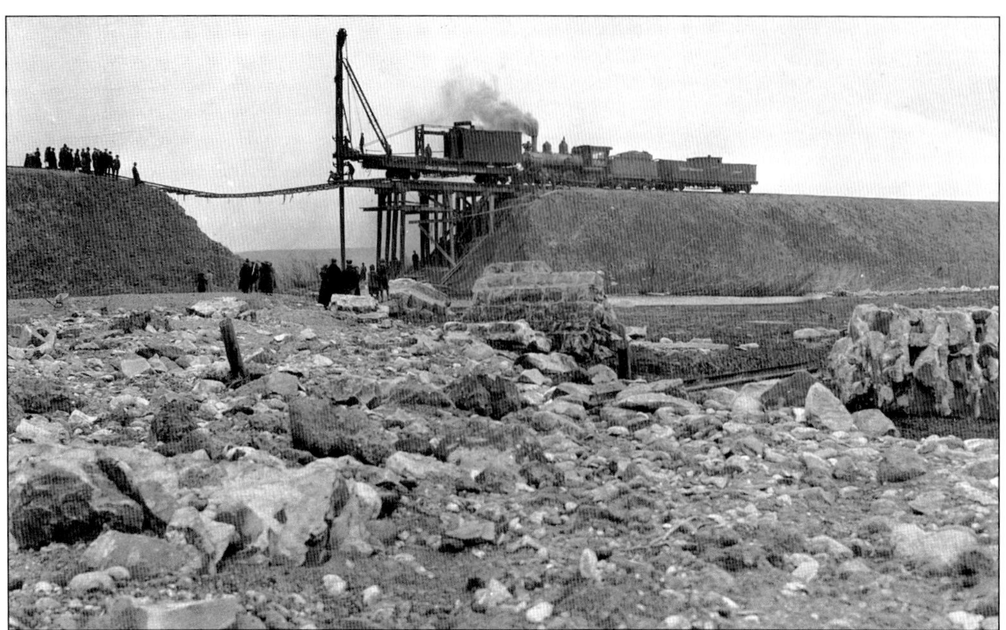

On the night of May 12, 1920, heavy rains washed out a culvert and the surrounding embankment beneath the Great Northern Railroad tracks northeast of town. A neighbor living near the area noticed the washout and contacted railroad officials. Fortunately, the 6:00 a.m. train leaving Huron was stopped before it met with disaster. Workmen built a wood bridge across the gap in five days to keep the trains running.

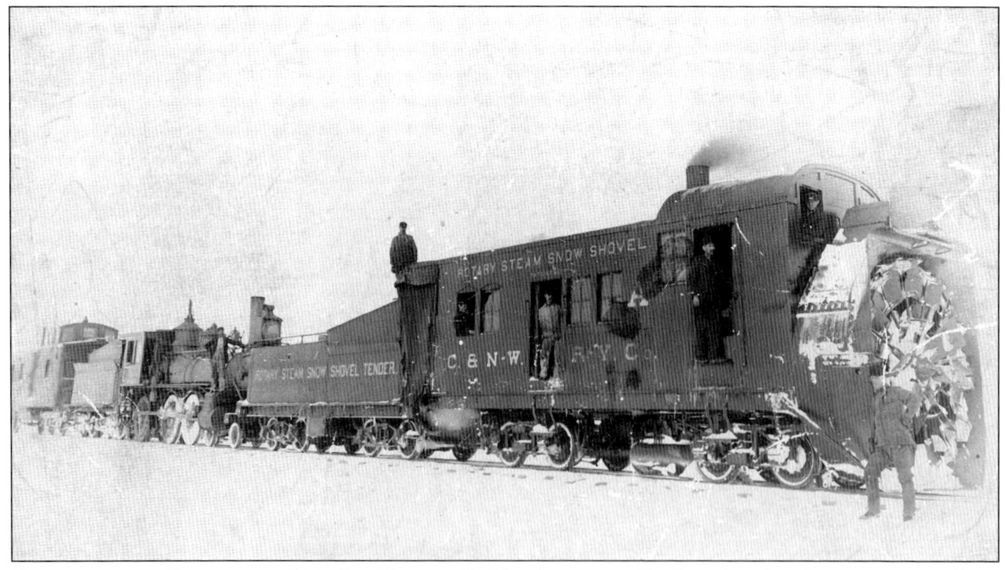

During years of heavy snowfall, the Chicago & Northwestern Railroad utilized rotary snow plows to clear the tracks. The plows had large circular blades on the front that rotated to cut through the deep snow pack instead of pushing the snow to the side like the wedge blades. Locomotives were used to push the rotary plow through the snow because the plow itself was not self-propelled.

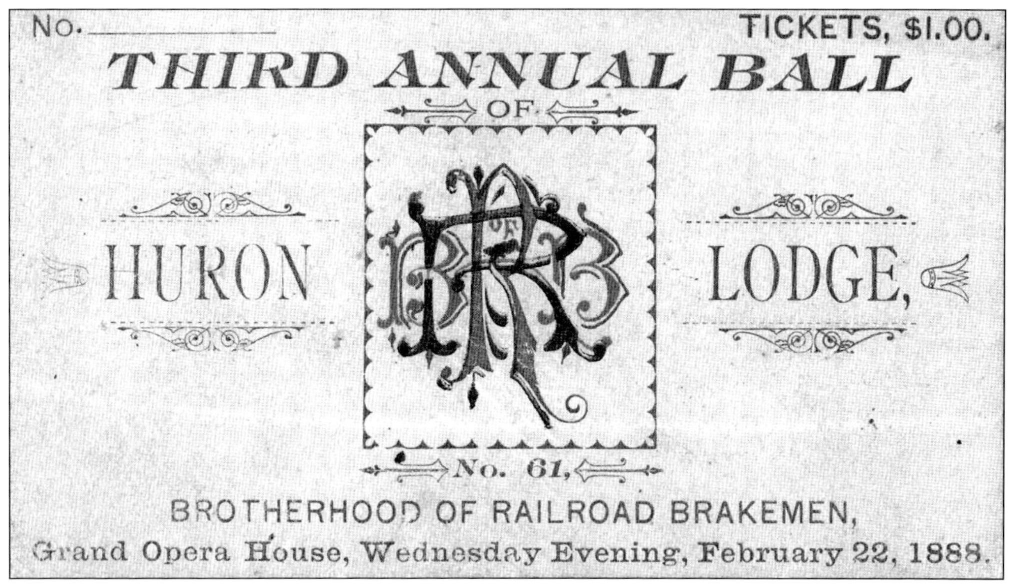

No.__________ TICKETS, $1.00.

THIRD ANNUAL BALL

OF

B of R T

HURON LODGE,

No. 61,

BROTHERHOOD OF RAILROAD BRAKEMEN,

Grand Opera House, Wednesday Evening, February 22, 1888.

Huron Lodge 61 of the Brotherhood of Railroad Brakemen was chartered on February 3, 1885. The organization represented trainmen employed by the Chicago & Northwestern Railroad during contract negotiations and helped resolve disputes between members and employers. Other benefits of membership included social events like this ball held downtown at the Grand Opera House on February 22, 1888.

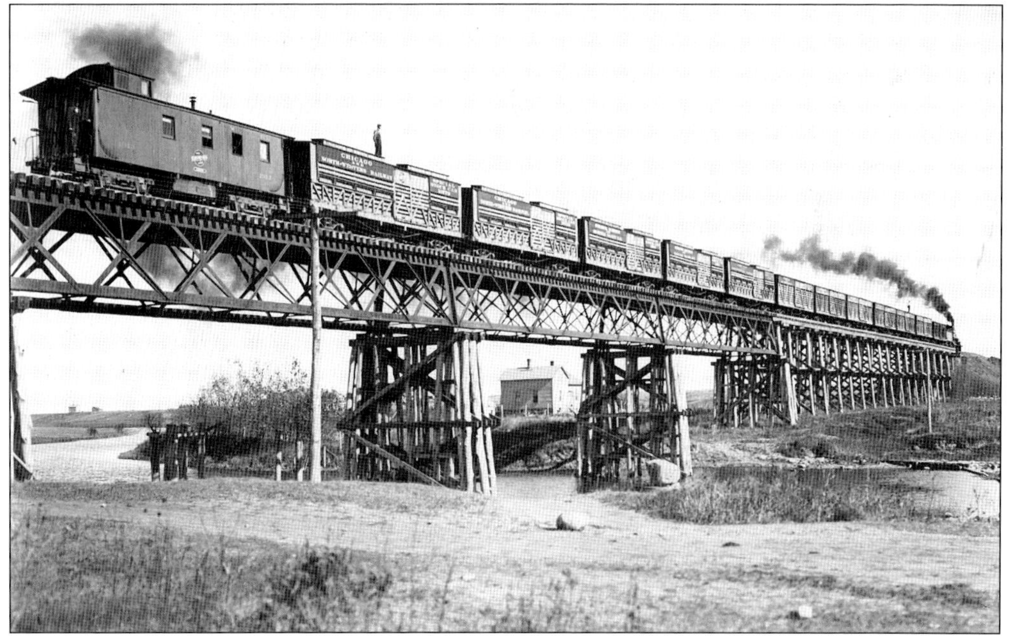

The Chicago & Northwestern train seen here is hauling livestock. It is interesting to note that the caboose is longer than usual. The cowboys, or drovers, who accompanied the livestock rode in this car. The men rode for free and were on hand to load, unload, and deal with any stock issues along the way.

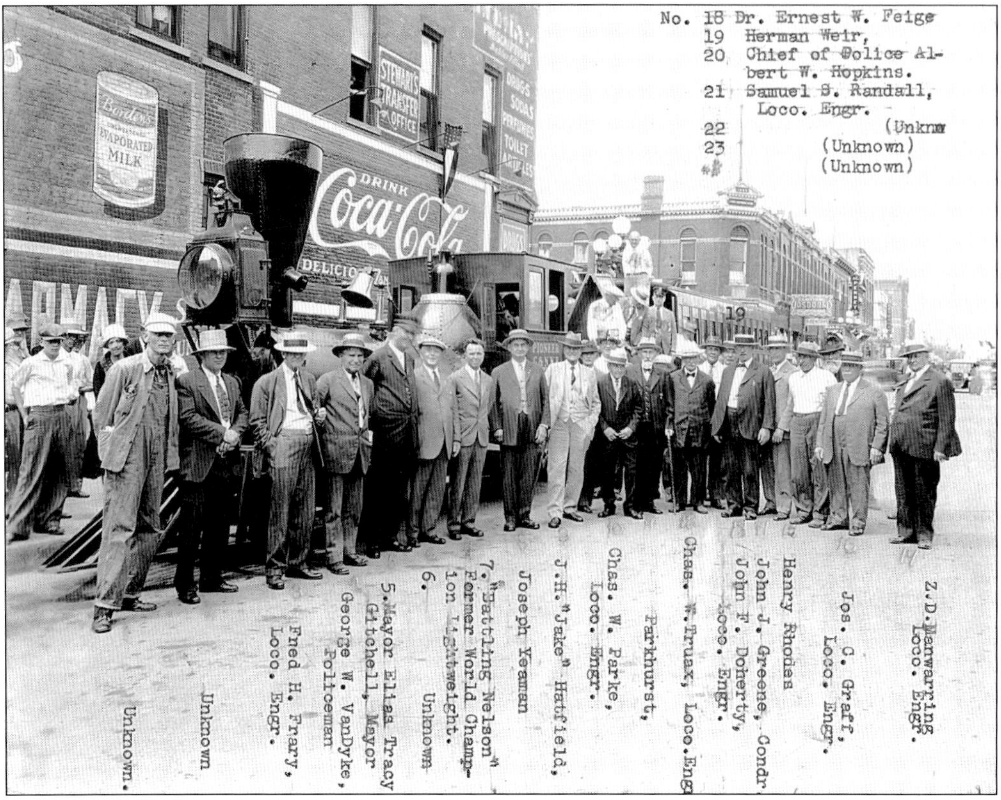

Huron celebrated its 50th anniversary on July 4, 1930. To commemorate the event, local railroad engineers and businessmen posed for a photograph in front of a store on the corner of Third Street and Dakota Avenue. Several notable men in the photograph are Mayor Elias Tracy Gitchell, chief of police Albert W. Hopkins, Dr. Ernest W. Feige, and Oscar "Battling" Nelson (1908 World Lightweight Champion). (Courtesy of Huron Public Library.)

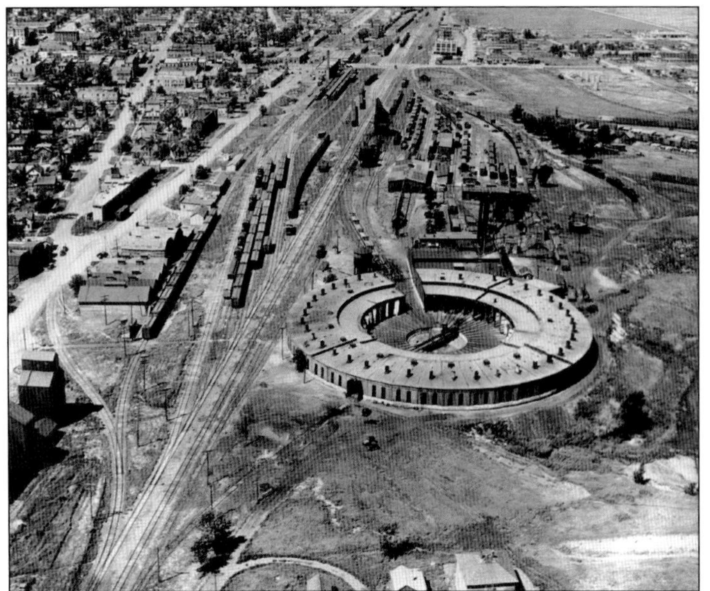

This aerial photograph was taken in the 1940s and shows the extensive railroad yard. Dakota Avenue can be seen across the top of the photograph from left to right. Surrounding the roundhouse in the center of the photograph are the railroad's storage and maintenance buildings. (Courtesy of NorthWestern Energy.)

Two

From the Ground Up

Although Huron only began in 1880, it quickly developed into a modern community with all the latest amenities.

During the first few months, government services arrived such as the post office, the land office, and the weather bureau, originally the US Signal Corps. Major infrastructure projects were undertaken. Electric streetlights were installed in 1883 and operated from dusk to midnight except on dance nights. The city paid $1 an hour after midnight to keep the lights on and the revelers safe. Western Union opened a branch in 1883 and in the first month sent 1,642 messages. By 1886, Huron boasted a world-champion fire department. Huron was growing by leaps and bounds.

The first means of public transportation were horse-drawn streetcars. The tracks ran along Dakota Avenue past the Chicago & Northwestern depot then on Third Street west to the fairgrounds. The other route went from the Great Northern depot along Fifth Street to Kansas Avenue then south to Ninth Street. The streetcars, which were heated and lighted, met the trains at night and ran every 15 minutes to the opera house. The fare was 5¢.

The citizens were obsessed with becoming the state capital, and the ensuing campaigns nearly led to ruin. But even with the hardship of severe indebtedness, Huron was able to continue providing services to its people.

Federal agencies were soon headquartered in Huron, especially any related to the Department of Agriculture. There were so many that one federal employee called Huron Little Washington, DC. The Federal Building was erected in 1977 to house all the federal offices, and the federal government continues to be one of the largest employers in Huron.

Huron has also produced several prominent political leaders both at the state level and reaching the national stage. Among them were a vice president of the United States, four US senators (two of them women), a governor, a leader in the suffrage movement, and the first woman sheriff in South Dakota. Huron may be the only city in the nation to claim this many dignitaries as citizens.

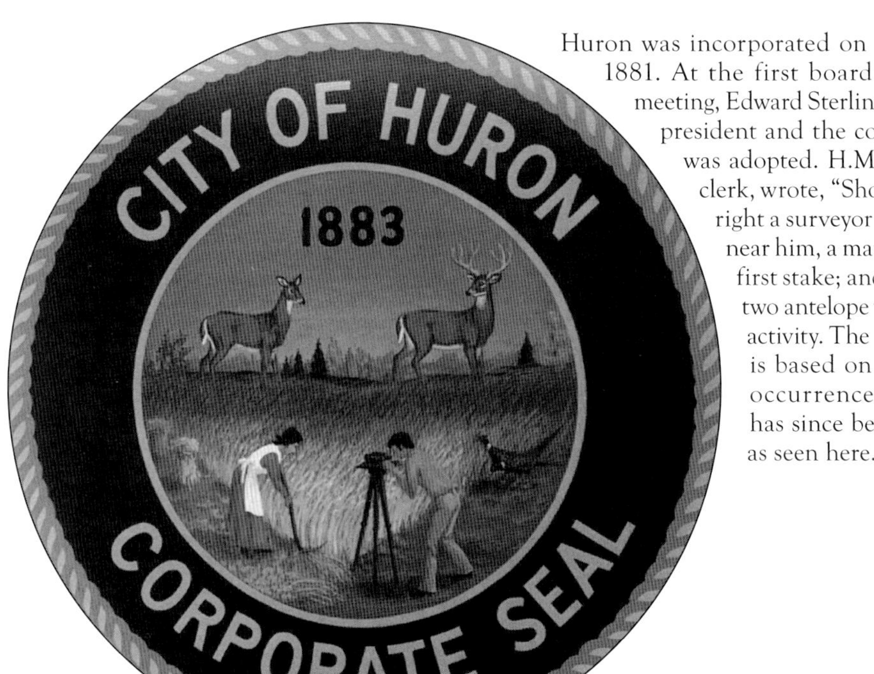

Huron was incorporated on February 1, 1881. At the first board of trustees meeting, Edward Sterling was elected president and the corporate seal was adopted. H.M. Jewett, the clerk, wrote, "Showing on the right a surveyor with tripod; near him, a man driving the first stake; and on the left, two antelope watching the activity. The above design is based on a historical occurrence." The seal has since been modified as seen here.

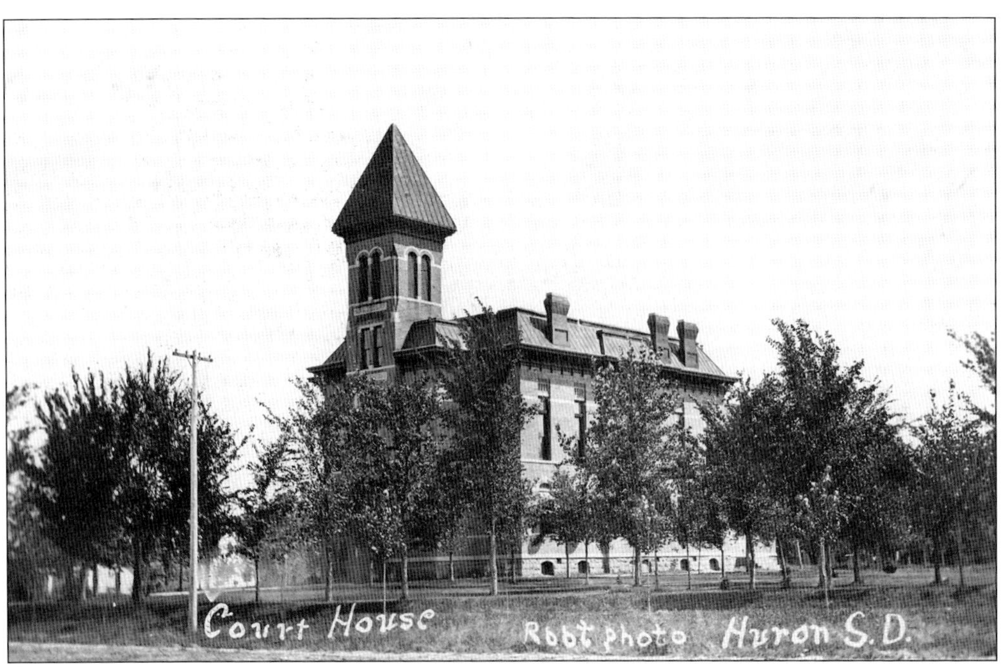

The first town election in 1881 saw voters approve the issuance of bonds to finance a county courthouse and jail. The Chicago & Northwestern Railroad donated the land for the courthouse along with the land for Capitol Hill. It later donated four blocks for the Huron College campus, 85 acres for the state fairgrounds, and land for several churches. (Courtesy of Jennifer Littlefield.)

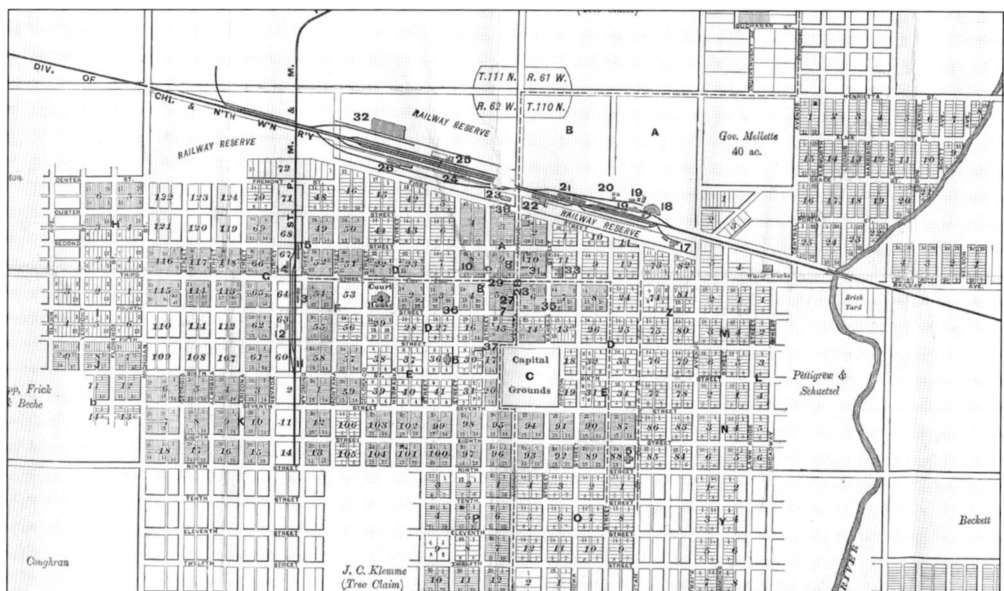

This open area was set aside for the capitol. It extended from Fifth to Seventh Streets and from Oregon to California Avenues. Dakota Avenue, which begins at the bottom right, did not extend through this area. When Pierre won the vote, Capitol Hill was divided into lots and sold except for two parcels designated East and West Parks, now known as Winter and Campbell Parks.

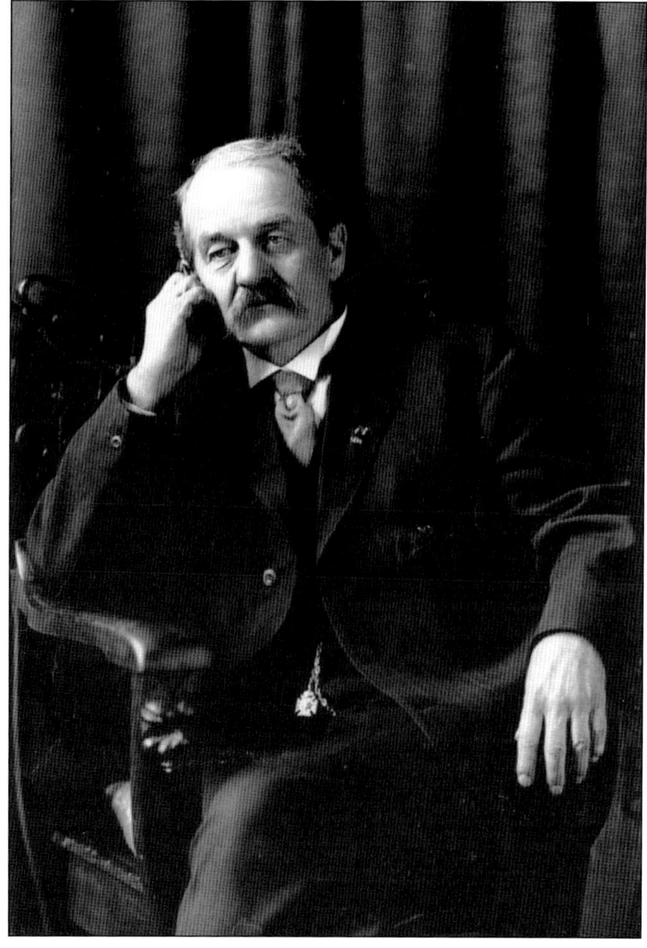

Huron became a city on March 8, 1883. In 1887, Mayor H.J. Rice led a campaign for the state capital that nearly bankrupted the city. Huron's bonded indebtedness was $143,000 before the fight and was still more than $300,000 twelve years later. During the subsequent lean years, one business was lost to fire when there was no money to replace a rotten fire hose.

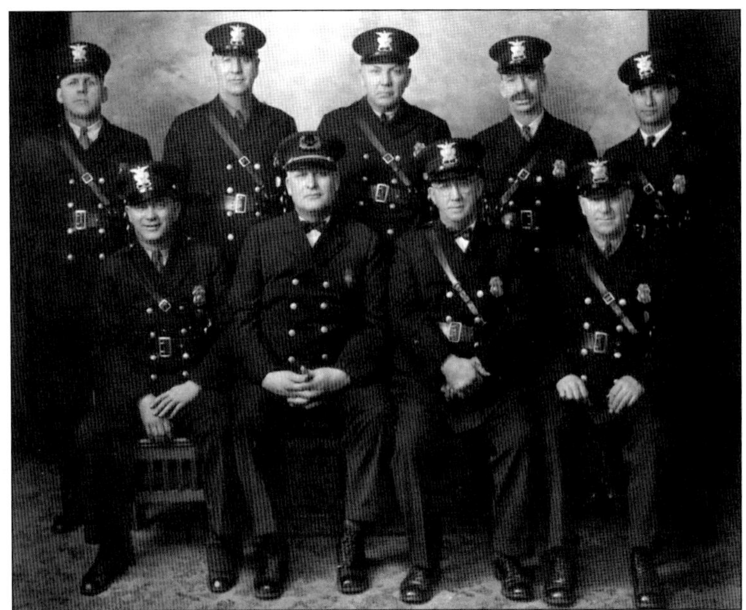

The 1935 police officers were, from left to right, (first row) Louis Matson, Chief J.S. Nilson, A.D. McRay, and J. Louis Anderson; (second row) E.A. Anderson, John Peterson, Guy Bevier, Walt Peterson, and Earl Pellant. In 1920, Vern C. Miller was hired as a policeman. He was elected sheriff within months, but by 1922, he had been convicted of embezzlement, and his later crimes included murder.

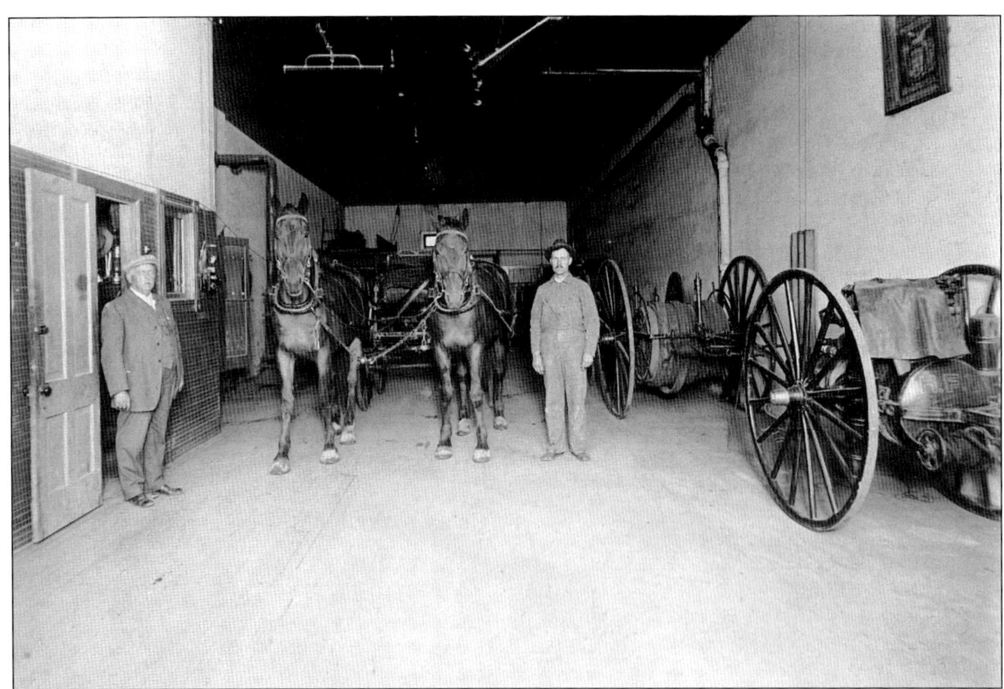

The Pioneer Hook and Ladder Company was formed on June 1, 1882. The motto of the fire department was "We come to conquer." It consisted of 30 volunteers, a horse-drawn water wagon, and two-wheeled hose reels pulled by men. Shown here are Chief William Ritchslag (left) and Fireman Barker with horses Tom and Jerry.

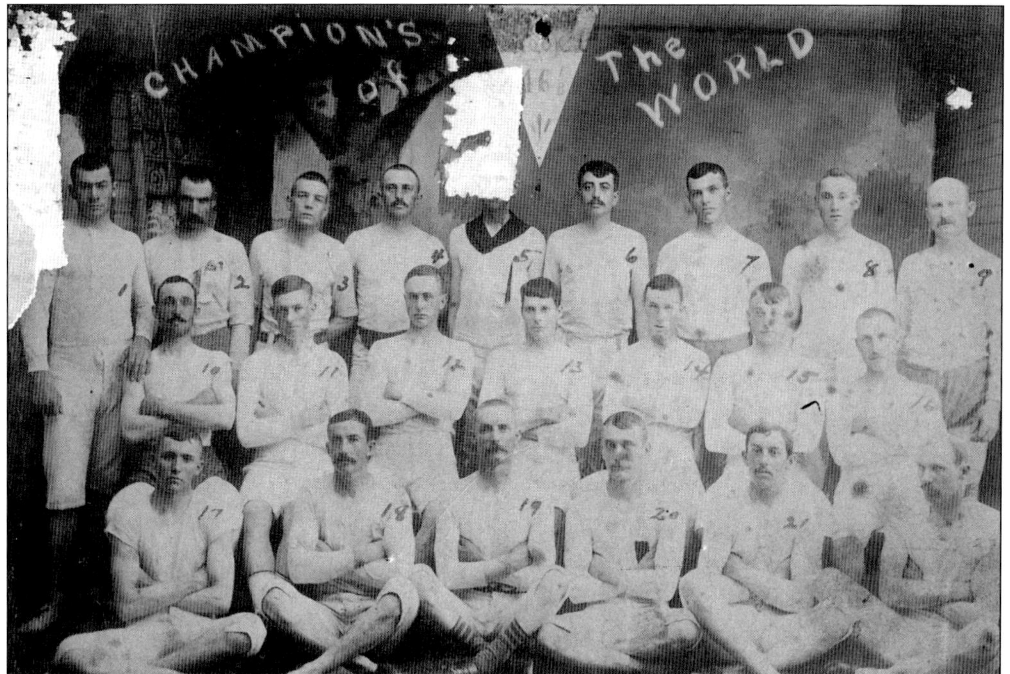

In 1886, the Huron Hose Team, captained by Con Huntley (seated far right), became world champions when they broke the record in the 300-yard contest, posting a time of 38 seconds. A two-wheeled chemical cart was purchased at one of these tournaments in Pierre when the Huron team, captained by J.H. Finch, was selected to demonstrate its use. They were so impressed that Chief Ritchslag bought it on the spot.

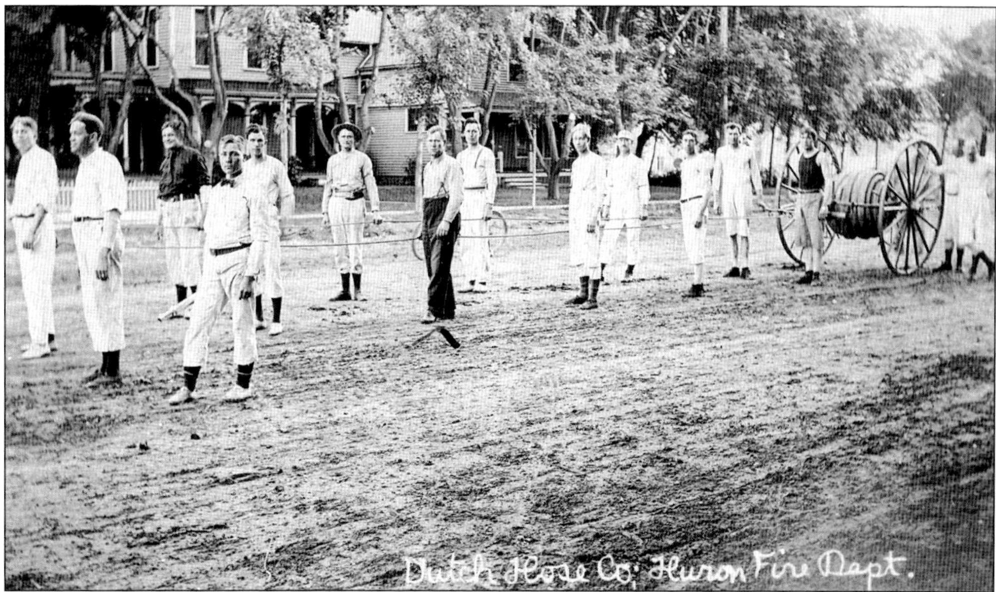

The Dutch Hose Company, made up entirely of Dutchmen, was formed in 1889. A hook and ladder wagon was purchased that year, and later a four-wheeled chemical cart replaced the two-wheeled outfit shown here. It proved to be too heavy to be pulled by hand, so the first teamster to the fire station would haul it to the fire. The job paid $1 per fire.

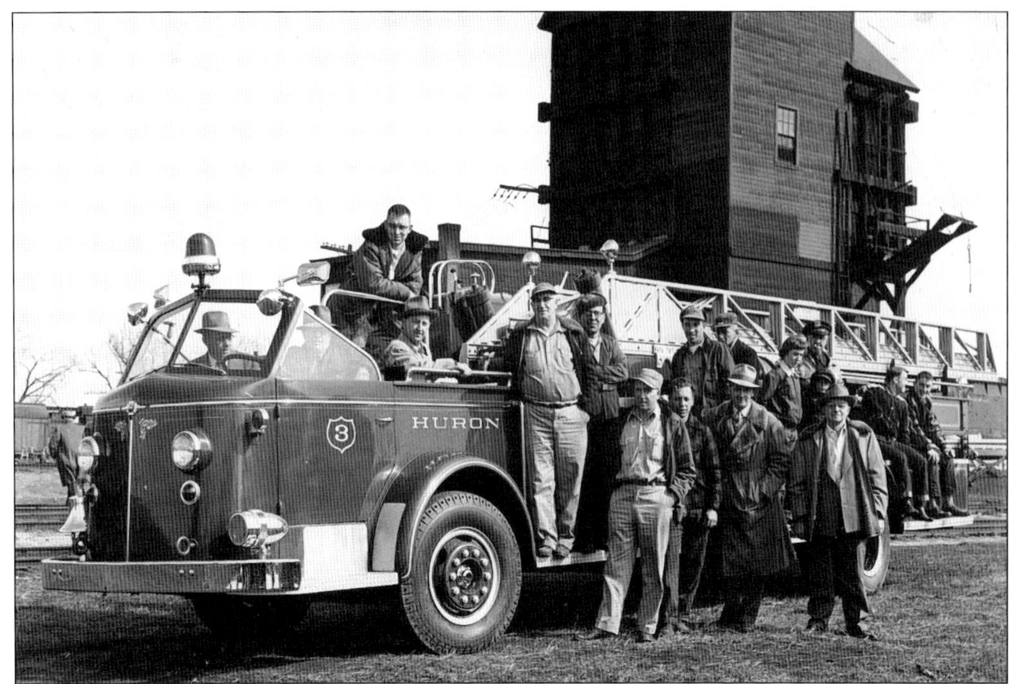

Huron acquired a modern American LaFrance hook and ladder truck in the late 1940s. When it was delivered, 13 members of the volunteer fire department, along with a representative from the American LaFrance Company, posed for this photograph near the railroad tracks. The driver of the engine was Harold Cantonwine. (Courtesy of Huron Fire Department.)

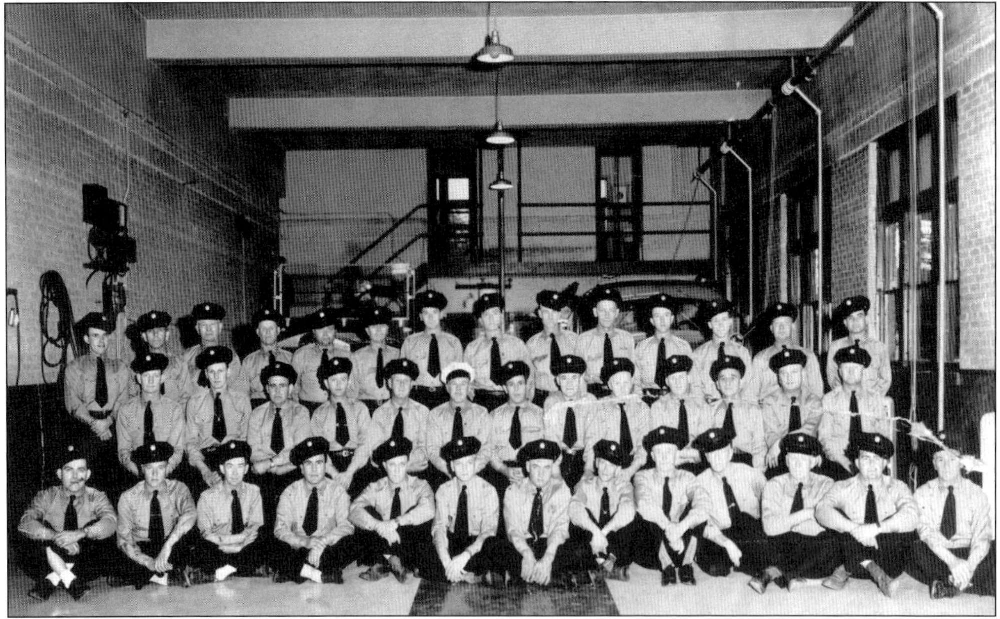

By 1949, Huron had two fire stations and boasted a large fire department of 40 professional firefighters, shown here in the central station. Modern trucks and equipment can be seen parked behind them, replacing the horse team of Tom and Jerry and the hand-pulled hose reels and carts used in the early years. (Courtesy of Huron Fire Department.)

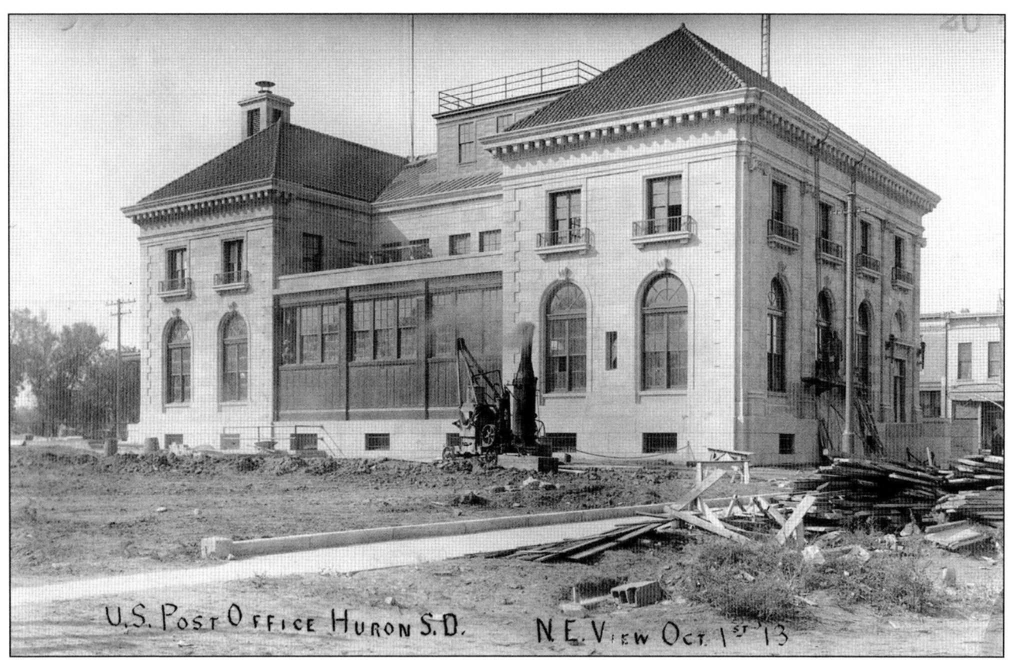

The post office opened on July 13, 1880, with John Cain as the postmaster. It was housed in the first building in Huron. By 1883, it was the largest in Dakota Territory and paid the highest salaries. In January 1914, the current building at Dakota Avenue and Fourth Street was completed. This photograph was taken from the back on October 1, 1913. (Courtesy of US Postal Service.)

To accommodate the continued growth of the city, an addition was added to the back of the post office in 1937. The first free mail delivery began in 1887 after the city commission reworked the system of streets and avenues into four quadrants and added house numbers. Those first mail carriers earned $600 a year. (Courtesy of US Postal Service.)

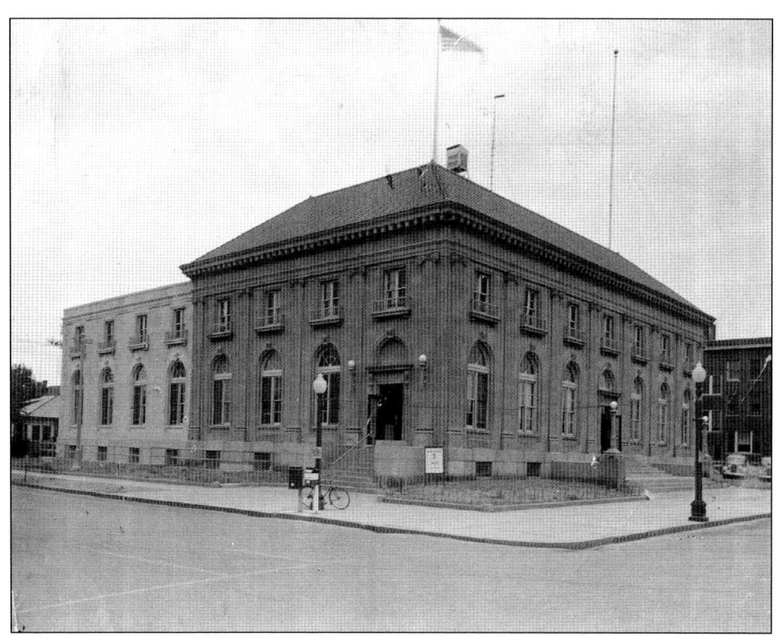

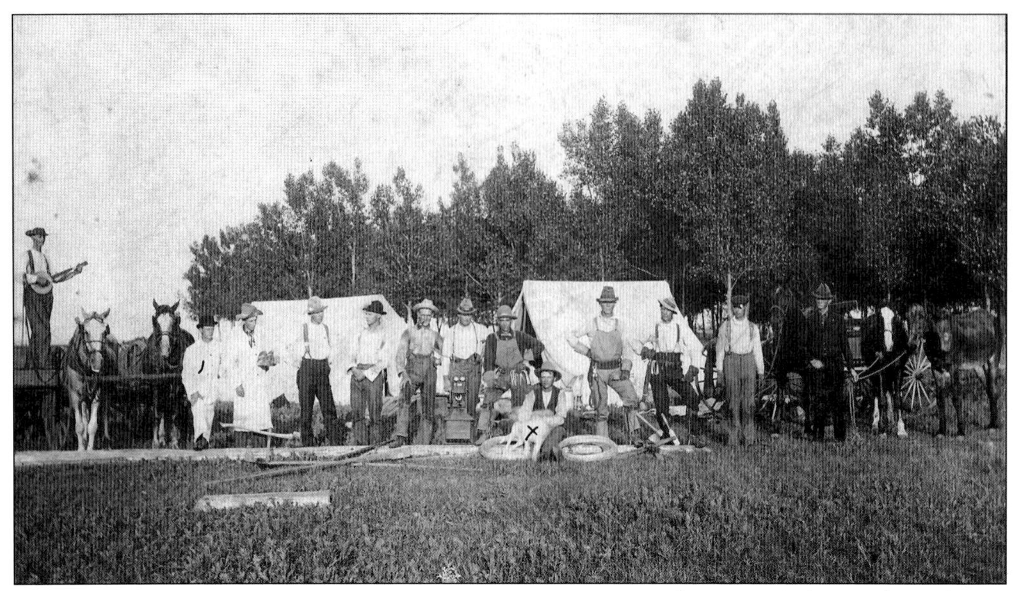

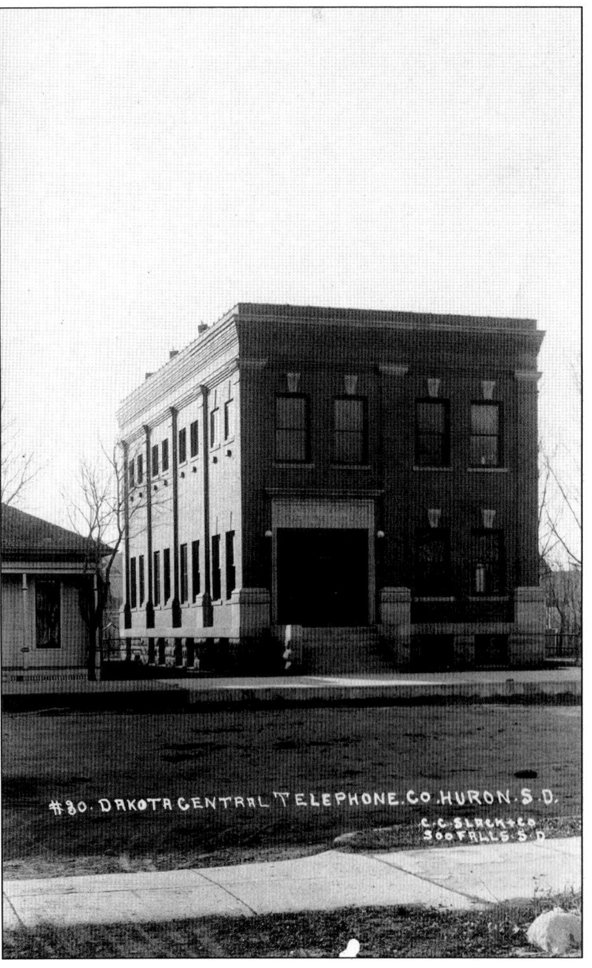

Southwestern Dakota Telegraph and Telephone Company began telephone service in November 1882 and soon had 55 subscribers. In 1898, J.L.W. Zietlow established a telephone exchange in city hall. These facilities became part of the Dakota Central Telephone Company. Pictured above is one of the first construction crews of the Dakota Central Telephone Company erecting poles and stringing wire. The crew foreman was Julius Feige. Also on the crew was Dr. C.A. Feige. At left is the telephone building, which housed the switchboard and operators in 1904. Crank telephones and party lines were gradually replaced with rotary dial phones when direct dial service began in 1910.

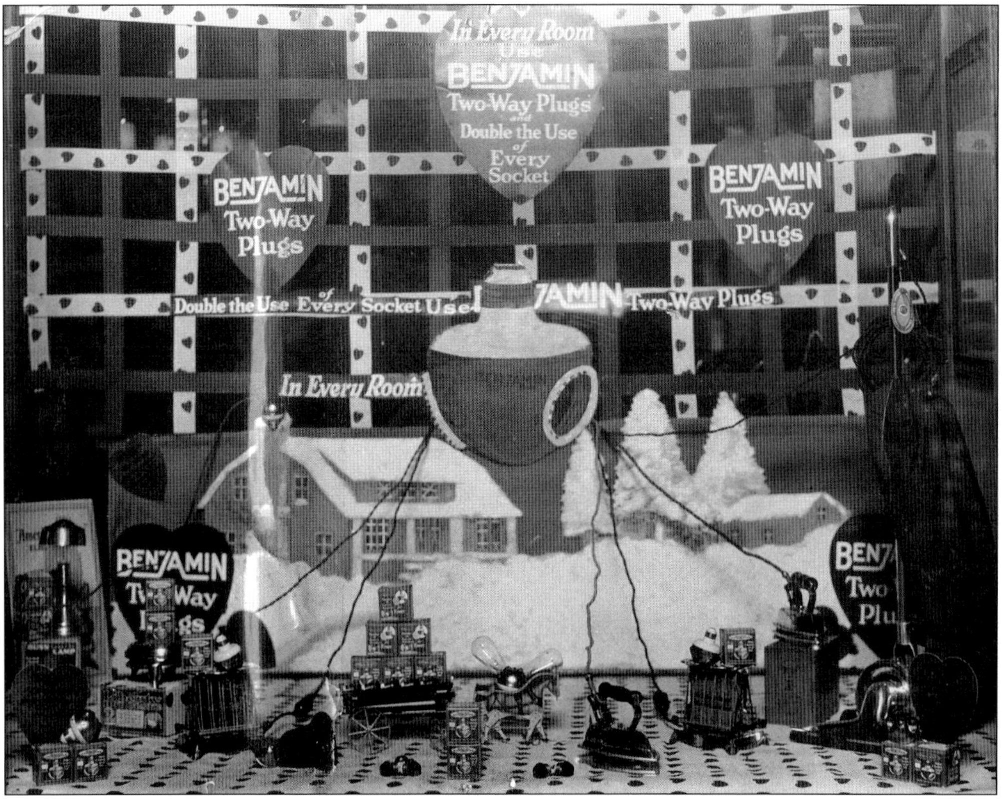

Elbert Bowe started a steam-generated electric power plant in 1883. Fuel for the boilers came from local livery stables. It operated from dusk until midnight. As demand for electric appliances grew, so did the need for more connections. This window display from 1935 advertised a plug that would double the socket space. Bowe's power station became Huron Light and Power in 1907 and Northwestern Public Service in 1924.

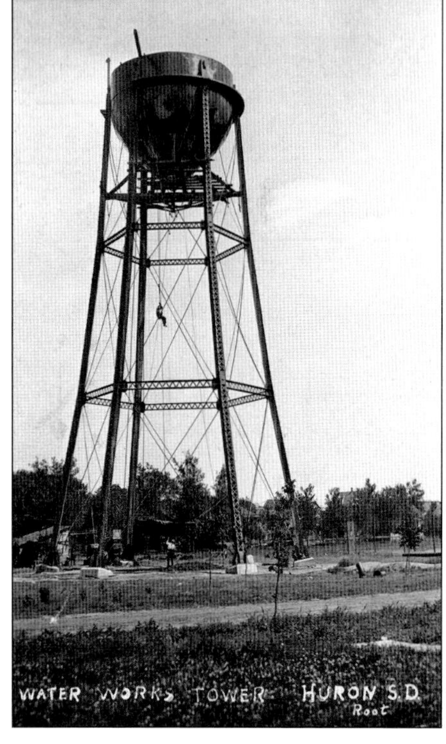

In 1883, the first water mains and plant were constructed. The *Huronite* reported in 1884 that water was filtered through 50 feet of gravel. The first city wells were located at Dakota Avenue and Second Street and on Third Street at Kansas Avenue and Wisconsin Avenue. The first water tower was erected in 1913 in East Park, which is now known as Winter Park. (Courtesy of Connie Greene.)

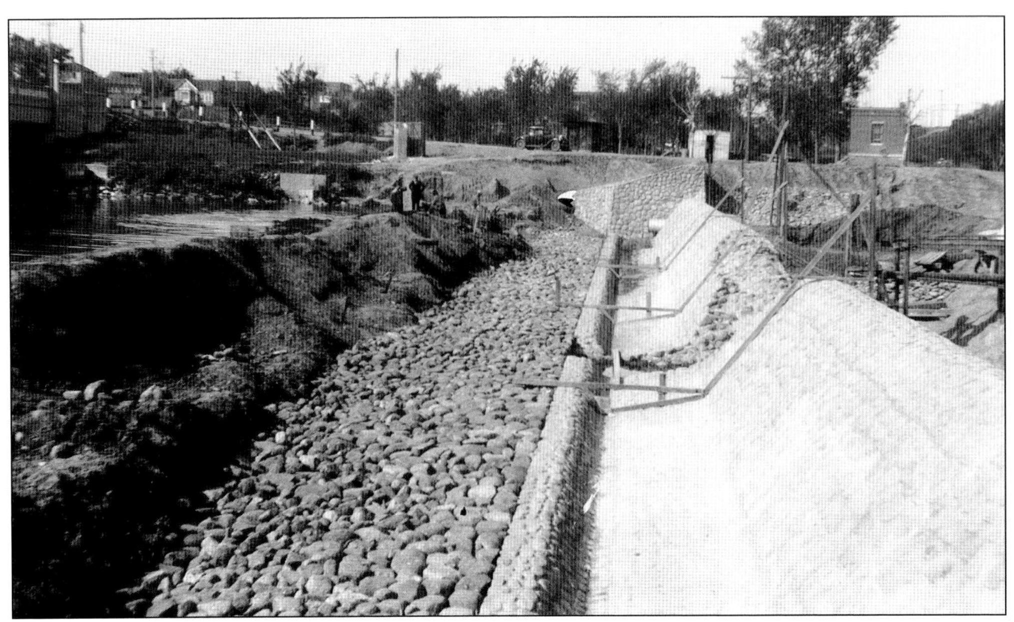

The James River has the distinction of being the longest unnavigable river in the world. It meanders for 750 miles to join the Missouri River just 250 miles south. It is the slowest moving river with an average gradient of only four inches per mile. Huron was dependent on the river for its water, but it would often dry up in shallow areas. The Works Progress Administration had the James River Dam, also known as the Third Street Dam, built in 1934 to ensure a steady supply of drinking water for Huron. It was constructed by the Civilian Conservation Corps Camp SDS 4 Company 2770, located at Huron. Above is a photograph taken during construction, and below is the dam after completion. This company constructed many other projects around Huron during the Great Depression.

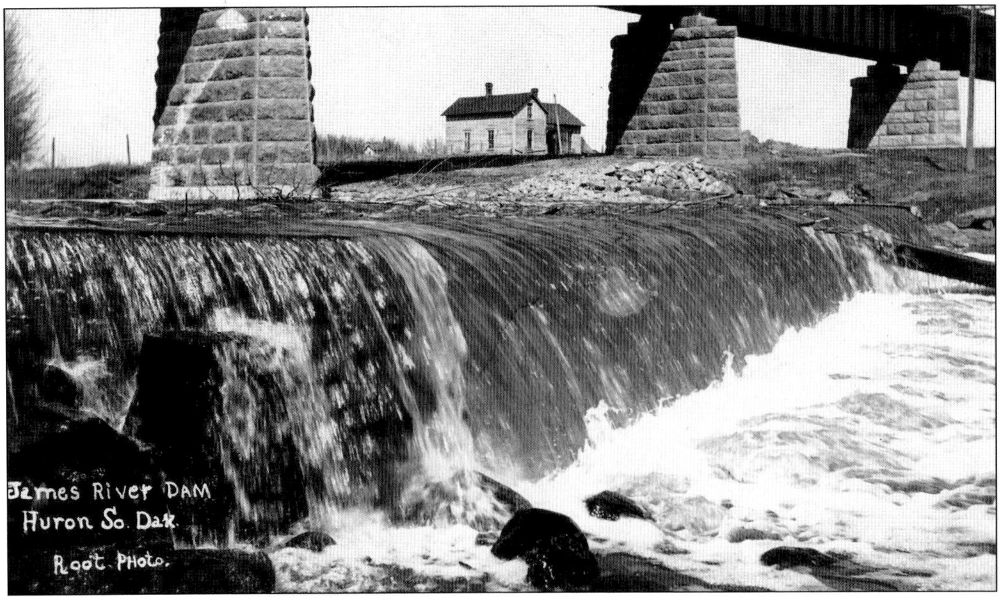

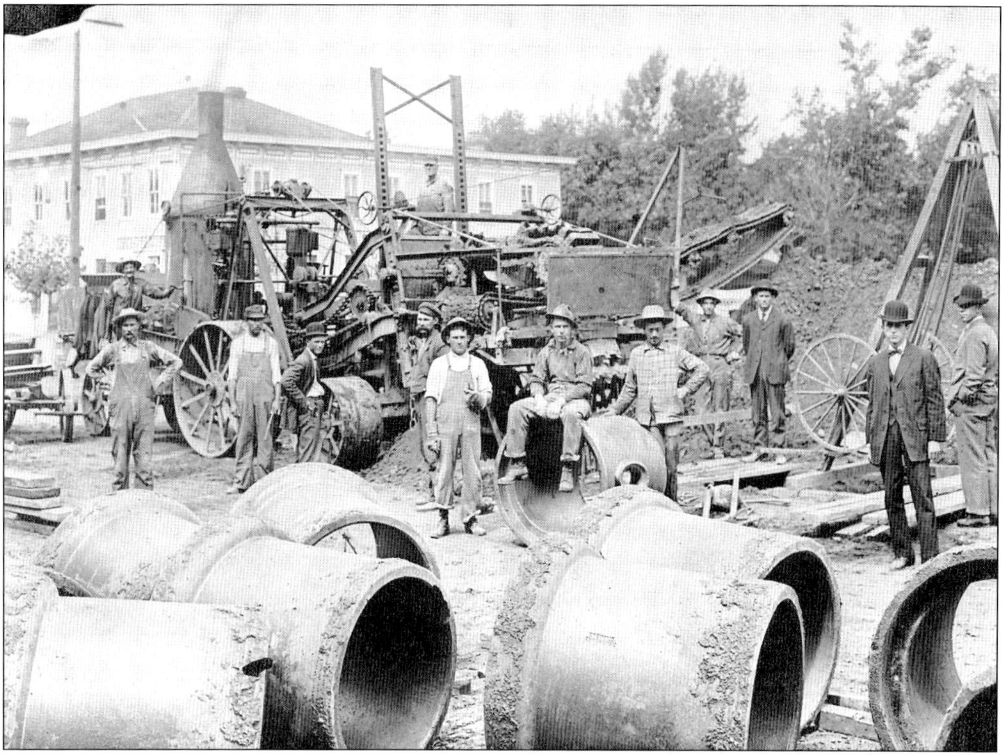

The first sewer in Huron, known as the Great Drain, was installed in 1883 in conjunction with the construction of the county courthouse. From the courthouse, located in the west part of the city, it ran east across town and ended just past Kansas Avenue. The area east of Kansas Avenue was a slough at the time.

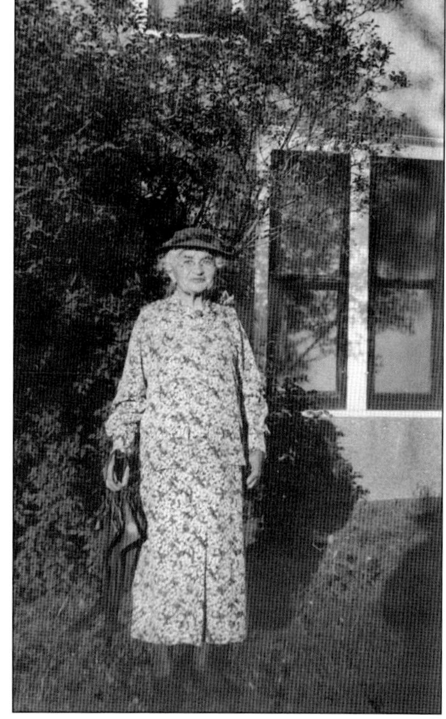

Medical practitioners have been part of Huron since before it was founded. A dentist was among those witnessing the driving of the first stake. Pictured here is Dr. Frieda Feige VanDalsem, the first woman doctor in Huron. She arrived in 1887 and set up an active homeopathic practice, which two of her sons later joined.

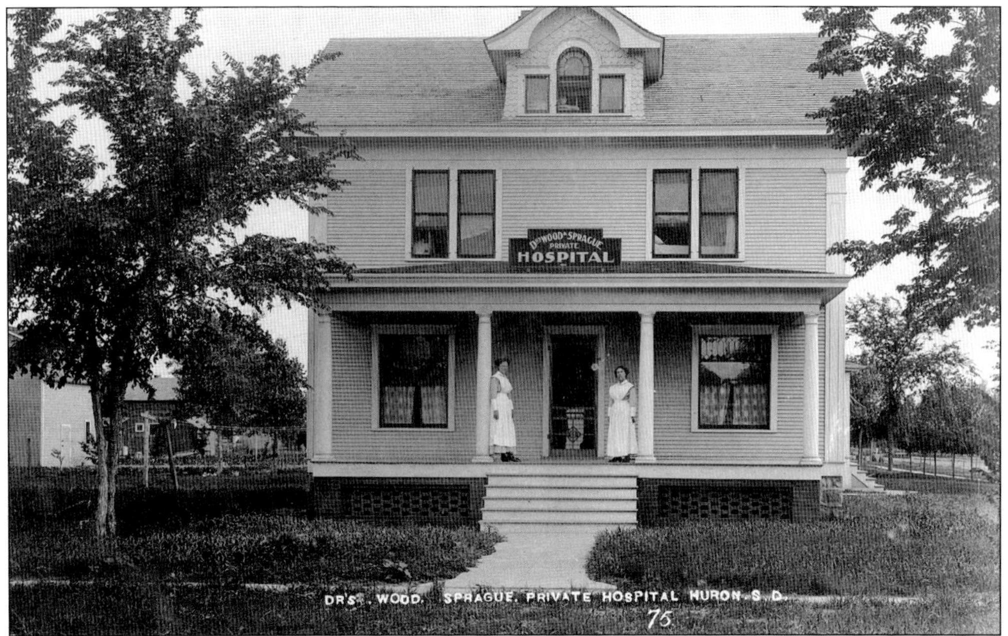

Dr. Tillson Wood practiced in Huron from the 1890s until 1953. Wood and Dr. B.H. Sprague opened the Huron Hospital, also known as the Wood Hospital, at 70 Seventh Street around 1908 with 10 beds. Nurses lived on the third floor, and the basement housed the kitchen and laundry. Eventually, this hospital was moved to a large house on Lawnridge Avenue between Fifth and Sixth Streets.

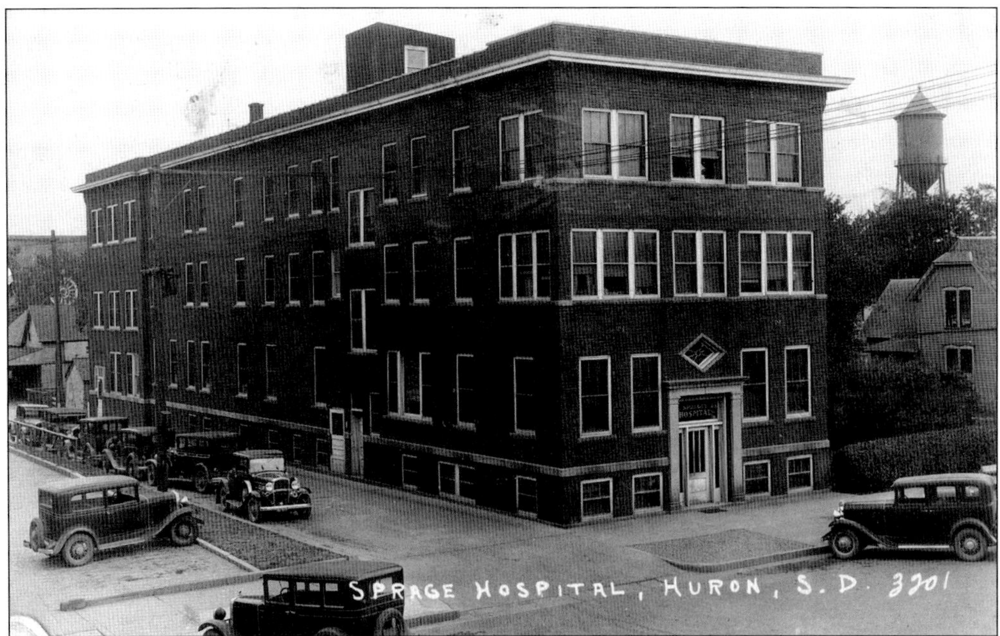

Dr. B.H. Sprague built the Sprague Hospital at 450 Dakota Avenue South in 1915. It could accommodate 57 patients. He added the Sprague School of Nursing in 1917 and opened a clinic in the hospital in 1922. When the hospital closed in 1947, the clinic moved to a new building at Fourth Street and Kansas Avenue and became the Huron Clinic. (Courtesy of Connie Green.)

Dr. John Tschetter, at right, converted the former John Campbell house at 720 Dakota Avenue South into a hospital in 1923. Samaritan Hospital contained 28 beds and an operating room. The third floor had rooms for the staff. He convinced his brothers Joe and Paul Tschetter and nephews Theodore and Paul Hohm, all doctors, to join him in organizing the Tschetter Hohm Clinic. It opened on June 1, 1945, in the Samaritan Hospital. The clinic remained there after the hospital closed in 1947 until a new building was completed at 455 Kansas Avenue. It opened on December 24, 1949, and closed in July 2022. (Both, courtesy of Huron Public Library.)

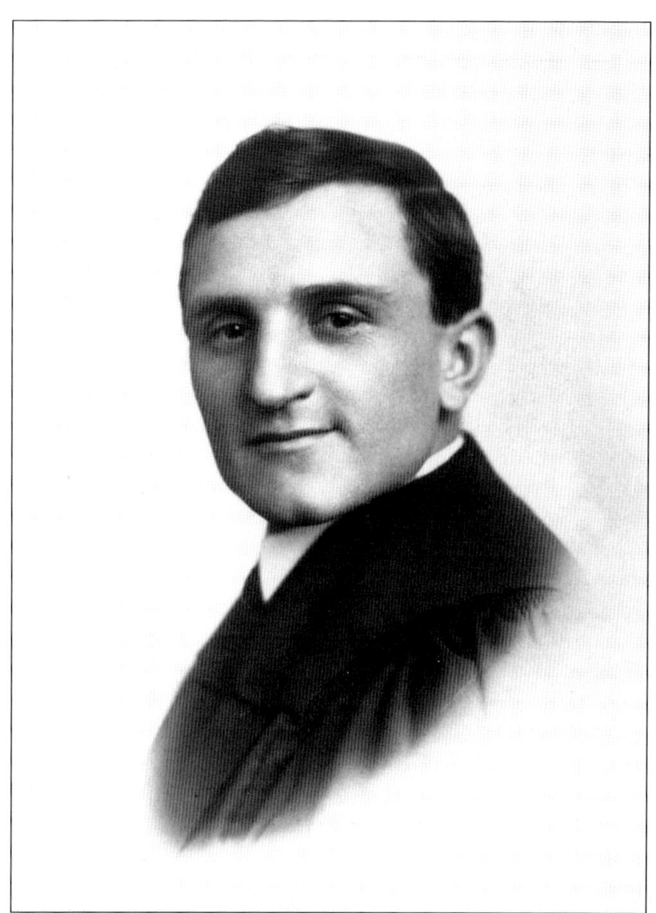

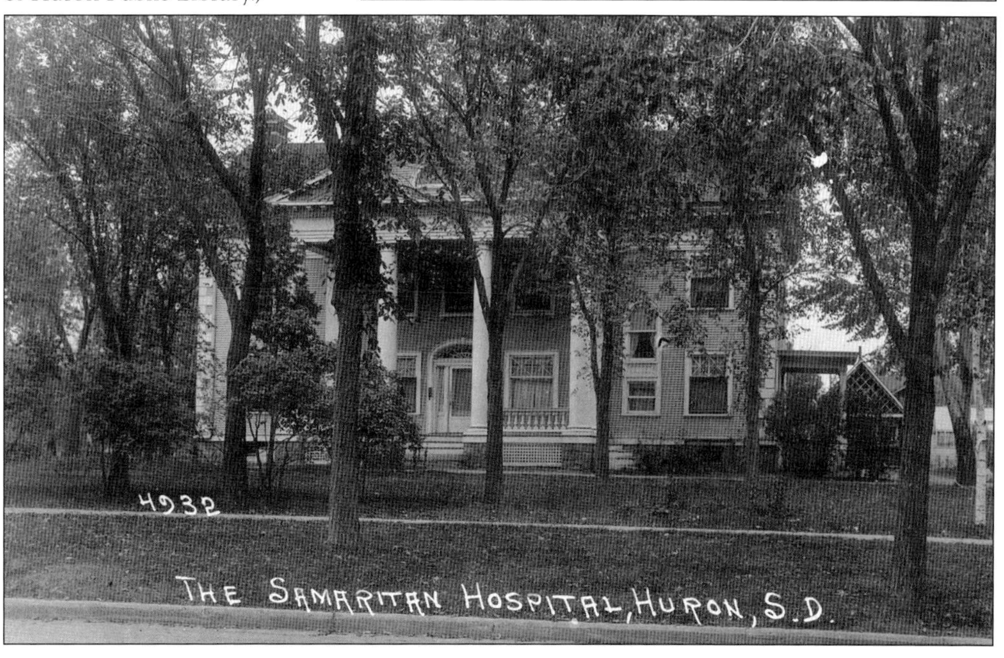

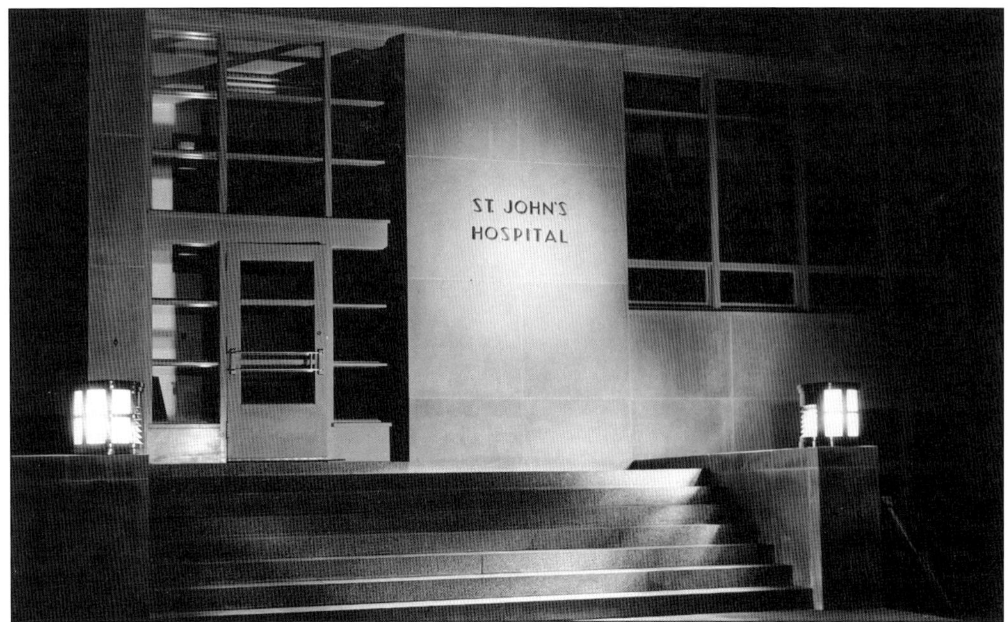

When St. John's Hospital opened on November 22, 1947, the other hospitals closed. St. John's had 150 beds and the latest equipment. It was also home to St. John's School of Nursing. It was maintained by the order of Franciscan Sisters for 30 years. It was purchased by a local nonprofit organization in 1977 and renamed Huron Regional Medical Center. It has expanded to encompass several specialty clinics and services. (Photograph by Sid Glanzer.)

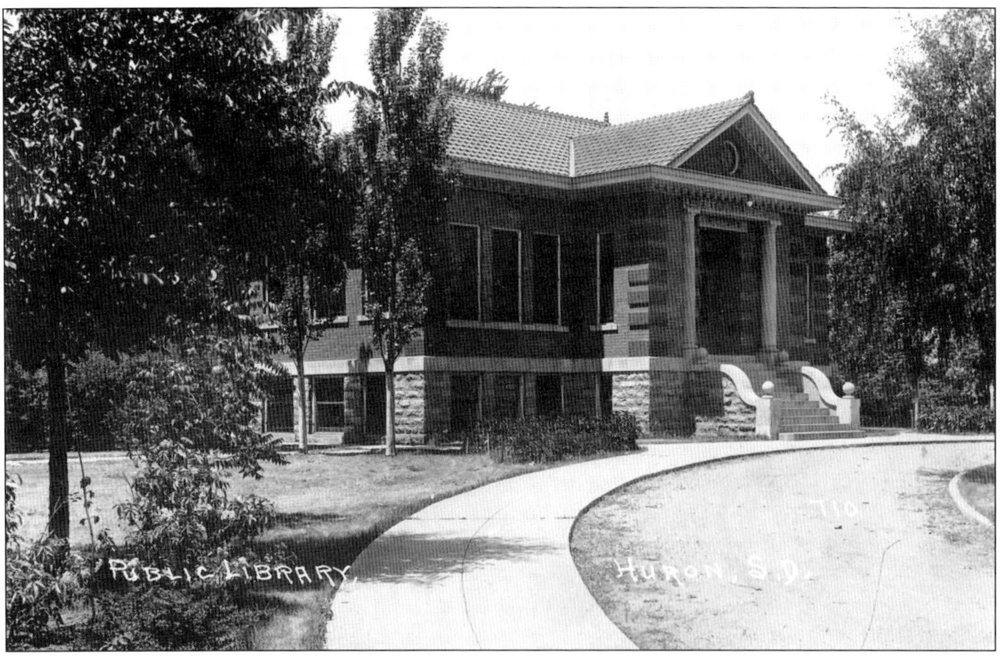

The Huron Public Library began as a reading room. As it grew, the community needed to find a permanent location. The city voted in 1907 to establish a Carnegie Library. It passed by only two votes. The north end of Campbell Park was chosen for the location, and the library opened in September 1909. It was razed and replaced with a new building in 1965.

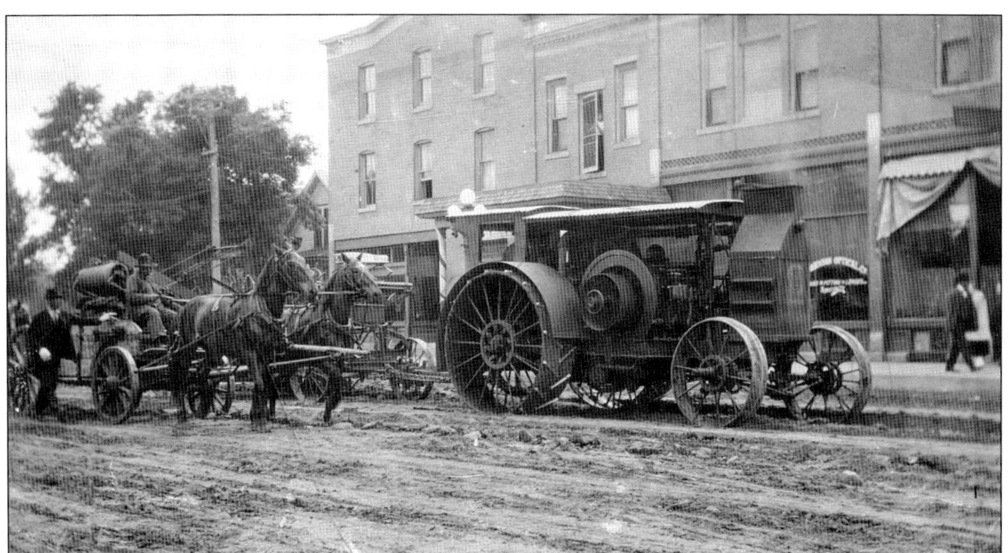

In 1916, Huron began to pave its streets. The photograph above, taken on July 16, shows a paving crew in front of Daum's Opera House. The photograph below shows a city street sweeper in the 1920s. Dan Wagner, standing, became city commissioner for street and public property in 1918. Running the sweeper is Harry Schaller. As roads improved, bus and truck usage increased. In 1930, commercial bus lines came to Huron. Well into the 1950s, Greyhound and Jack Rabbit Lines serviced Huron as well as a local intracity line called Huron City. Trucking firms could offer door-to-door service, and William Wilson began Wilson Forwarding in 1935. Moving operations followed in 1946 when Ellis Ross opened Huron Transfer and Storage as an agent of Allied Van Lines.

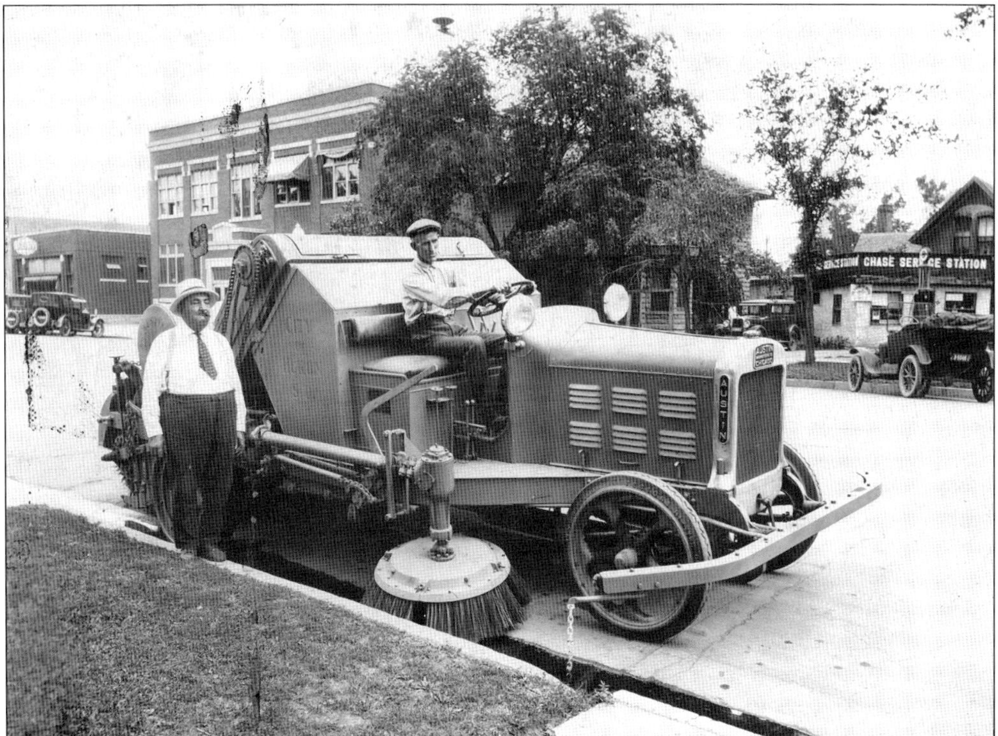

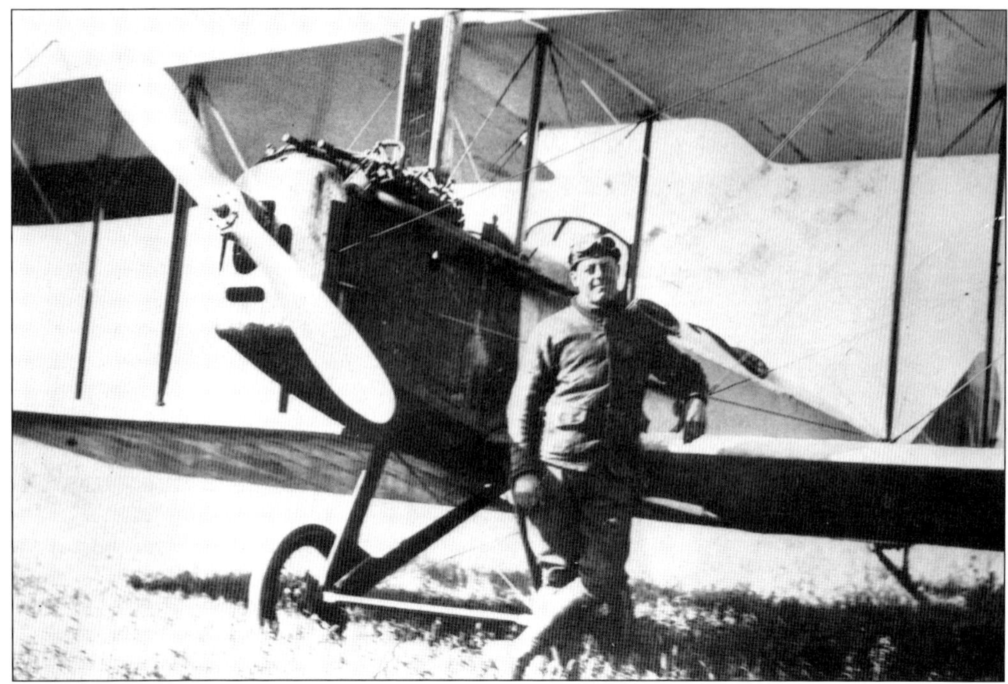

Airplanes came to Huron even earlier than buses. In June 1919, Aero Rapid Transit was formed with Clyde Ice becoming the first pilot to fly mail and passengers to and from Huron. The following year, its name was changed to Huron Aerial Rapid Transit. The first airfield was at the fairgrounds on Ninth Street. By 1921, Huron had built Mayer's Field south of the fairgrounds. (Courtesy of Huron Regional Airport.)

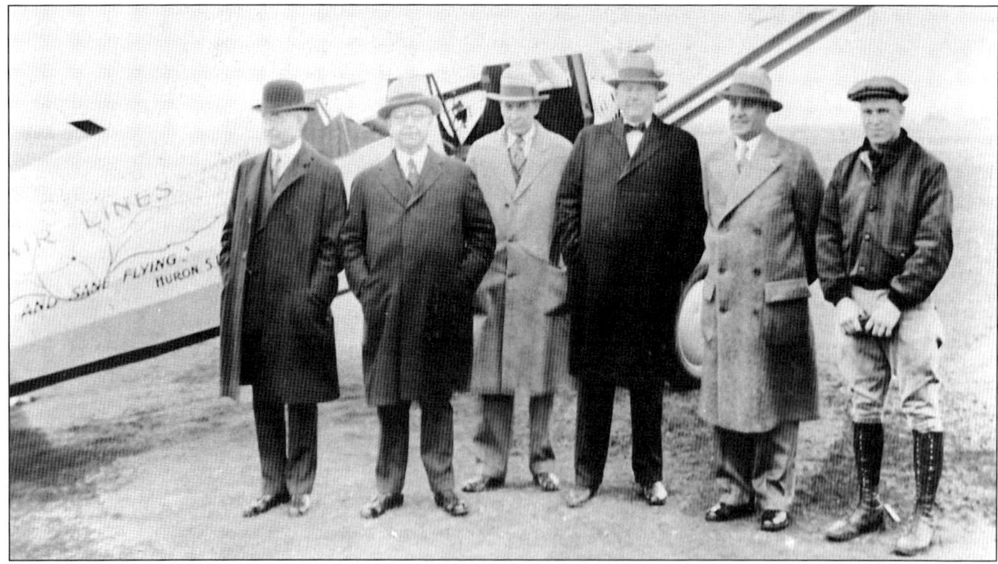

In 1928, the airport north of Huron was completed with four runways. Rapid Airlines began daily passenger service to Rapid City. Shown minutes before the inaugural flight on May 1, 1929, are, from left to right, W.R. Leahy, Chicago; H.J. Wagen, Winona, Minnesota; C.J. Heyman, Huron; Huron mayor Don Madbery; T.B. Prew, Huron; and pilot Ed Hefley. Flight time was 3 hours and 30 minutes, while the train took 10 hours and 30 minutes. (Courtesy of Huron Regional Airport.)

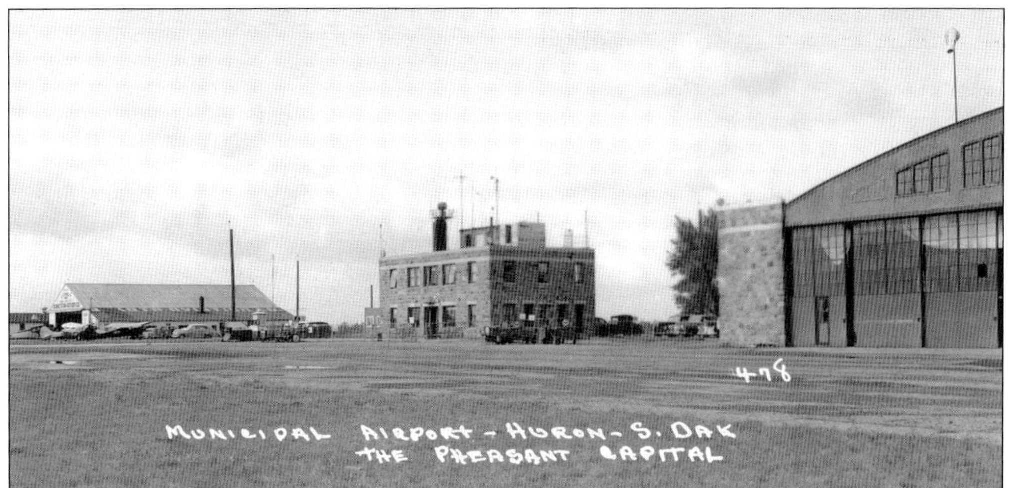

In 1934, the Works Progress Administration instructed the Civilian Conservation Corps to begin work on a hangar constructed of fieldstone at a cost of $67,000. A combined terminal and administrative building, repair shop, and improved runways completed the project. Hanford Airlines, based in Sioux Falls, began scheduled passenger service to Huron on July 3, 1934. (Courtesy of Jennifer Littlefield.)

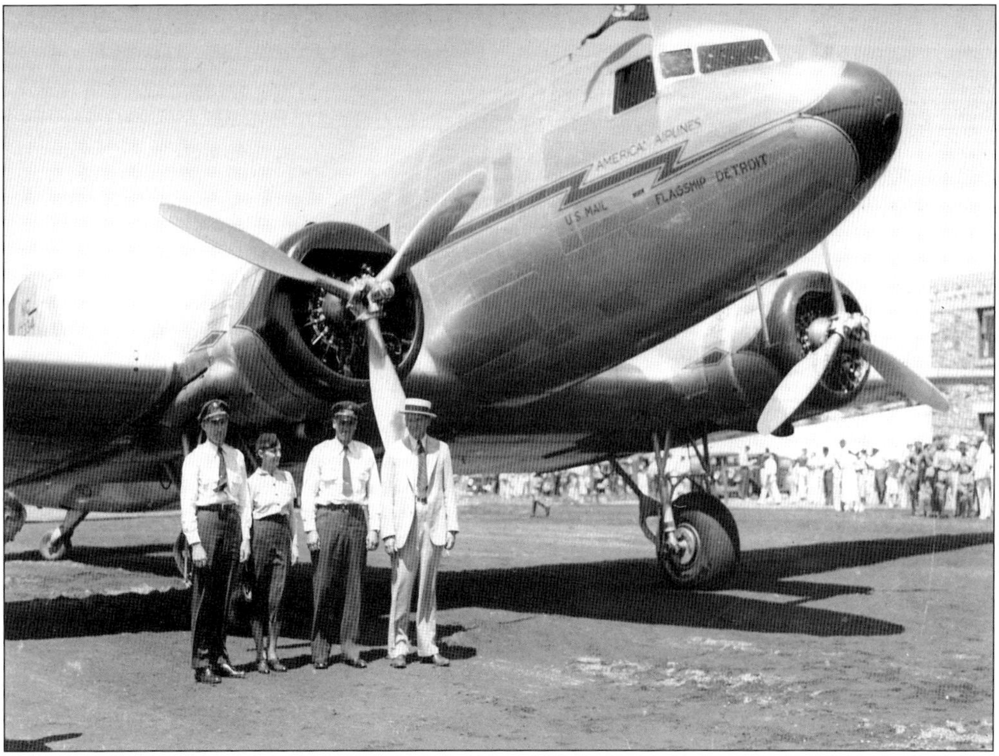

The W.W. Howes Municipal Airport was dedicated on July 5, 1935. Part of the festivities included this American Airlines aircraft and flight crew. The airport was named in honor of a Huron attorney and avid aviation enthusiast who was appointed assistant postmaster general by Pres. Franklin Roosevelt. The main speaker at the ceremony was Capt. Eddie Rickenbacker, the most successful flying ace in World War I.

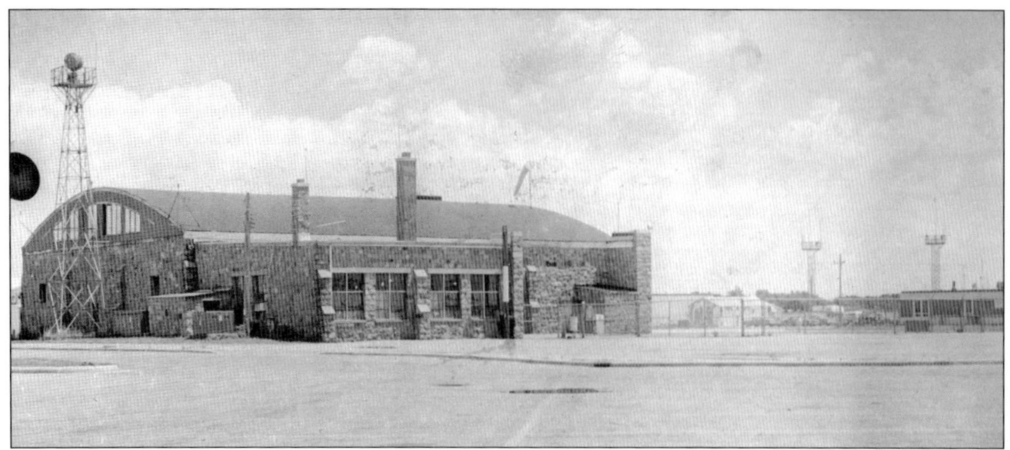

Thomas Ryan purchased Hanford Airlines in 1937. He moved the headquarters to Huron when the US Bureau of Commerce directed the airline to discontinue service at all airports in South Dakota except Huron's, the only facility it considered safe. Huron quickly became the hub of east-west and north-south air travel and had the only passenger service in the state for a considerable length of time. (Courtesy of Huron Regional Airport.)

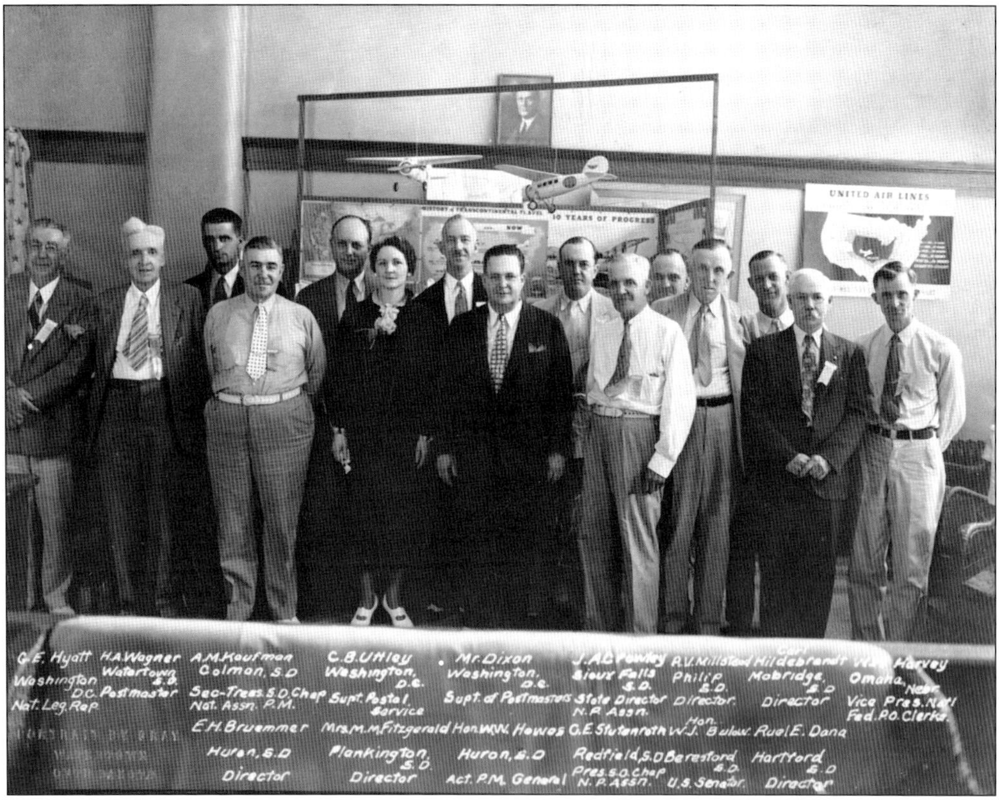

The US Postal Service instituted Air Mail as a special class of mail in 1937. Those attending the inaugural ceremony held at Huron included three postal dignitaries from Washington, DC, a US senator, the vice president of the National Federation of Post Office Clerks from Omaha, and representatives from 10 South Dakota post offices. All Air Mail for the state was routed through Huron.

By 1940, Huron Flying Service was the oldest and largest service in the state. It was awarded a government contract to train military pilots 30 at a time. Later known as Dakota Aviation, it became the leading Aeronca dealer in America, selling 46 new aircraft in the first six months of 1948. Crop spraying began in 1946 when Aerial Weed Control was formed by Bill Hebron.

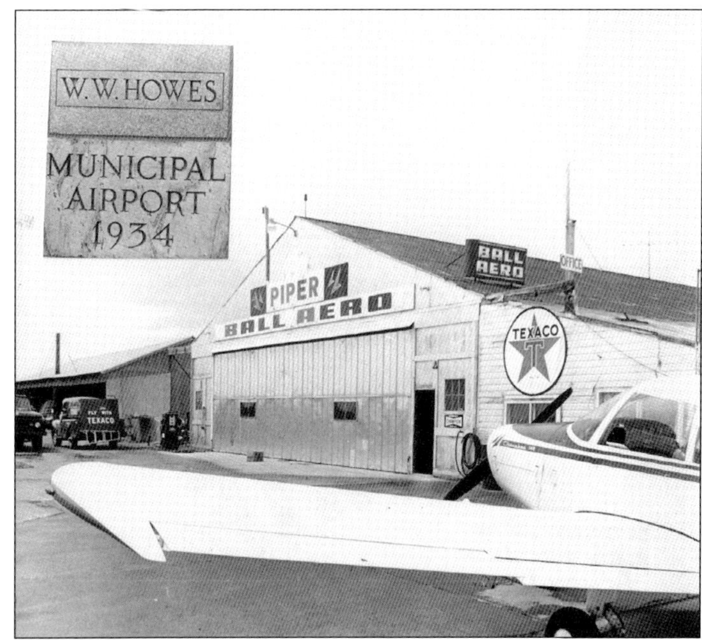

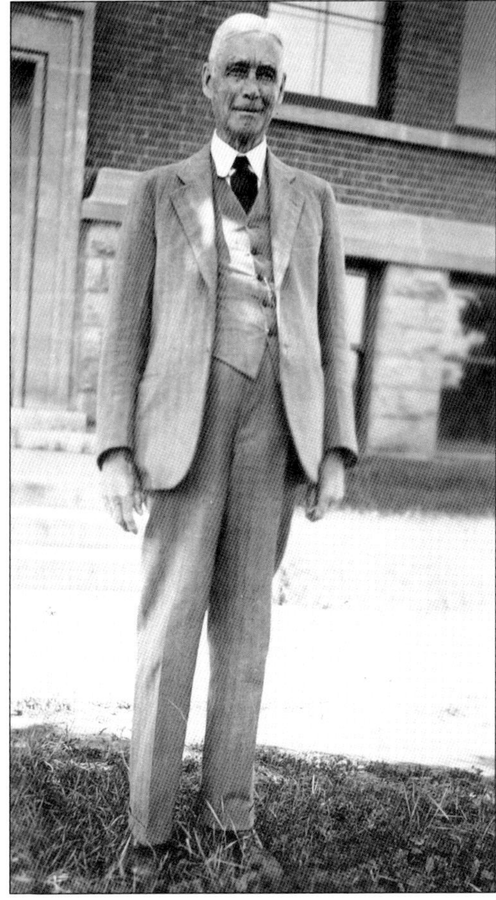

Coe Crawford moved to Huron in 1897. He was a member of the first South Dakota state senate and served as attorney general. He was elected governor in 1906, the sixth to hold that office, and then to the US Senate in 1910. After returning home, he continued his law practice and served as a trustee of Huron College. (Courtesy of Huron College.)

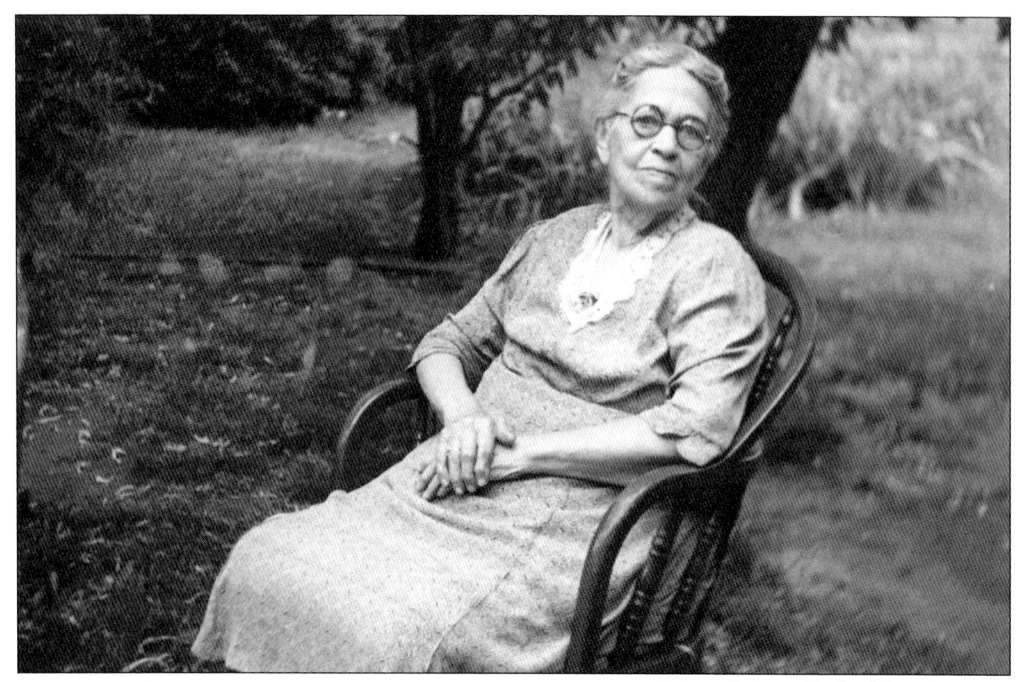

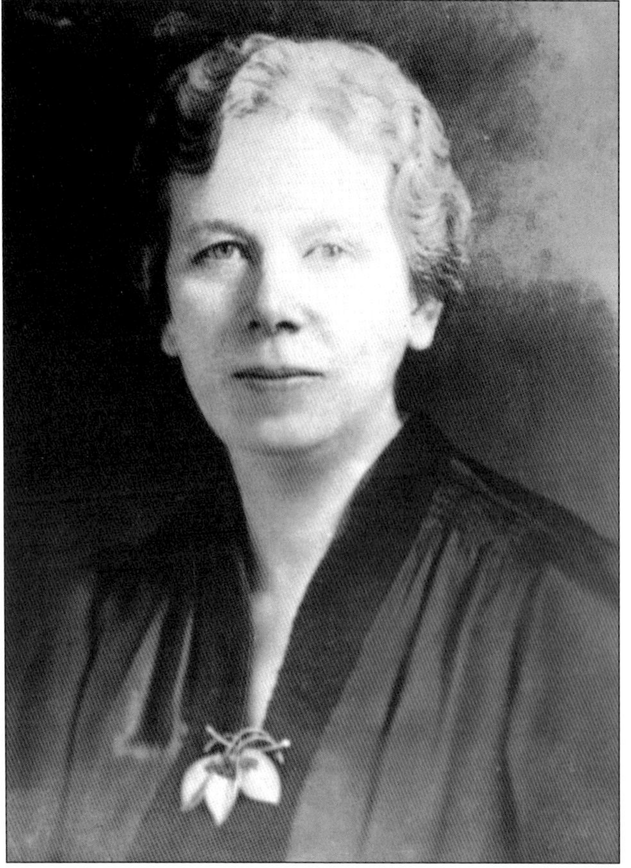

Mary "Mamie" Shields Pyle was a key player in South Dakota's suffrage movement. She was instrumental in getting the vote for women in 1918 and the 19th Amendment ratified in South Dakota. She was president of the S.D. Universal Franchise League, which became the League of Women Voters, from 1910 to 1920. She was the first woman in the United States to be a presidential elector in 1922.

Gladys Pyle was the daughter of Mamie and John L. Pyle. As a woman, she achieved many firsts in the state. She was elected to the state legislature (1923–1927), appointed deputy secretary of state, and then elected secretary of state. She went on to become the first woman in the United States to be elected to the US Senate in 1938.

Huron resident Lydia Larsen became the first woman sheriff in South Dakota when she was elected on November 2, 1926, in Beadle County. She defeated two male opponents by a large majority. Prior to this, she was the jailer. Five masked men executed a daylight robbery of the Farmers and Merchants Bank on June 8, 1927. Larsen tracked down and arrested the men two weeks later in St. Paul.

A person instrumental in the building of Huron was architect Frank Charles William Kuehn. He was responsible for designing many of the early structures around town, including the acoustically excellent bandshell located at the south end of Campbell Park, the original city hall, and the Lyric Theatre, which stood downtown on Dakota Avenue. He was well known for designing schools throughout South Dakota.

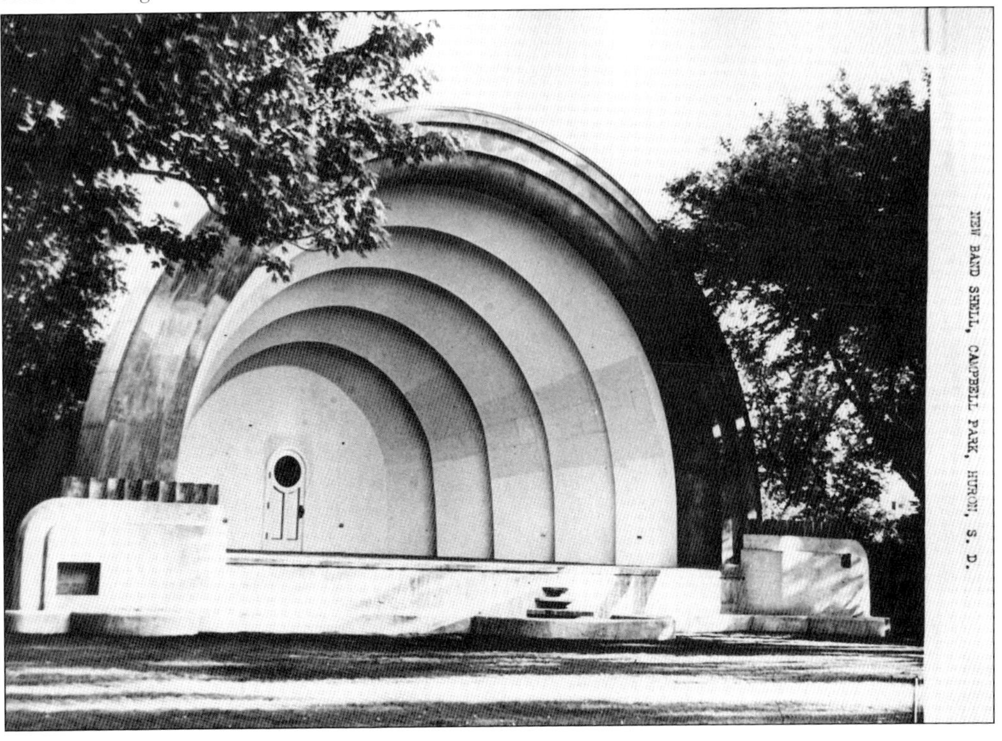

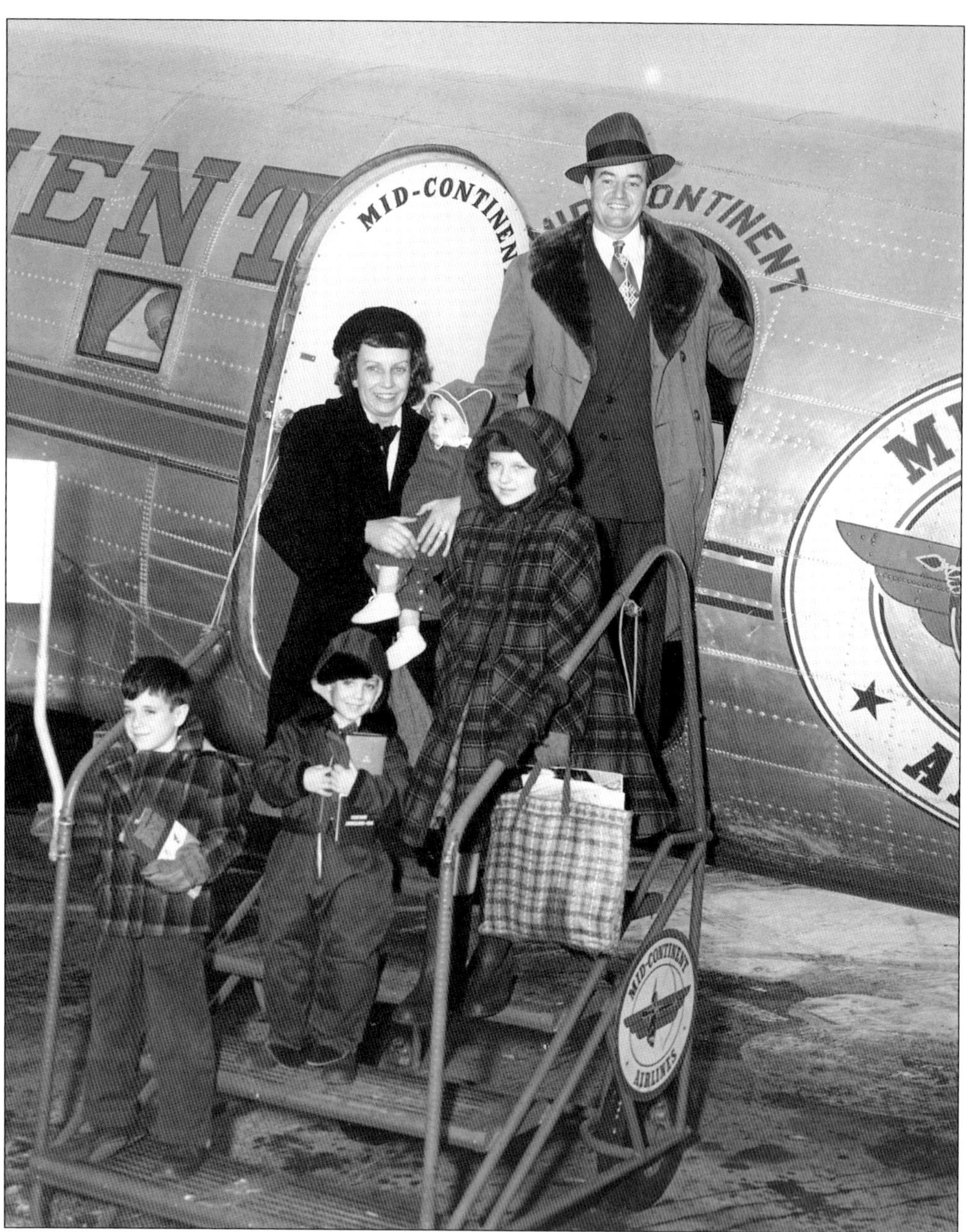

Hubert and Muriel Humphrey with their family are shown here during a visit to Huron. Hubert H. Humphrey Jr. rose to the office of vice president of the United States. He grew up in Huron working as a pharmacist in the family business, Humphrey Drug Store. After moving to Minneapolis, he began his political career, first as mayor, then as US senator, and finally as vice president from 1965 to 1969. He returned to the Senate in 1976. Huron native Muriel Buck married Hubert Humphrey in 1936. She became the second woman US senator to come from Huron when she was sworn into office in 1978 to complete her husband's term after his death. She is the only second lady of the United States to ever serve in the Senate, and Huron may be the only city in the nation to have two women senators.

Three

Building a Community

Construction of businesses downtown began as soon as the Chicago & Northwestern Railroad tracks were built across the James River. With a population of 164 in 1880, business on Dakota Avenue consisted of a store, restaurant, pool hall, saloon, and livery barn. During this time, a building lot could be purchased for less than $1. Many of these early buildings were brought in from other locations because new construction materials were costly and difficult to obtain. Early settlers braved blizzards, fire, and a shortage of food, water, and supplies to establish Huron.

Fortunately, Huron's location put the city in a beneficial economic position within the state. Located in the center of Beadle County, Huron was easily accessible from all directions. Being a railroad hub meant products were quickly and easily shipped across the state and to large cities like Minneapolis, Chicago, and Omaha.

Huron soon attracted manufacturers and wholesale distributors. Great quantities of meat, dairy, and poultry were shipped around the region first by railroad, then by trucks. Large companies like Standard Oil Company, Armour and Company, and Swift and Company designated Huron as their regional headquarters and distribution centers. These industries employed hundreds of people and invested millions of dollars in the development of the community.

The retail market also benefited from Huron's location. In 1928, there were 109 retail businesses in the downtown area. Department stores such as J.C. Penney, Gambles, Sears, and Montgomery Ward established stores here. Products were readily available, and the variety attracted shoppers from all over the eastern side of the state.

Huron saw tremendous growth and prosperity during the first half of the 20th century. The various forms of transportation made Huron highly accessible, which brought the community more products, lower prices, and increased profits. The businesses in turn invested their profits into helping build the community that Huron is today. The photographs in this chapter are a small fraction of the businesses in operation before 1950.

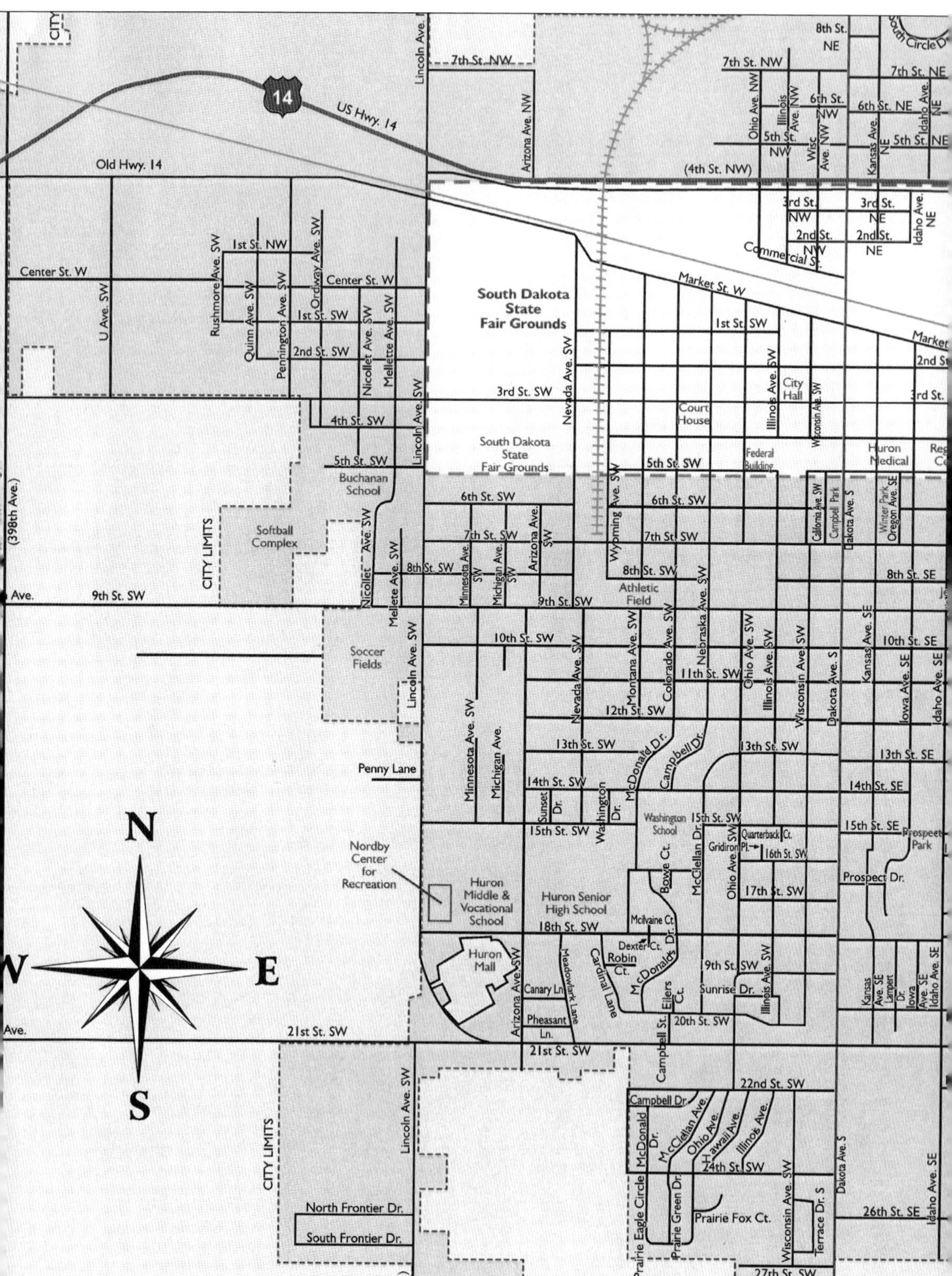

14
US Hwy. 14
Old Hwy. 14
7th St. NW
Lincoln Ave.
Arizona Ave. NW
8th St. NE
South Circle Dr.
7th St. NW
7th St. NE
Ohio Ave. NW
Illinois Ave. NW
6th St. NW
6th St. NE
Idaho Ave. NE
5th St. NW
Wisc. Ave. NW
Kansas Ave. NE
5th St. NE
(4th St. NW)
3rd St. NW
3rd St. NE
Idaho Ave. NE
2nd St. NW
2nd St. NE
Commercial St.
Market St. W
Market
1st St. NW
Center St. W
Center St. SW
U Ave. SW
Rushmore Ave. SW
Quinn Ave. SW
Ordway Ave. SW
Pennington Ave. SW
1st St. SW
2nd St. SW
Nicollet Ave. SW
Mellette Ave. SW
South Dakota State Fair Grounds
Nevada Ave. SW
1st St. SW
2nd St.
3rd St. SW
Lincoln Ave. SW
3rd St.
City Hall
Illinois Ave. SW
Wisconsin Ave. SW
Court House
4th St. SW
5th St. SW
South Dakota State Fair Grounds
5th St. SW
Federal Building
Huron Medical
Buchanan School
6th St. SW
6th St. SW
California Ave. SW
Campbell Park
Dakota Ave. S
Winter Park Oregon Ave. SE
(398th Ave.)
Softball Complex
CITY LIMITS
Nicollet Ave. SW
7th St. SW
Wyoming Ave. SW
7th St. SW
Arizona Ave. SW
Mellete Ave. SW
8th St. SW
Minnesota Ave. SW
Michigan Ave. SW
8th St. SW
8th St. SE
Athletic Field
Nebraska Ave. SW
Ave.
9th St. SW
9th St. SW
Soccer Fields
Lincoln Ave. SW
10th St. SW
Montana Ave. SW
Colorado Ave. SW
Ohio Ave. SW
Illinois Ave. SW
Wisconsin Ave. SW
Kansas Ave. SE
10th St. SE
Nevada Ave. SW
11th St. SW
Dakota Ave. S
Iowa Ave. SE
Idaho Ave. SE
12th St. SW
Minnesota Ave. SW
Michigan Ave.
13th St. SW
McDonald Dr.
Campbell Dr.
13th St. SW
13th St. SE
Penny Lane
14th St. SW
Washington Dr.
McDonald Dr.
14th St. SE
Sunset Dr.
Washington School
15th St. SW
15th St. SE
Prospect Park
15th St. SW
Quarterback Ct.
Gridiron Pl.
16th St. SW
Ohio Ave. SW
Bowe Ct.
McClellan Dr.
Nordby Center for Recreation
Huron Middle & Vocational School
Huron Senior High School
17th St. SW
Prospect Dr.
18th St. SW
McIlvaine Ct.
Dexter Ct.
N
Huron Mall
Arizona Ave. SW
Meadowlark Lane
Cardinal Lane
Robin Ct.
McDonald's Dr.
19th St. SW
Illinois Ave. SW
W
E
Canary Ln.
Eilers Ct.
Sunrise Dr.
Kansas Ave. SE
Lampert Dr.
Iowa Ave. SE
Idaho Ave. SE
Pheasant Ln.
Campbell St.
20th St. SW
Ave.
21st St. SW
21st St. SW
S
Lincoln Ave. SW
22nd St. SW
Campbell Dr.
McDonald Dr.
McClellan Ave.
Ohio Ave.
Hawaii Ave.
Illinois Ave.
CITY LIMITS
24th St. SW
Dakota Ave. S
Idaho Ave. SE
Prairie Eagle Circle
Prairie Green Dr.
Wisconsin Ave. SW
Terrace Dr. S
North Frontier Dr.
Prairie Fox Ct.
26th St. SE
South Frontier Dr.
27th St. SW

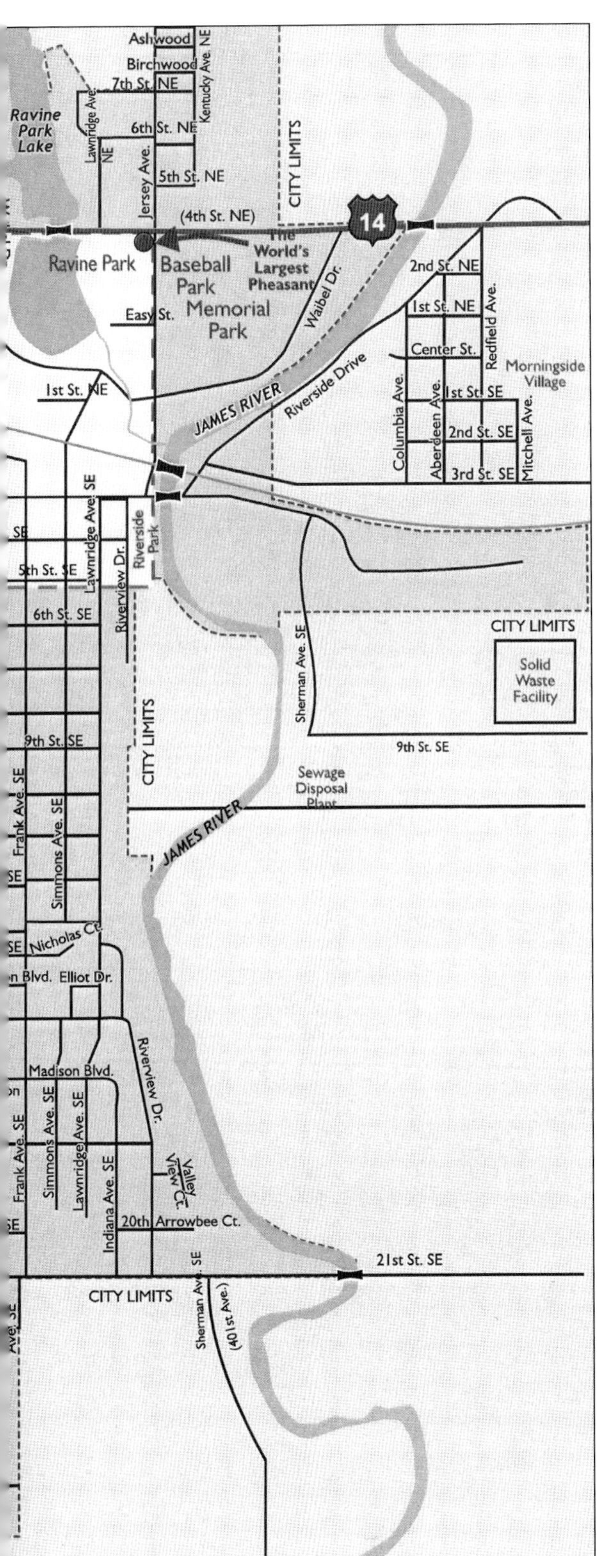

The Huron Chamber and Visitors Bureau provided this 2023 map showing the city's current boundaries. The majority of the businesses referred to in this chapter can be found near Dakota Avenue, running north and south in the middle of the page, and Third Street, running east and west toward the top of the page.

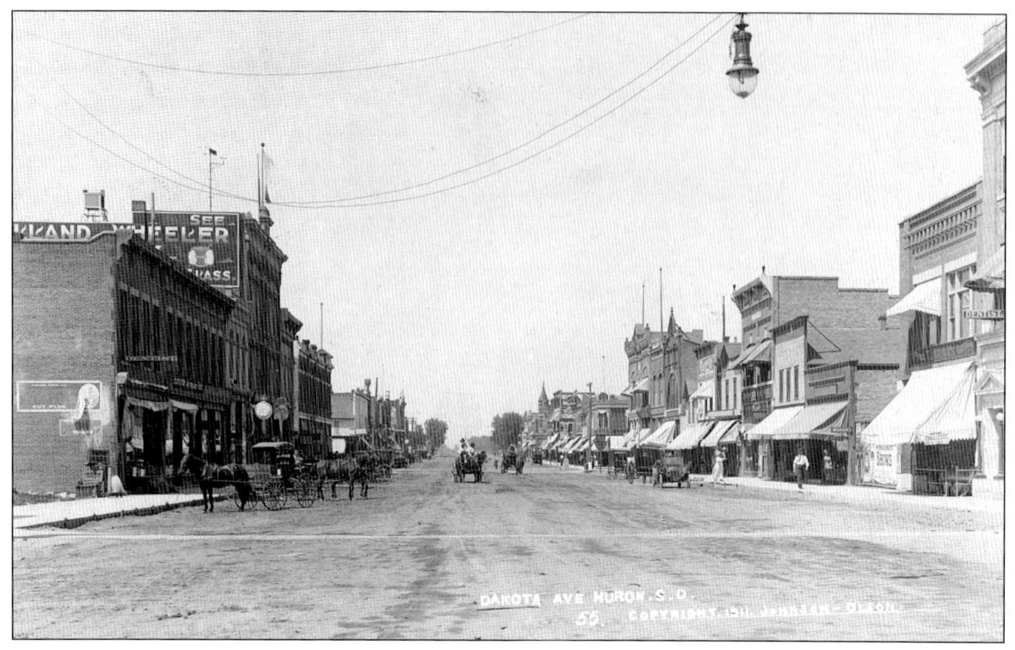

Dakota Avenue was one of the first streets established in Huron. It started as four blocks running north and south and steadily expanded as the city grew. The above photograph from 1911 shows Dakota Avenue from Fourth Street looking north. Businesses in this section of downtown included the National Bank of Huron, T.J. Curry Clothier, Costain Brothers Music Store, Smith Jewelry Company, Olson Clothiers, and Waibel Hardware. The photograph below was taken from Third Street in 1937. The National Bank and Costain Brothers Music Store are still there along with several new stores, including Red Owl and Humphrey's Drug Store.

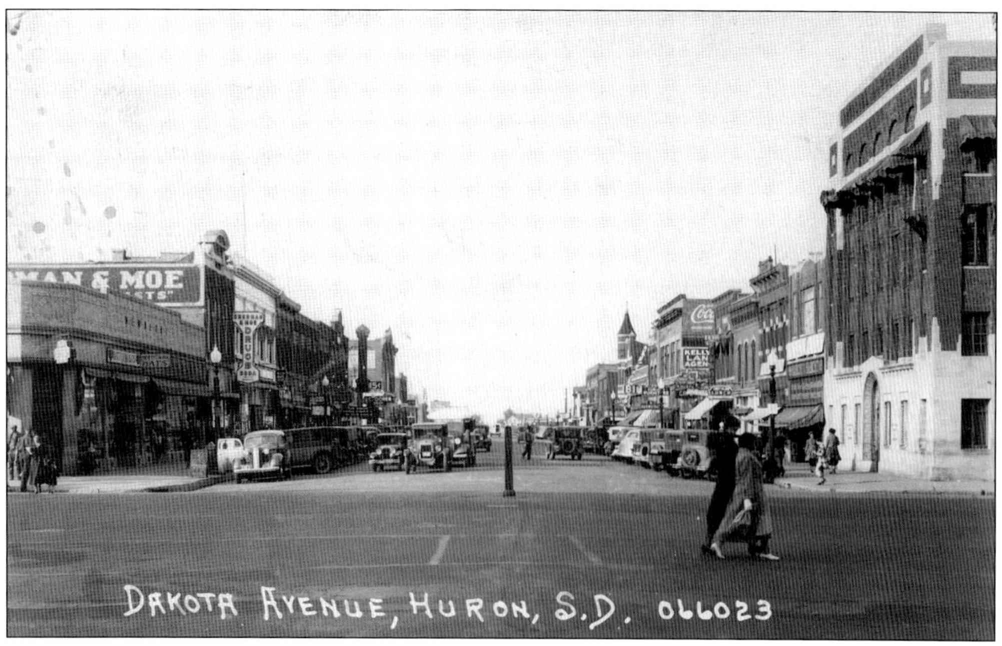

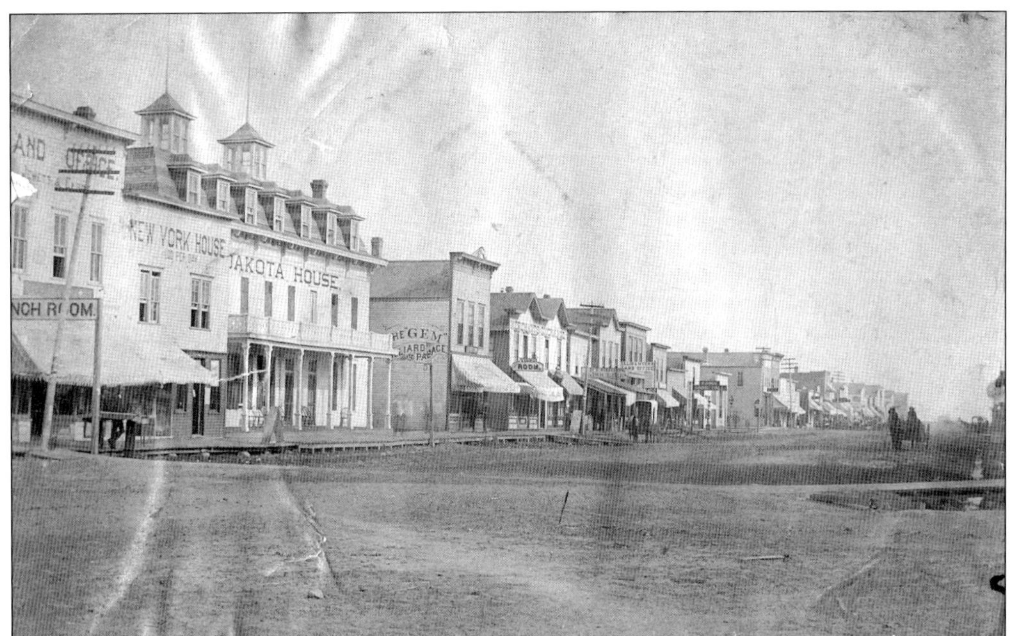

Among the first buildings erected in Huron was the Dakota House on the 100 block of Dakota Avenue. Michael Dinneen bought the building in 1880 and operated the hotel until the 1930s. This early photograph shows the Dakota House on the left. Several doors down is a billiard parlor called the Gem and multiple signs advertising rooms for rent.

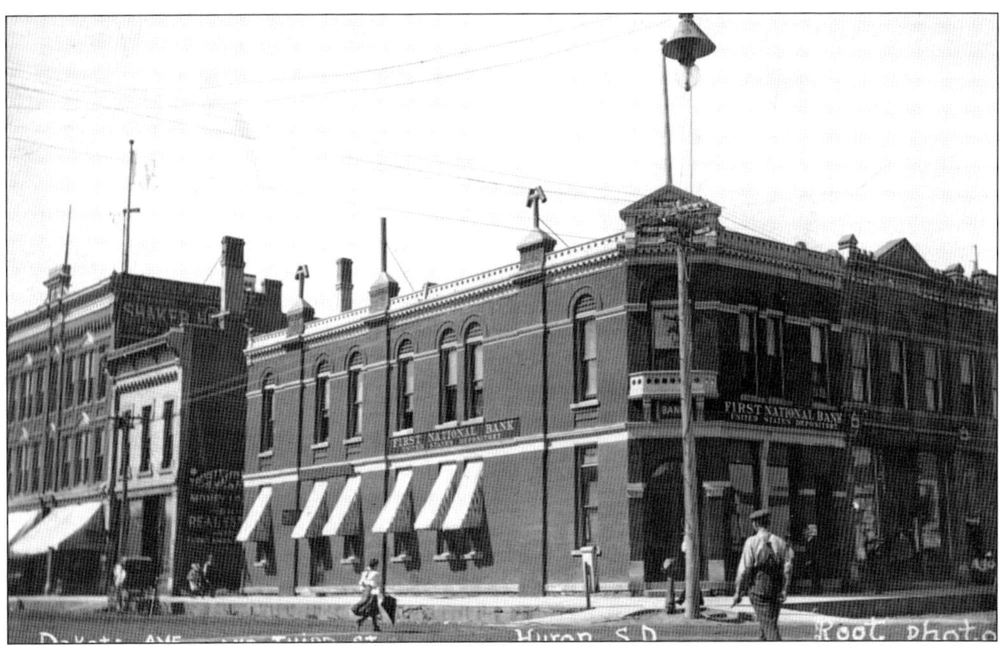

The first brick building constructed in Huron was the First National Bank, which opened in 1881. John W. Campbell was the owner and bank president. The building was located at the corner of Dakota Avenue and Third Street. The bank was temporarily used as a school and a meeting place for the Congregational church until additional buildings were constructed.

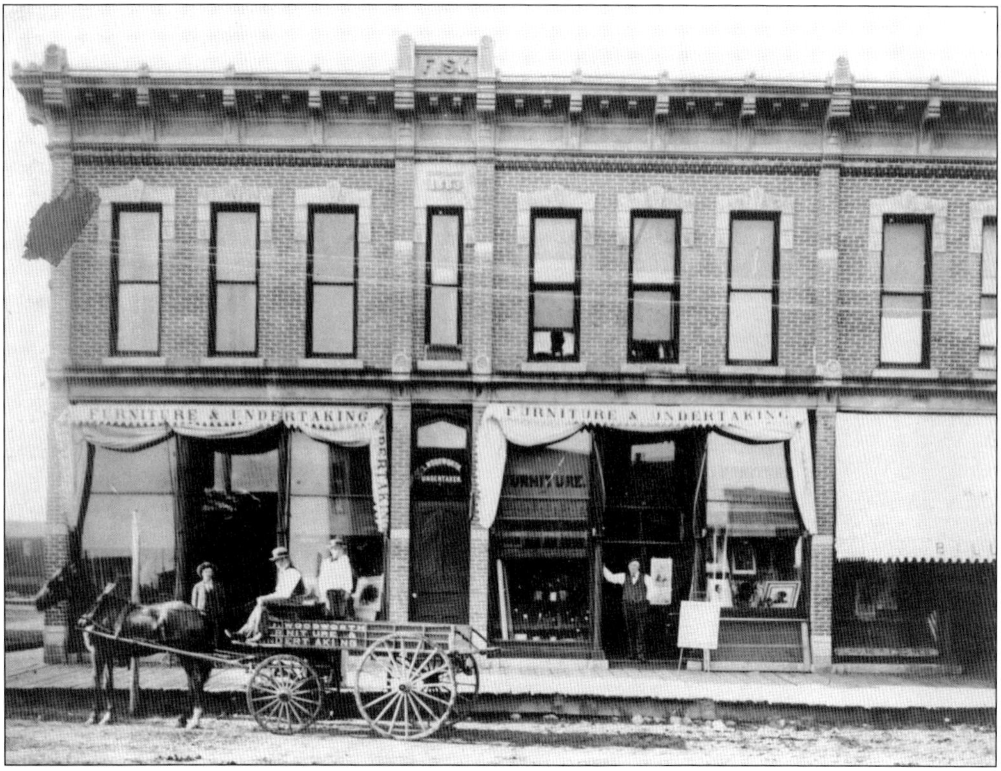

Leonard Woodworth was a veteran of the Civil War. He brought his family to Huron in 1882. Using money from his veteran's pension, Woodworth started a business as an undertaker and furniture salesman. The store was located in the Fisk building on Third Street and Wisconsin Avenue. Here he is standing in front of his store with three of his sons in 1900.

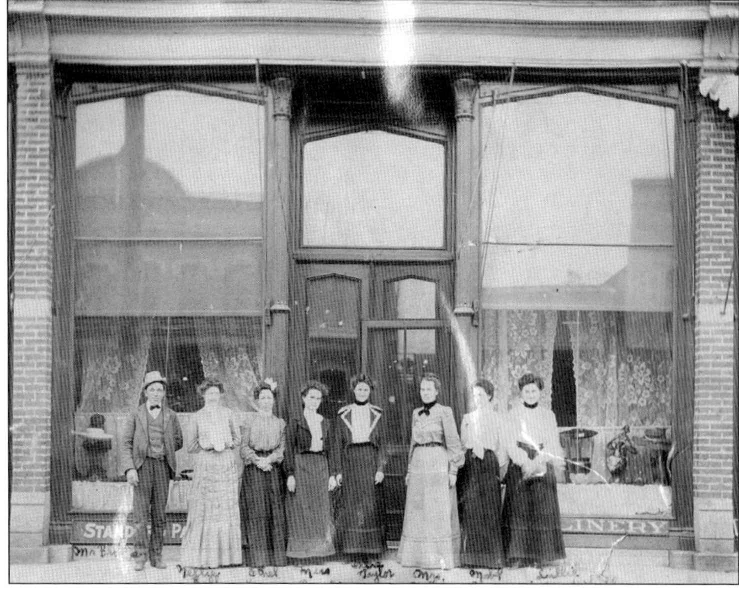

Ellen Dickey's millinery store was located on the north side of Third Street between Dakota Avenue and Wisconsin Avenue. This photograph from 1900 shows the women who worked in the store. From left to right are George Browne, Nellie Bell, Ethel Kenyon, Elizabeth Boughton, Ollie Taylor, Ellen Dickey, Mabel Moyer, and Lillie Underhill. (Courtesy of Huron Public Library.)

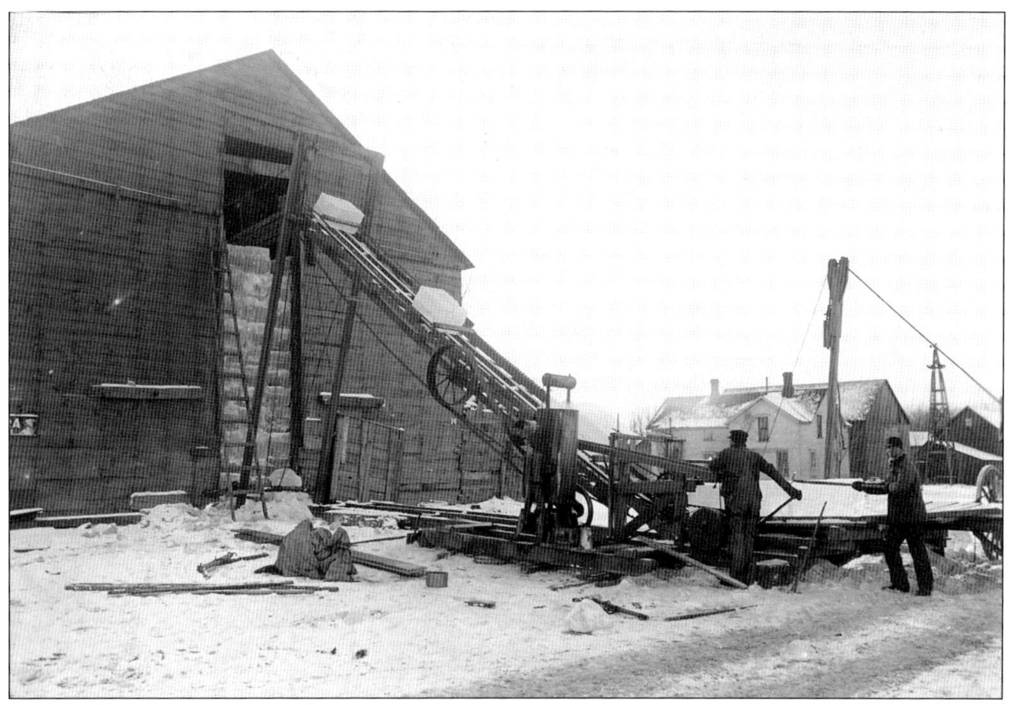

The Holton brothers started Huron Ice Company in 1888. Before refrigeration, blocks of ice were cut from the James River and used to preserve and transport food. Fred Holton is seen here operating a conveyor belt to move ice into the icehouse for storage. At one time, Huron had 14 icehouses, including those owned by the railroad.

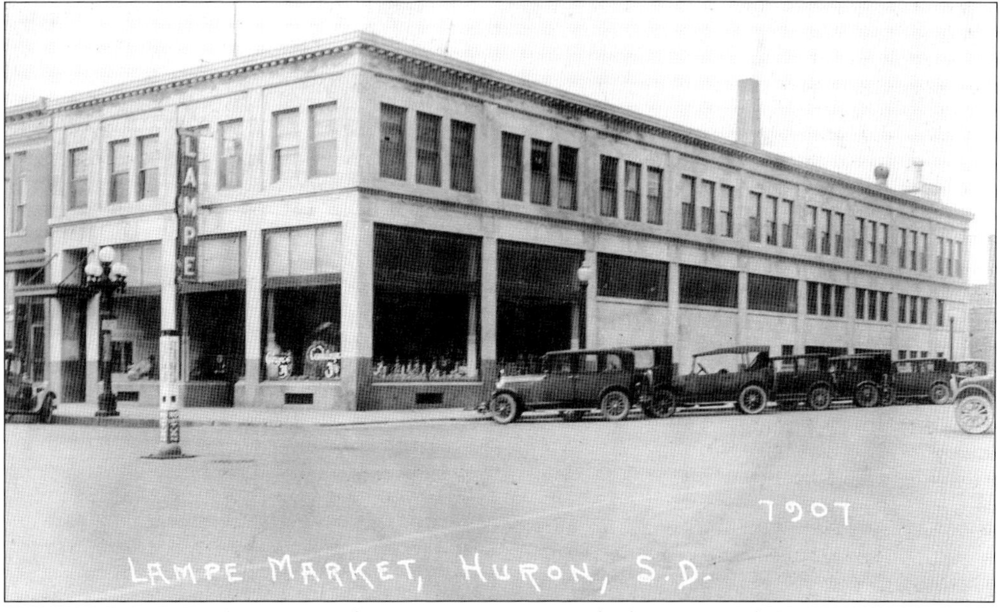

Albert Lampe opened a meat market in 1889, operating the business with his five sons. In 1927, the business moved to a larger location on the corner of Fourth Street and Dakota Avenue near the Marvin Hughitt Hotel. The Lampe family raised livestock and processed the meat to sell in their store.

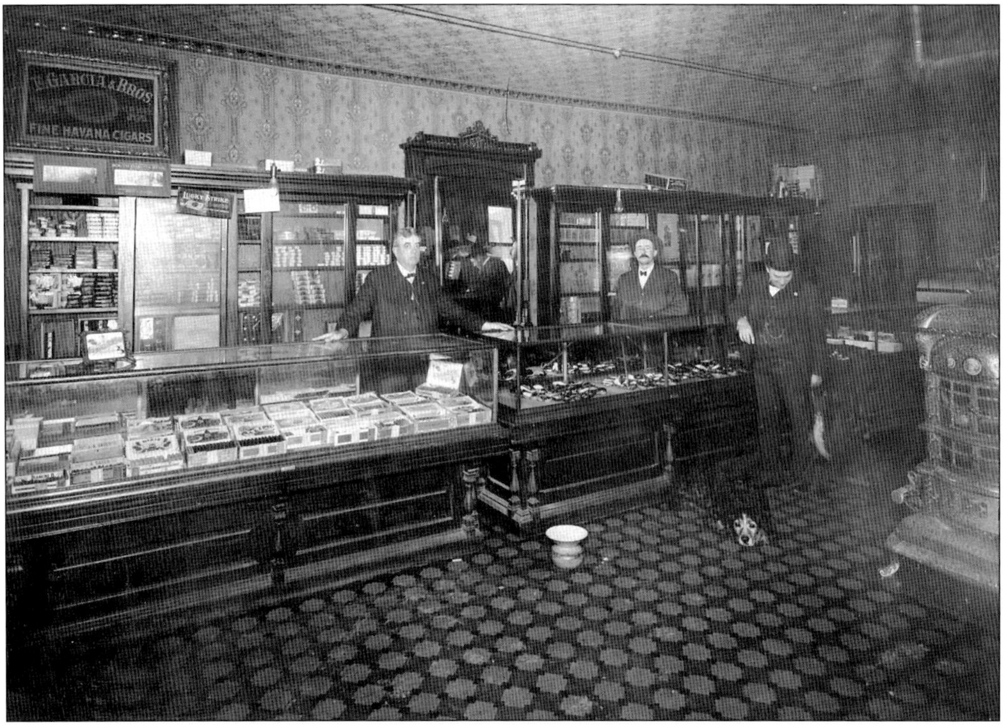

John Sauer's cigar factory was one of the first industries established in Huron. By 1900, it was the largest cigar manufacturing company in South Dakota. Sauer employed 60 people, sold one million cigars a year, and had salesmen in four states. He operated the company until he retired in 1934. The photograph above shows Sauer and Ed Barrett standing behind the counter in the Huron Store. The wagon in the photograph below is loaded with 30,000 cigars ready to be delivered across South Dakota. Sauer's cigars were hand-rolled using the best tobacco. His most popular brands were Our Best, Commandery, Fair City, and South Dakota Star. (Above, courtesy of Huron Public Library.)

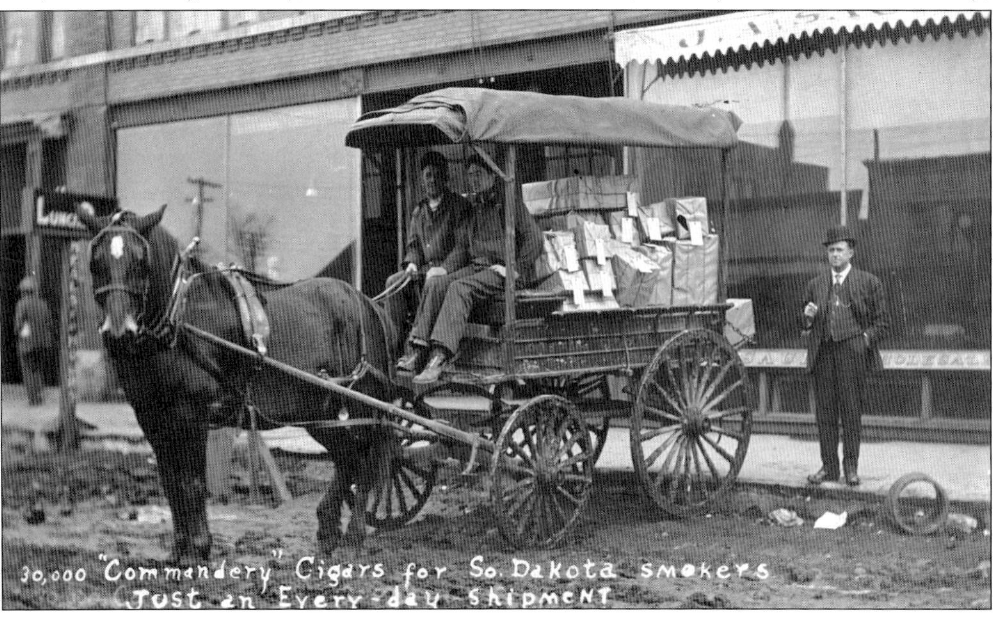

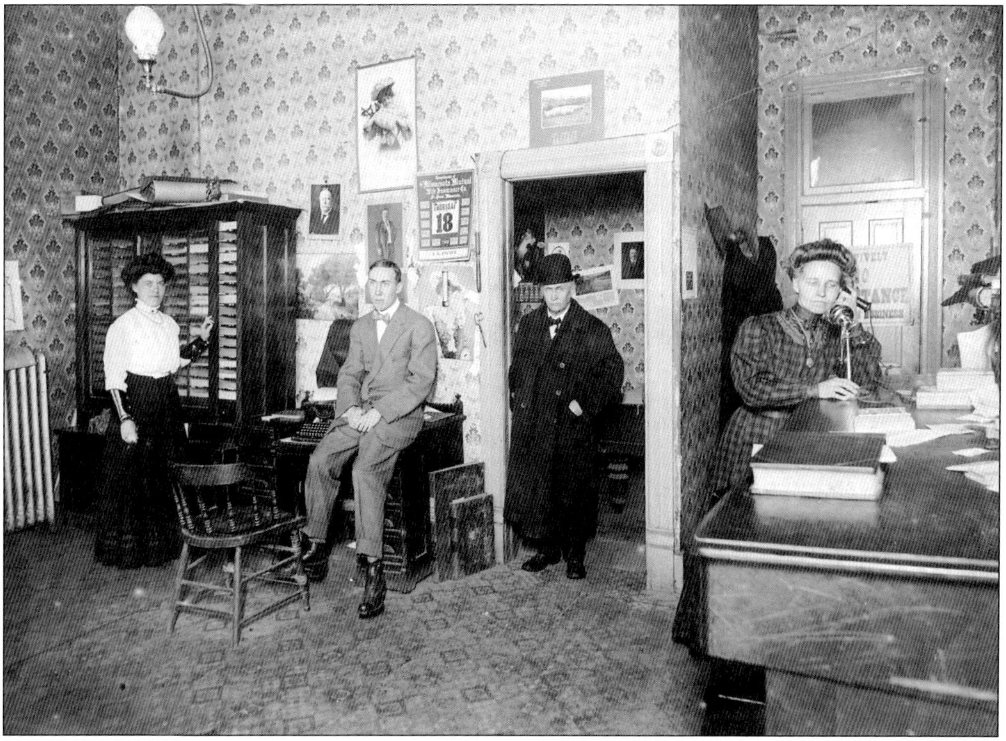

This photograph, taken in 1909, shows the newspaper office and staff of the *Huronite*. From left to right are Helen Parke Oviatt, George Bowen, W.S. Bowen, and Anna Payson. The Bowens owned and published the newspaper until it was sold in 1926 to the Huron Publishing Company, owned by Robert Lusk and Charles Mitchell.

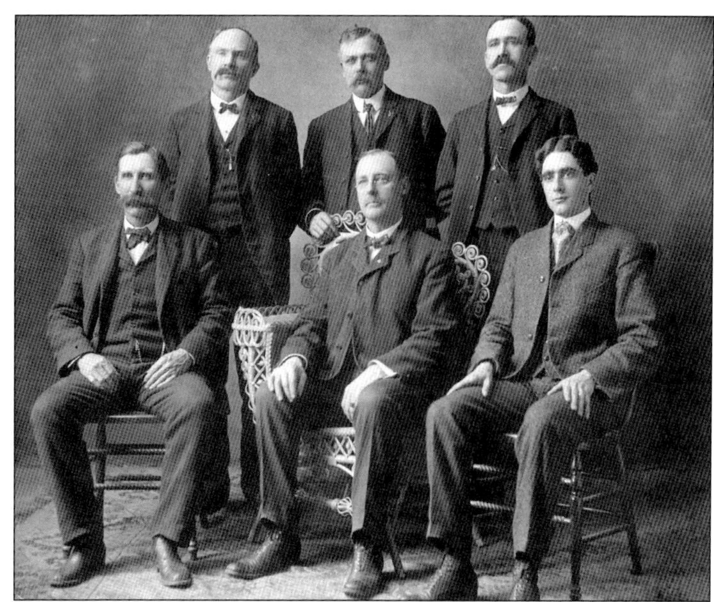

The James Valley Bank, located on the corner of Dakota Avenue and Third Street, was established in 1902 by a group of 40 well-known Huron businessmen. The individuals selected for the board of directors are, from left to right, (first row) Mike Tobin, William Waibel, and John Greene; (second row) Charles Bonesteel, George Hutchinson (bank president), and Frank Sauer. By 1924, the bank had run into financial difficulties and closed.

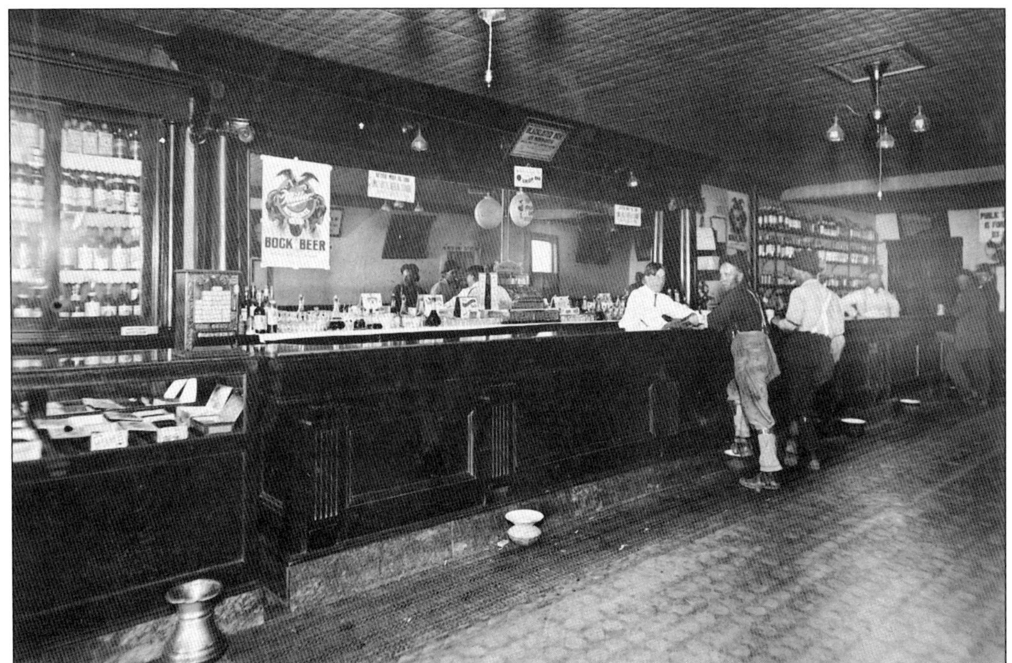

Warren Hurst opened the White Front Saloon in 1903. The wood structure was located on the corner of Dakota Avenue and Second Street. This photograph shows the interior of the bar in 1909. In 1926, the wood building was replaced by a brick building and renamed Hurst's Corner. (Courtesy of Hurst's Corner.)

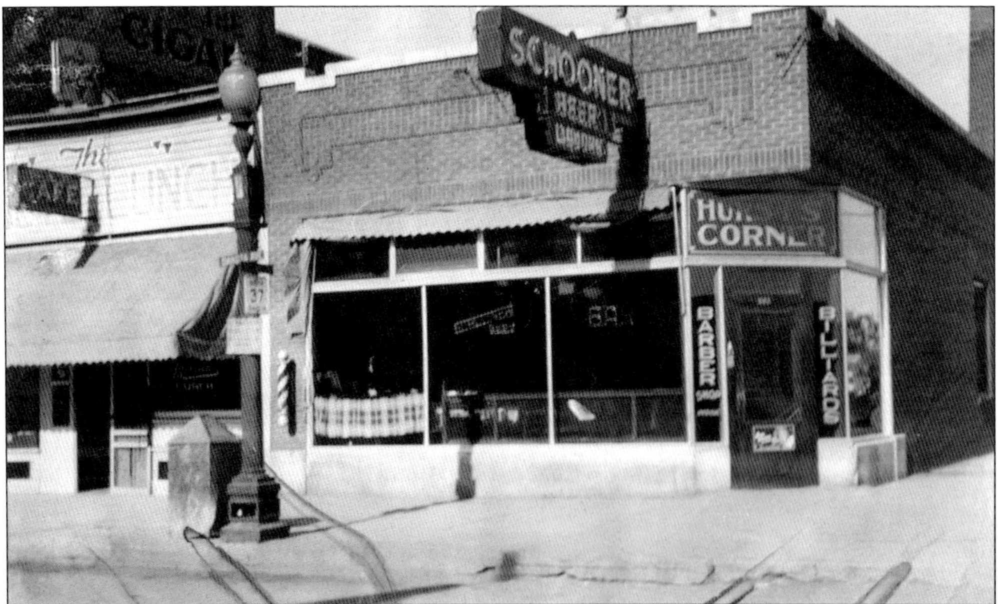

Hurst's Corner, the oldest business in Huron still in operation, has remained in the same location and has been run by the same family for over four generations. Several changes were made over the years, including the addition of a pool hall and lunch on Fridays. This photograph from the early 1950s shows the exterior of the building, which had changed very little since its construction in 1926. (Courtesy of Hurst's Corner.)

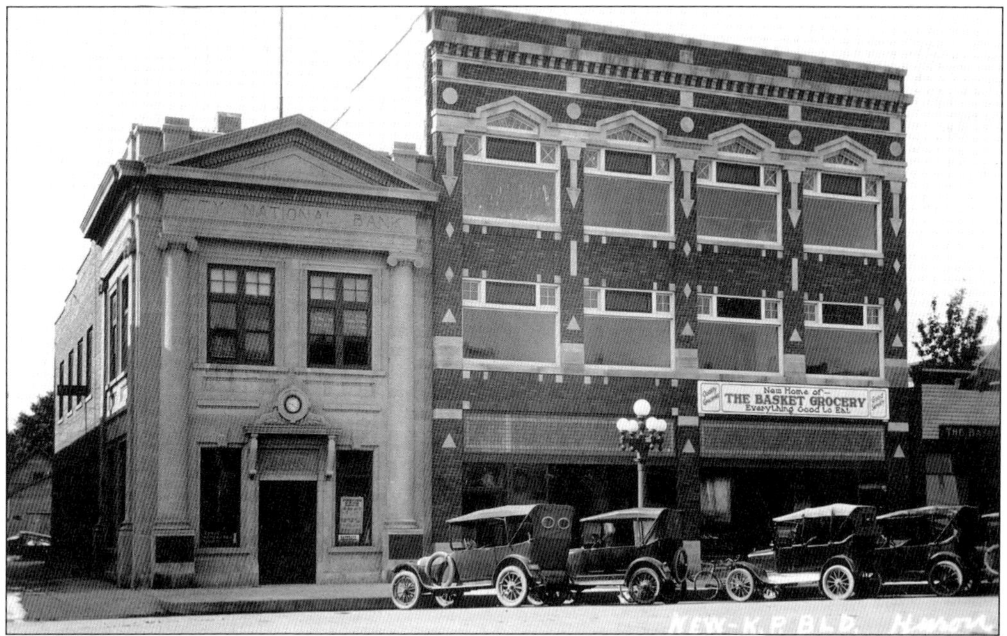

R.H. Maag opened the Basket Grocery store on Third Street in 1910. It was a new and unusual shopping experience compared to other grocery stores in town. The Basket Grocery only accepted cash and only made deliveries for orders over $5. Operating the business in this manner allowed for a greater selection of goods and lower prices.

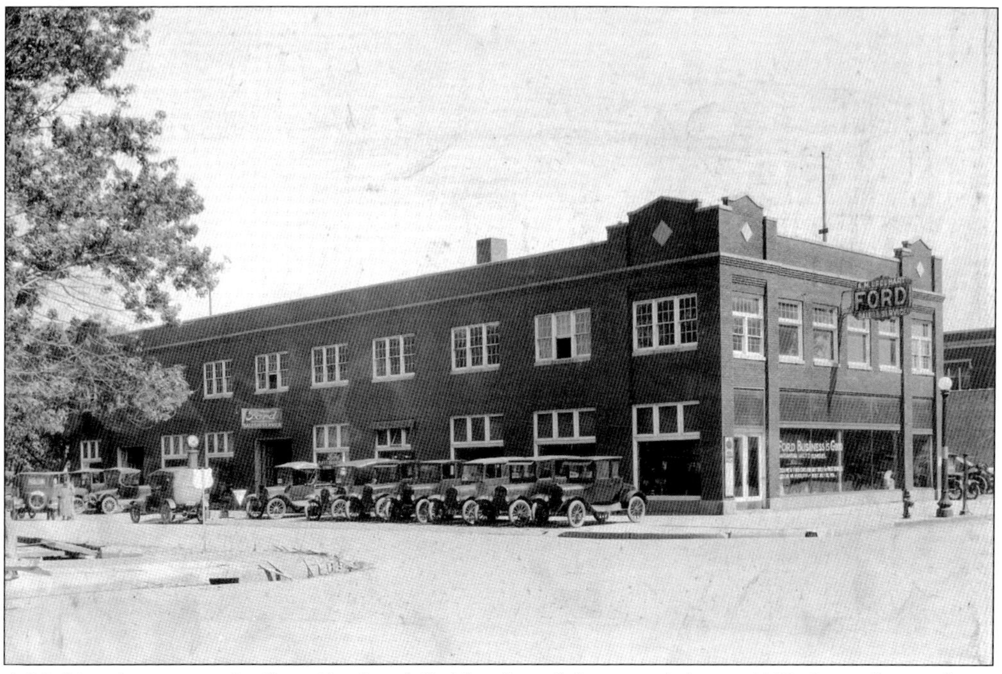

A.M. Urquhart started selling Ford and Oakland model automobiles in 1910. Several years later, he moved his business into this two-story building at Third Street and Kansas Avenue. The front portion of the first floor contained offices and a showroom. The back portion housed a service garage for repairs. The remainder of the building was used for work areas and storage.

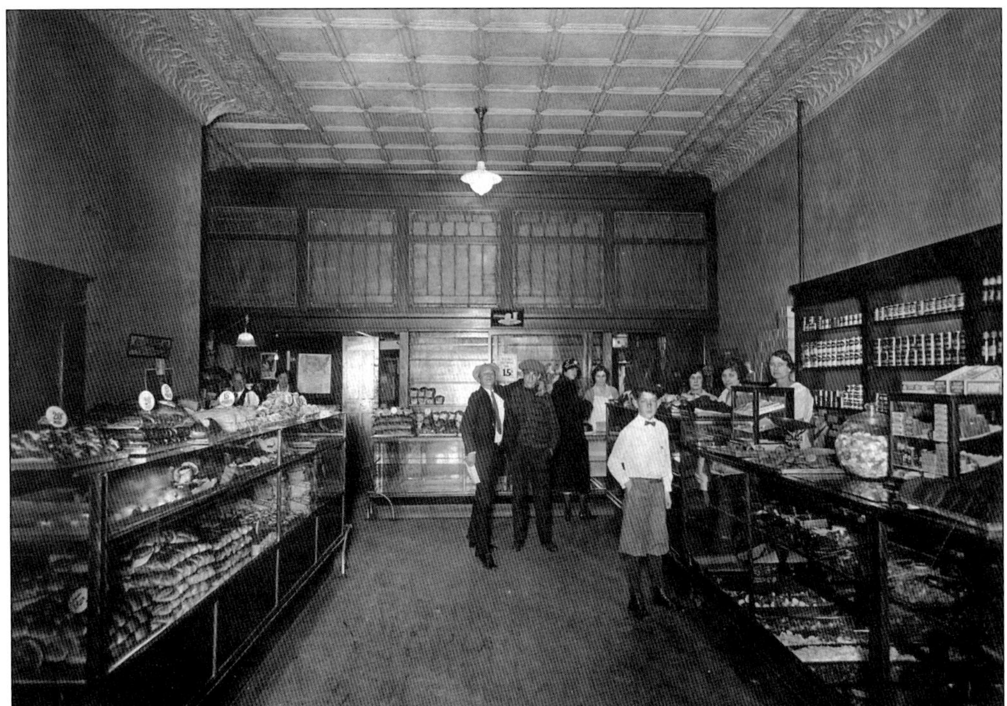

Alfred Hopkins arrived in Huron from Redfield in 1914 and opened Hopkins Bakery on Third Street. He sold a variety of baked goods and pastries. Unforeseen challenges arose, however, and Hopkins closed the store in 1926 after 12 years of dedicated service. He declared bankruptcy and had the equipment sold at an auction.

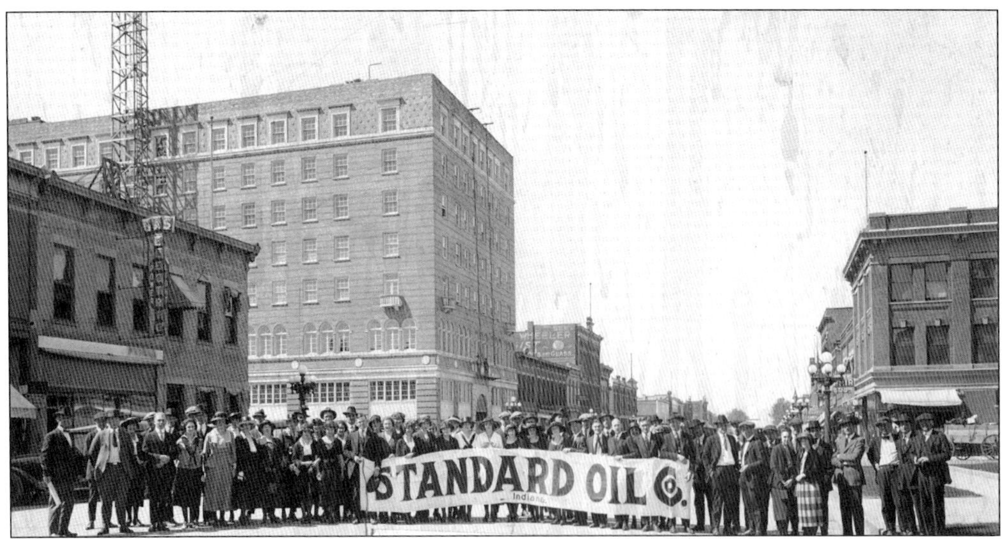

In 1918, the Standard Oil Company of Indiana opened a sales division office in Huron to serve North and South Dakota. The office was located at Third Street and Iowa Avenue. This district office became one of the largest industrial employers in Huron until the late 1950s, when the office was closed.

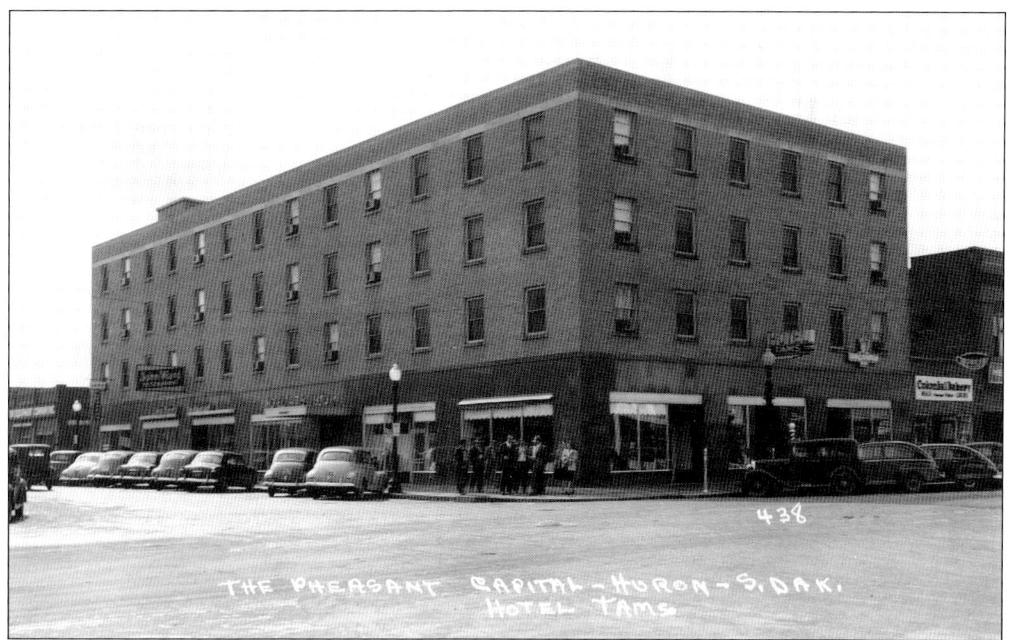

August and Anna Tams purchased the Royal Hotel on Third Street and Wisconsin Avenue in 1920. They operated the hotel until the building was destroyed by a fire in 1943. Despite wartime supply restrictions, Anna had a new, modern, four-story hotel and restaurant constructed in the same location. The new building was named Tams. (Courtesy of Jennifer Littlefield.)

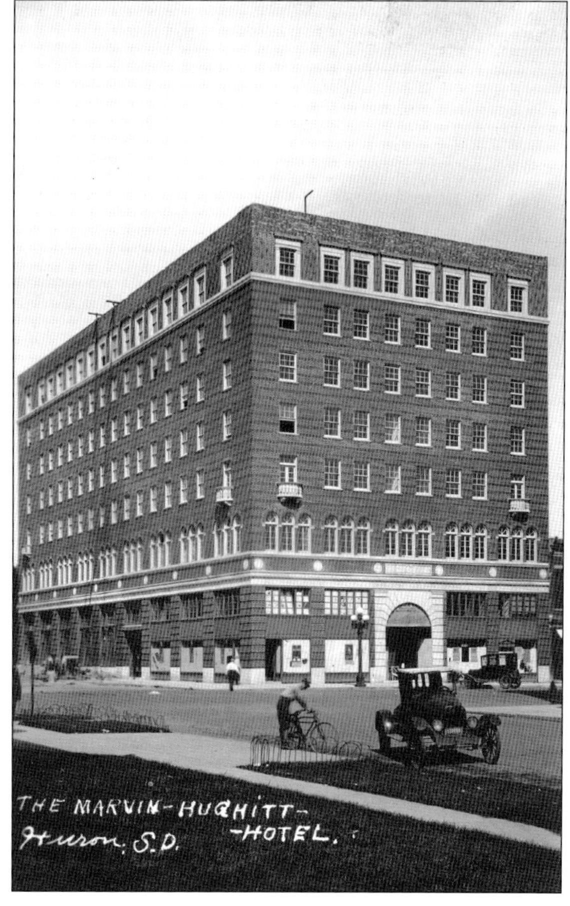

The Marvin Hughitt Hotel was constructed in 1920 by the Huron Elks Lodge No. 444 on the corner of Fourth Street and Dakota Avenue. The building provided 165 guest rooms with running water, dining rooms, the Elks lodge and ballroom, and its own ice storage in the basement. Today, the building contains senior apartments and several offices.

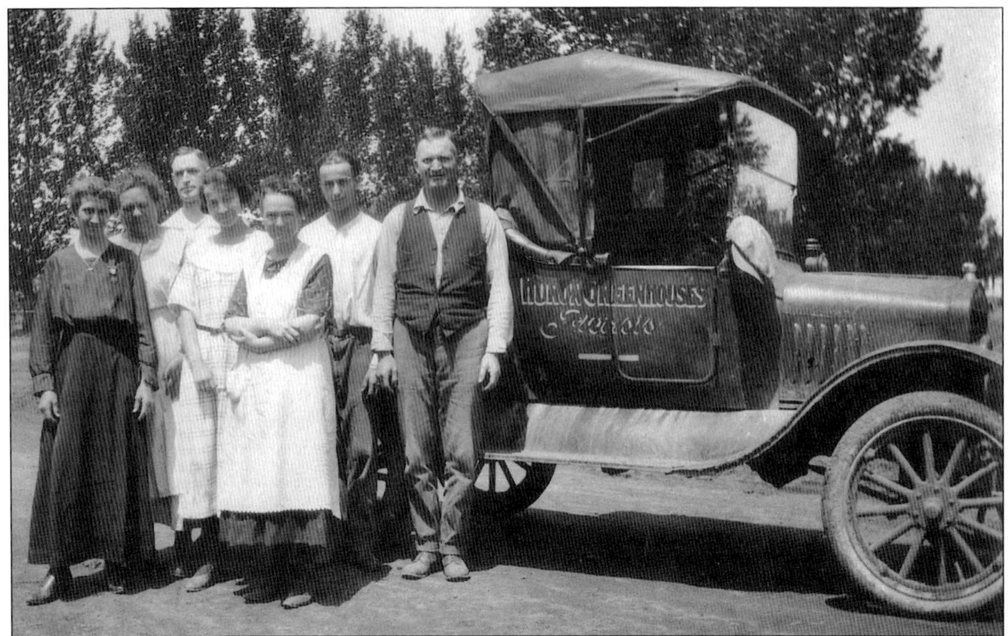

Clarence Walker started the first floral shop in 1923. The store was originally located on the lower level of the Marvin Hughitt Hotel. This photograph shows Walker and his employees. From left to right are Jennie Woodford, Lena De Land, Ernest Palm, Bertha Locker, Leona Schreck, Wenfred Morrison, and Clarence Walker. (Courtesy of Walker's Flower Shop.)

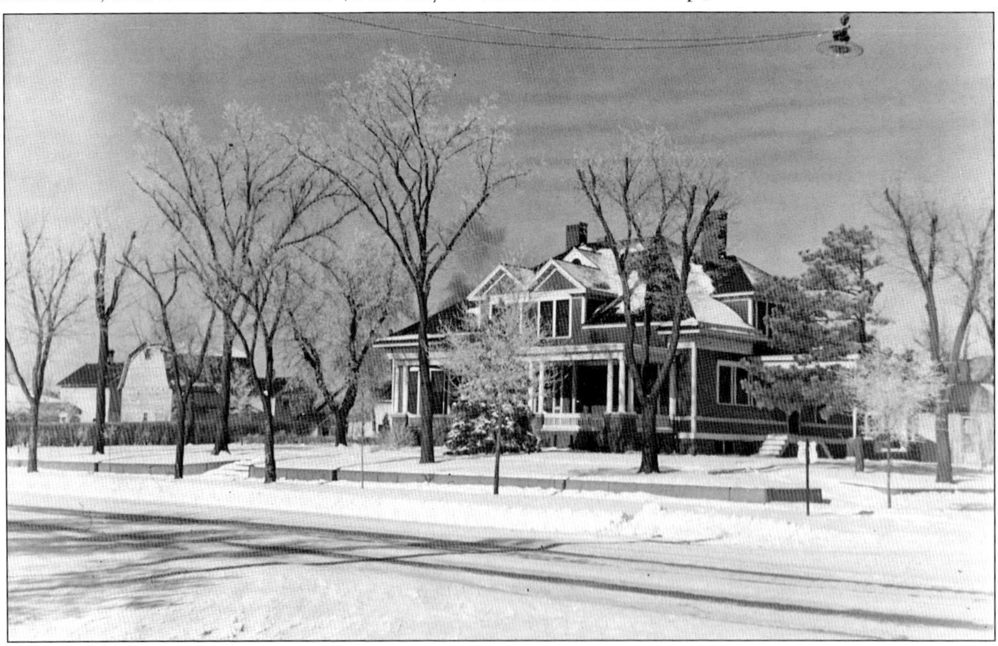

In 1925, William Welter began working as an undertaker at the Kinyon Funeral Home. Several years later, he opened his own business, located in the Tams Hotel. In 1948, Welter moved his funeral home into the former residence of Richard O. Richards on Third Street, seen here. The new location offered a spacious chapel, music room, and family room, all of which were air-conditioned. (Courtesy of Welter Funeral Home.)

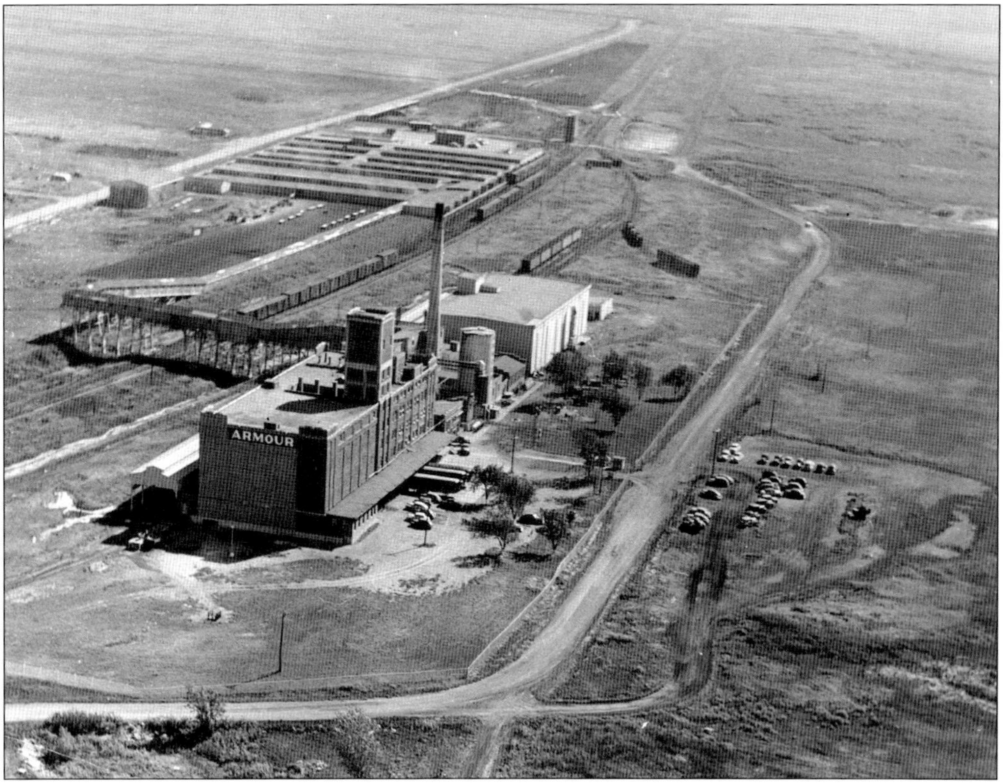

The meat-packing industry in Huron was established to meet the needs of farmers raising livestock. In 1925, Armour and Company purchased a farmer co-op processing plant east of the James River. It employed hundreds of people and invested millions of dollars into Huron's growth and development. This aerial photograph shows the processing plant and related facilities in 1952. The plant closed in 1983. (Courtesy of NorthWestern Energy.)

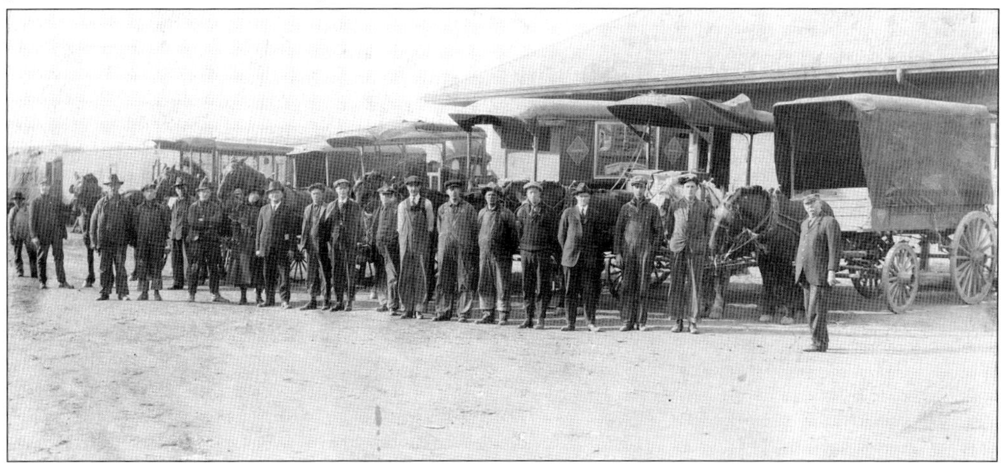

The American Express Company started as a nationwide express delivery company. The Huron office was located in the Chicago & Northwestern Railroad depot. During World War I, the demand for transporting supplies for the war effort rapidly increased. As a result, the company hired additional delivery drivers. The employees seen here worked around the clock in three shifts delivering products to and from the railroad station.

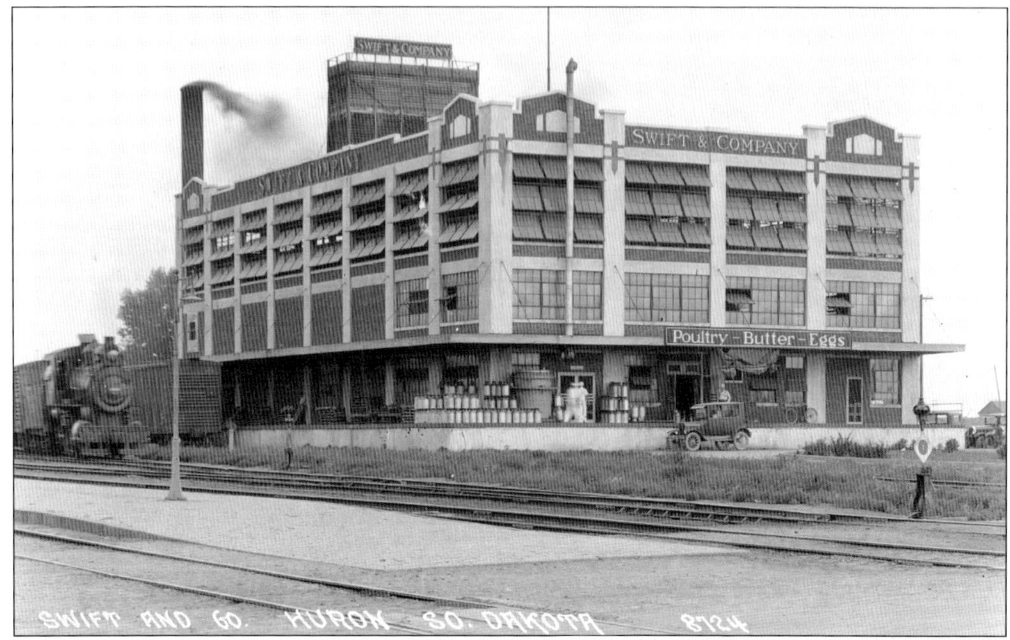

In 1925, Swift and Company of Chicago chose Huron as the location for a plant to produce high-grade chickens, eggs, butter, and cream. The plant was conveniently located next to the Chicago & Northwestern Railroad tracks, making it faster and easier for the company to ship fresh products. The creamery was located on the first floor of the building, and live poultry was housed on the third floor. Robert Johnston, seen below, was a delivery driver for the company for 25 years. During that time, he drove 800,000 miles without an accident. In June 1950, Johnson received a certificate and pin from the plant manager for his excellent driving record.

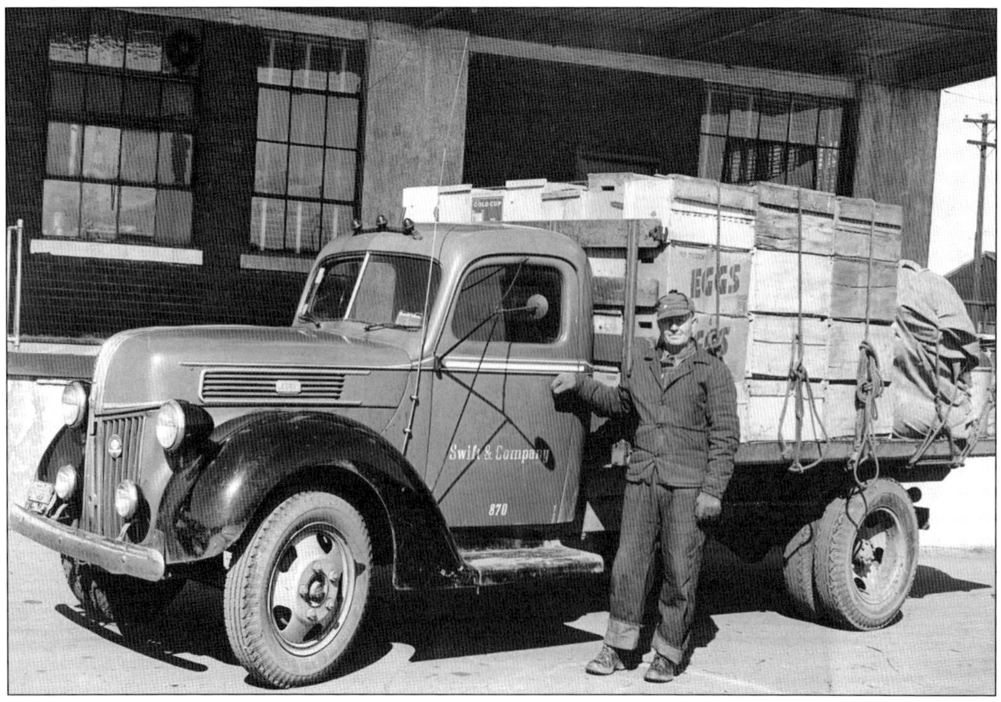

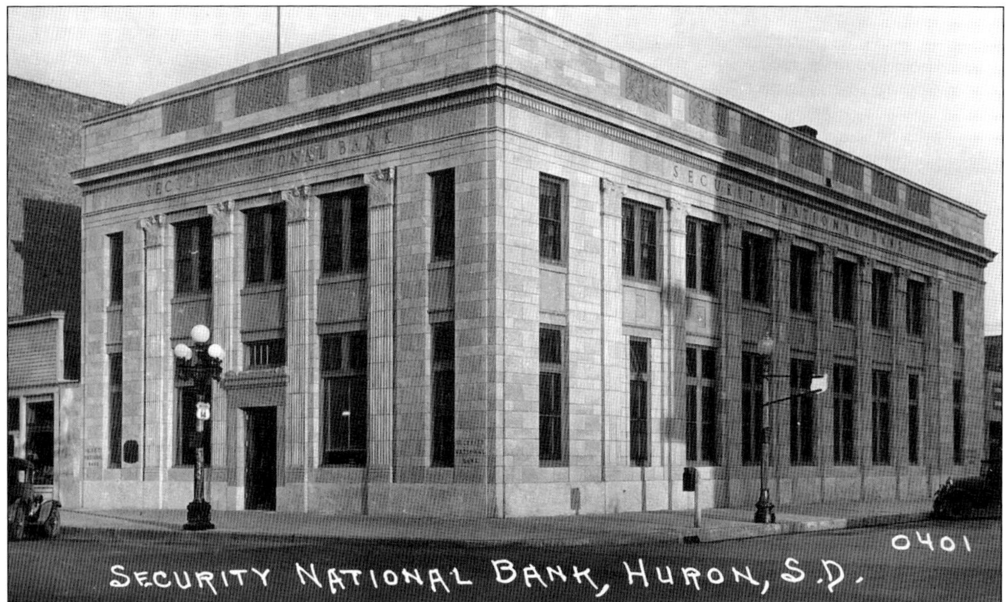

The Security National Bank was built in 1930 on the corner of Wisconsin Avenue and Third Street. It was advertised as the most modern and well-equipped bank in the region. One unusual feature was the construction of the vault. Despite weighing over 500 tons, the vault was moveable. If an addition was built, the vault could be moved into the expanded area.

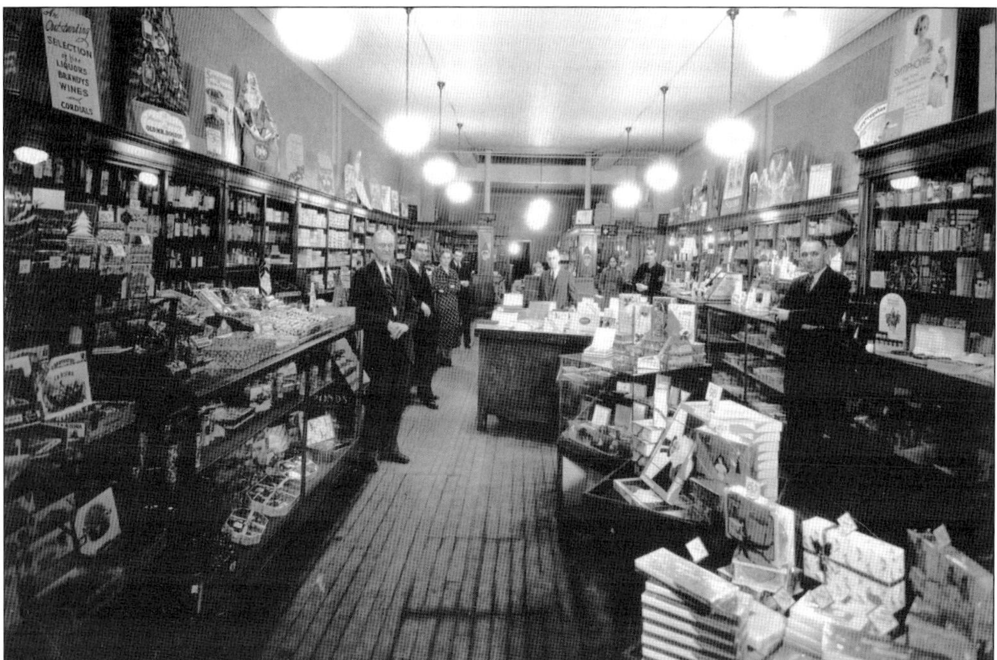

Holland Wheeler started the first drugstore in town. He received his pharmacy license in 1885 and mentored many of the other pharmacists in town. This photograph is of Wheeler Drug Store in 1934. From left to right are Holland Wheeler, Harold Osborn, Maxine Hunt, Jimmy Burns, pharmacist Wilford Gormley, Allison Wheeler Luddy, Kirke Wheeler, and John Wheeler. (Courtesy of Ron and David Wheeler.)

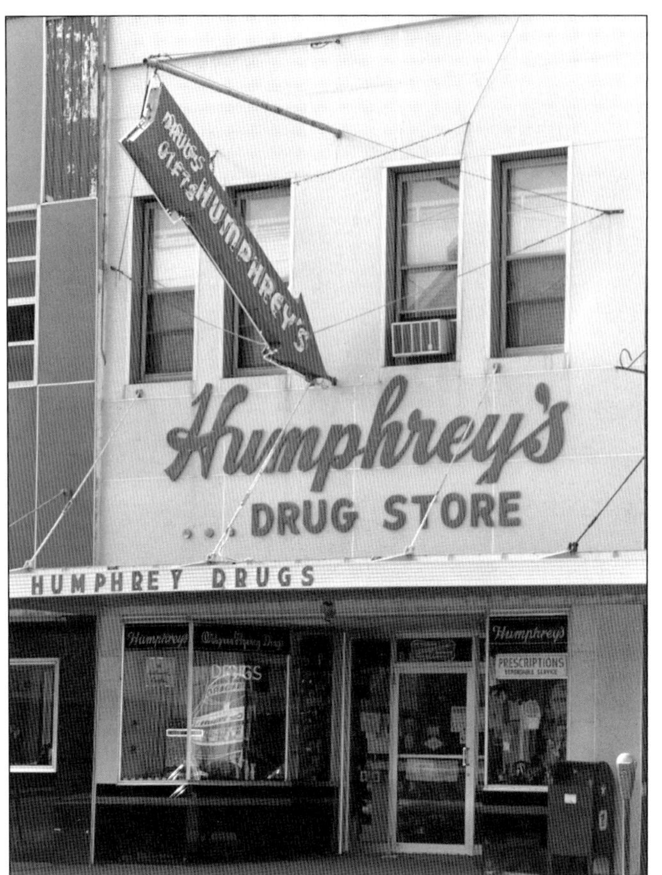

Humphrey's Drug Store, located at 233 Dakota Avenue, was easily identifiable by the iconic red arrow sign on the front of the building. Hubert Humphrey Sr. opened the drugstore in 1931. When his son became a US senator, and then vice president under Lyndon Johnson, the drugstore became a popular tourist destination. The store remained in the family until 2021.

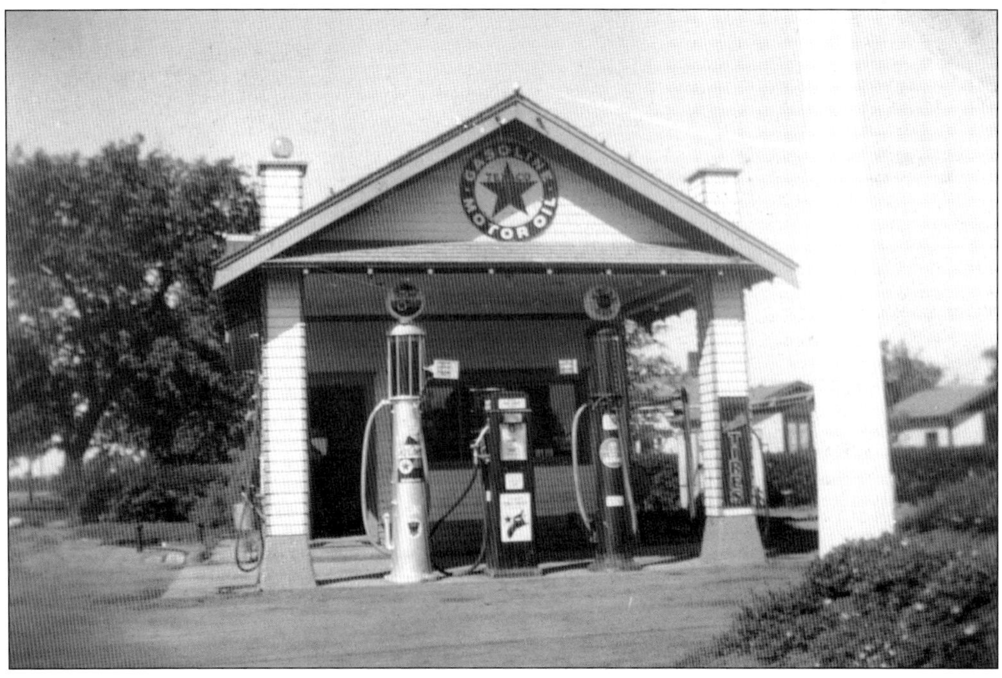

Lee Patrick purchased this full-service Texaco station in 1930 and moved it to Third Street and Lincoln Avenue. His family worked at the station pumping gas, cleaning headlights, and checking tire pressure. Lee built an addition to the building that included a pit for performing oil changes. (Courtesy of Leanne Gutormson.)

In 1946, Lee Patrick opened Lee's Café & Drive In north of his Texaco gas station. Lee's daughter, Leanne, was the first female carhop in Huron. The drive-in offered root beer made at the Patrick family's home and hamburgers using a recipe from NuWay Burgers. Burgers were sold for 15¢, fries for 20¢, and coffee for a nickel. (Courtesy of Leanne Gutormson.)

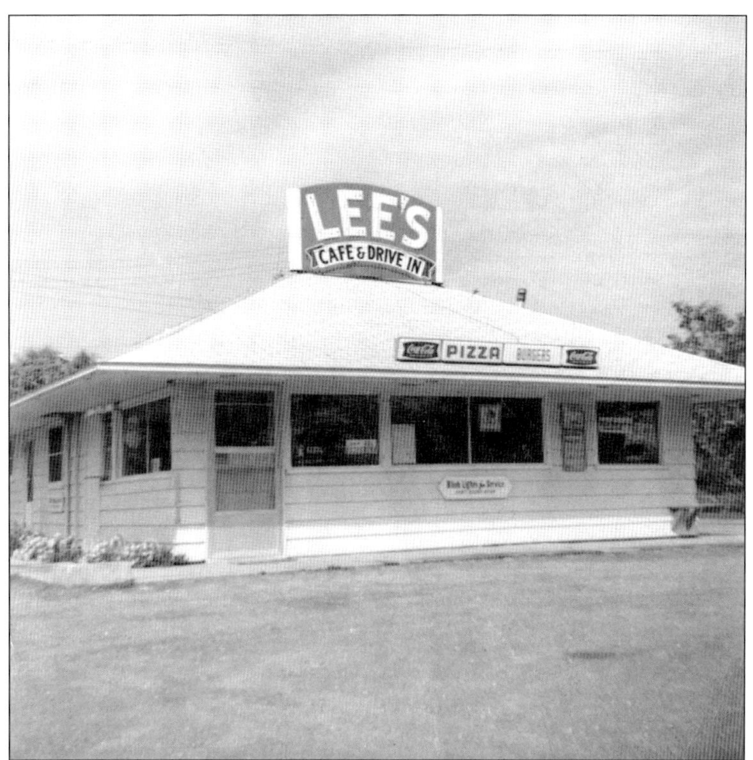

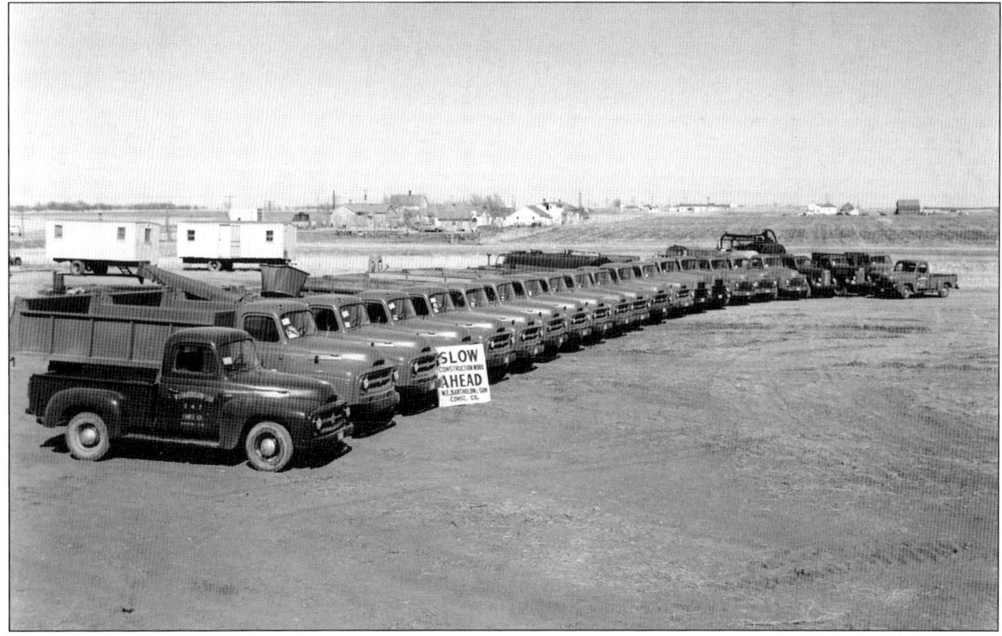

William Bartholow started the W.E. Bartholow and Son Construction Company in the 1930s. The company specialized in building roads made with asphalt. During this time, there was a great demand for constructing new roads, and Bartholow's company grew into one of the largest road-building firms in South Dakota. This photograph shows a line of work trucks owned by the company during the 1950s.

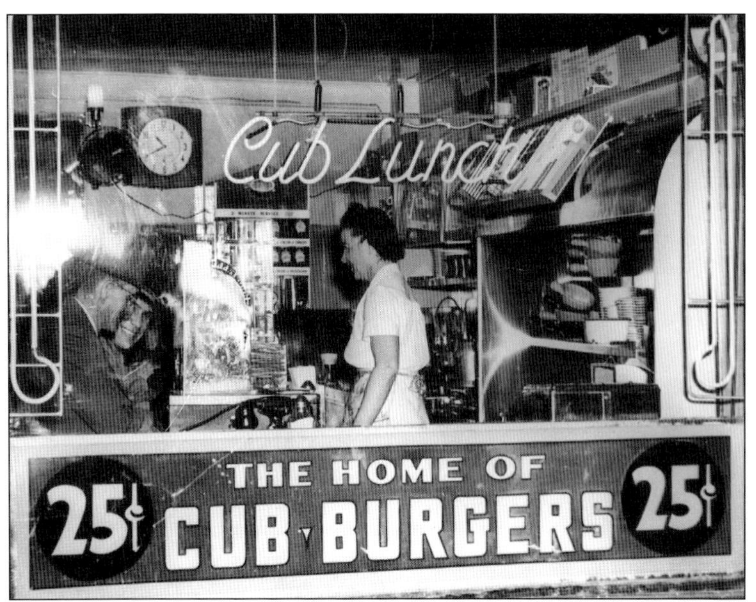

Cub Lunch was a diner that opened during the Great Depression in 1933. It was located on Third Street next to the Huron Theater. The diner offered fast and friendly service to fit even a meager budget. During the 1930s, hamburgers cost a nickel. Al and Claire Baird operated the diner until 1974.

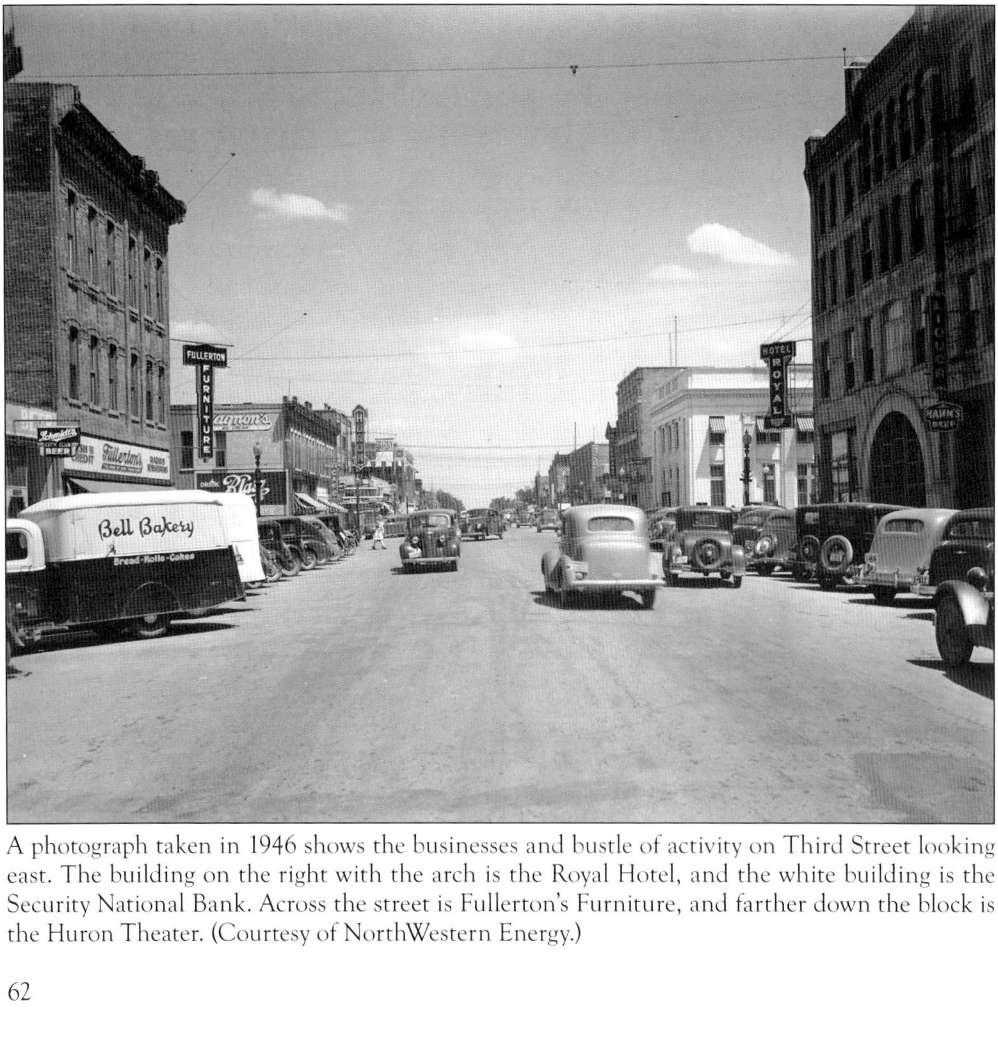

A photograph taken in 1946 shows the businesses and bustle of activity on Third Street looking east. The building on the right with the arch is the Royal Hotel, and the white building is the Security National Bank. Across the street is Fullerton's Furniture, and farther down the block is the Huron Theater. (Courtesy of NorthWestern Energy.)

Four

Reading, Writing, and 'Rithmetic

Beadle County experienced a large influx of people called the Great Dakota Boom between 1878 and 1886. People arrived in Huron on as many as 18 trains a day. In 1883, one week saw 1,000 passengers arrive in the city. Most of these new settlers came from established states in the east. They brought with them a respect for education and skills in managing and organizing rural schools.

The territorial superintendent of public instruction was Gen. William Beadle. Schools were built with the help of funds supplied by the territorial government and administered by Beadle's office. The first school in Huron was opened in the fall of 1880 on Wisconsin Avenue between First and Second Streets. It began holding classes three months after the first train of settlers arrived in Huron. The 15 students were taught by Watson Weed using a blackboard, whatever books the parents had brought with them, and his snake whip. The only furnishings were long benches and dry goods boxes for desks. These were replaced with wooden desks the following year.

Enrollment grew to 137 within the first year. In the summer of 1881, a two-room schoolhouse was built and a second teacher, Delia Rogers, was employed to teach the primary grades. During the fall, as enrollment grew, students were taught in classrooms in a store and in an old saloon on Kansas Avenue and First Street. Space was later found in the Congregational church at California Avenue and Fifth Street and in a bank on the corner of Dakota Avenue and Fourth Street.

In 1883, the Huron School District was established. Huron became known as the educational center of the Dakota Territory when the Dakota Educational Society was organized on June 2, 1884. It later became the South Dakota Educational Association. Meetings were held in Huron for the first three years of its existence.

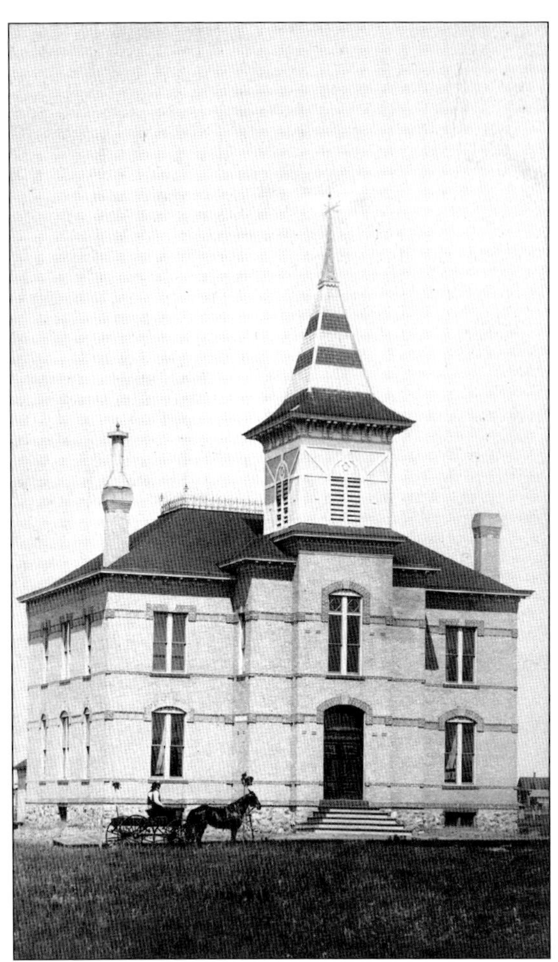

The first brick schoolhouse was the Illinois School. It opened in 1882 at Illinois Avenue and Fifth Street at a cost of $9,000. It housed 140 pupils with three teachers. By 1883, enrollment had increased to 300 students. Teachers were recruited locally, and two-thirds were women. All were certified by the county superintendent. Pay averaged $30 per month, including board, with male teachers being paid $5 more.

Pictured here is Miss Adams's class in 1883 on the front steps of Illinois School. The first school party was held in 1884 and was funded partially from fines collected from students who chewed gum or used slang. Each student donated 4¢ to buy a gift for the teacher.

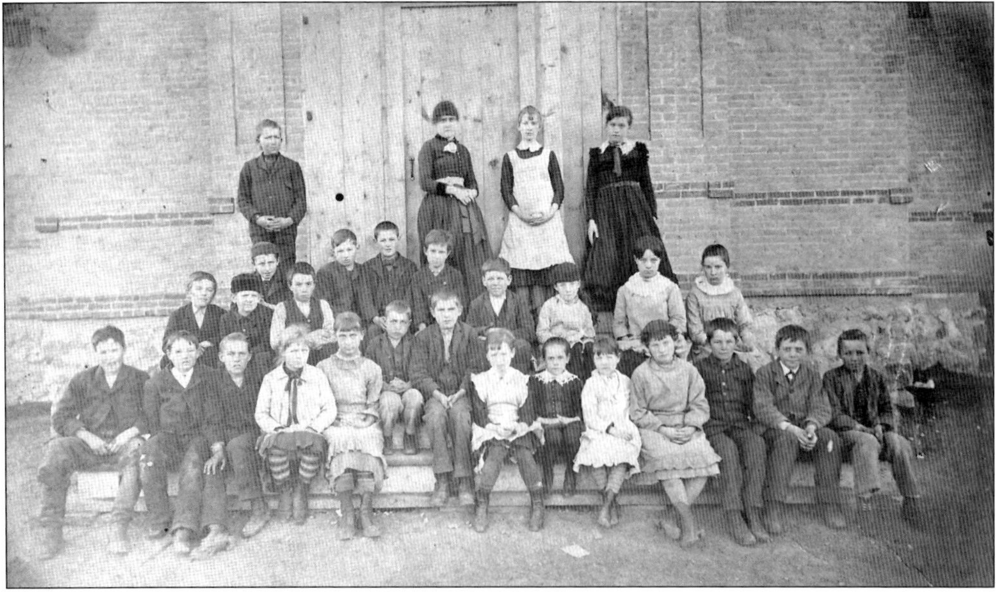

After the $10,000 Utah School was completed in December 1886, a two-room annex was added to the Illinois School and it became the high school. Utah School was called "the Castle" because of its fancy architecture, including a tower and turrets. It was located at Utah Avenue and Eighth Street. Huron now enrolled 410 students in 12 grades, and the curriculum included everything taught in the Eastern schools.

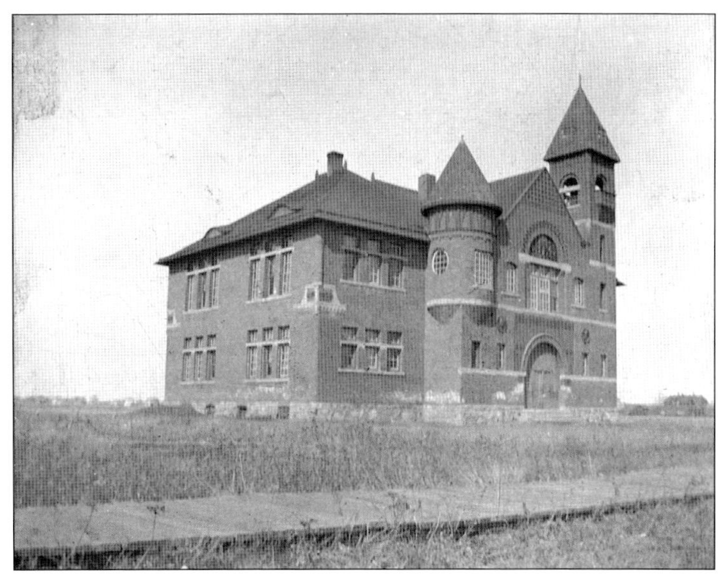

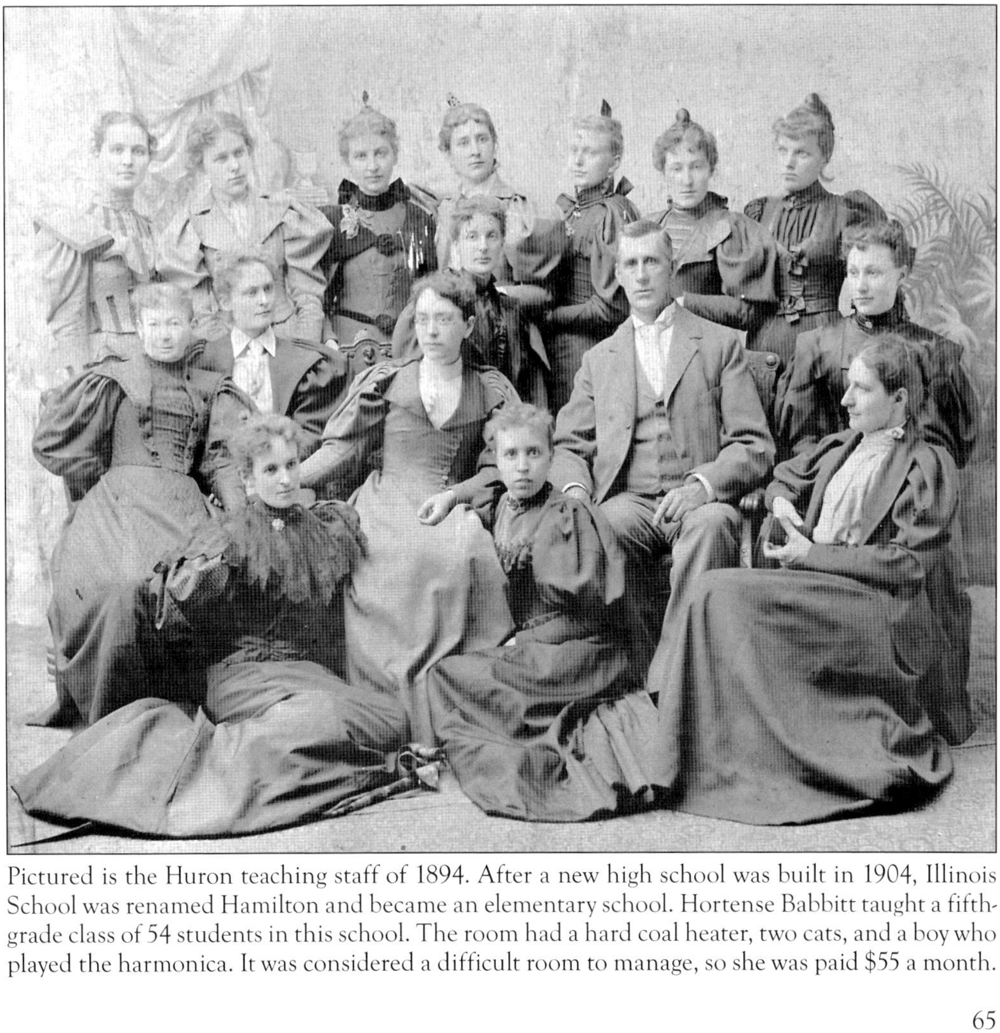

Pictured is the Huron teaching staff of 1894. After a new high school was built in 1904, Illinois School was renamed Hamilton and became an elementary school. Hortense Babbitt taught a fifth-grade class of 54 students in this school. The room had a hard coal heater, two cats, and a boy who played the harmonica. It was considered a difficult room to manage, so she was paid $55 a month.

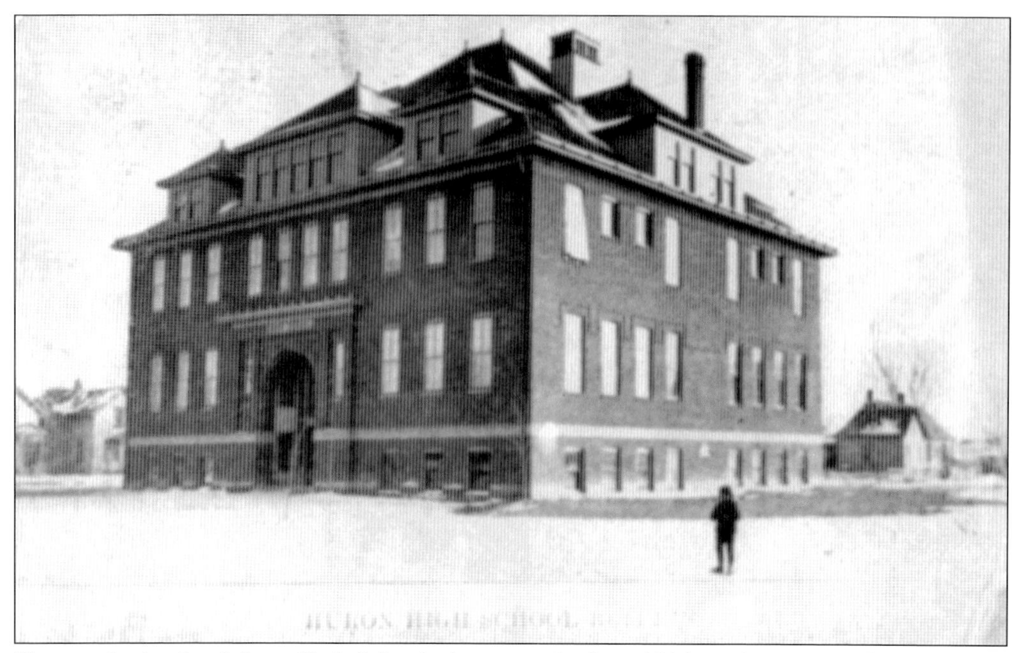

The new high school, Iowa High School, above, was built in 1904 on the corner of Iowa Avenue and Fourth Street. But because of growing enrollment, a larger building was soon needed. A newer high school, below, was built in 1914 just south of Hamilton School. The Iowa School was renamed Washington and became an elementary school. A fire destroyed the third story of Washington School in January 1925. The building was rebuilt that summer and continued to be used until 1939, when it was torn down. St. John's Hospital was built on that location in 1947. In 1918, Hamilton, which had been in service for 36 years, was demolished to make room for an addition to the high school, which now housed the junior high classes as well. Several documents were placed in the cornerstone of the addition, including a staff roster, a *Huronite* newspaper, and the superintendent's annual report.

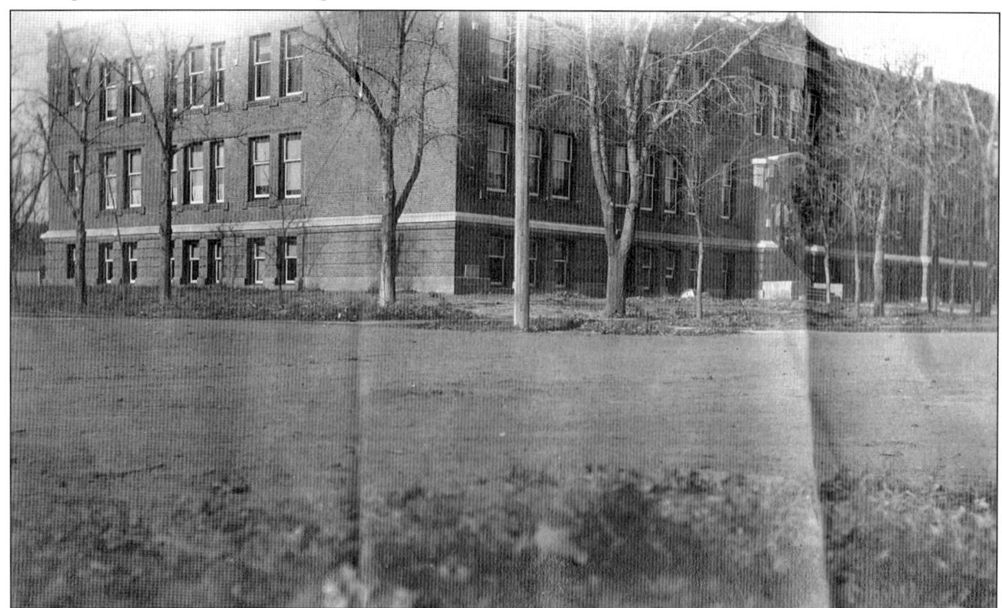

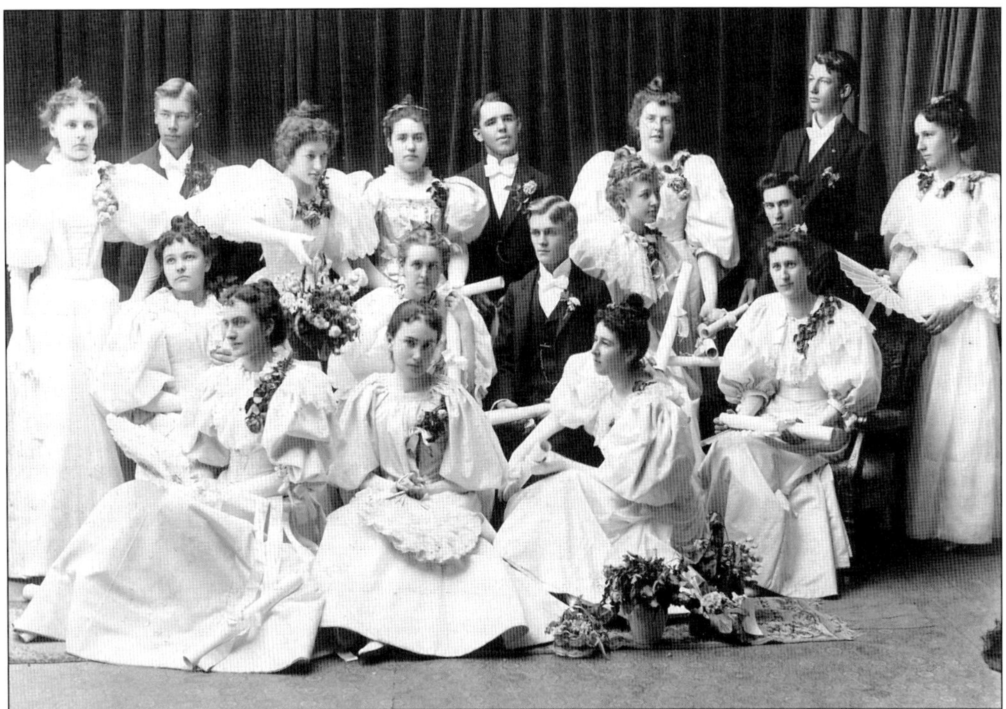

The commencement ceremony for the first graduating class of 10 seniors was held on June 3, 1887, in the Grand Opera House. The class of 1896, pictured here, included 17 graduates. Huron had the only high school in Beadle County for more than 20 years. By 1889, Huron had 680 students with an average of 52 pupils per class.

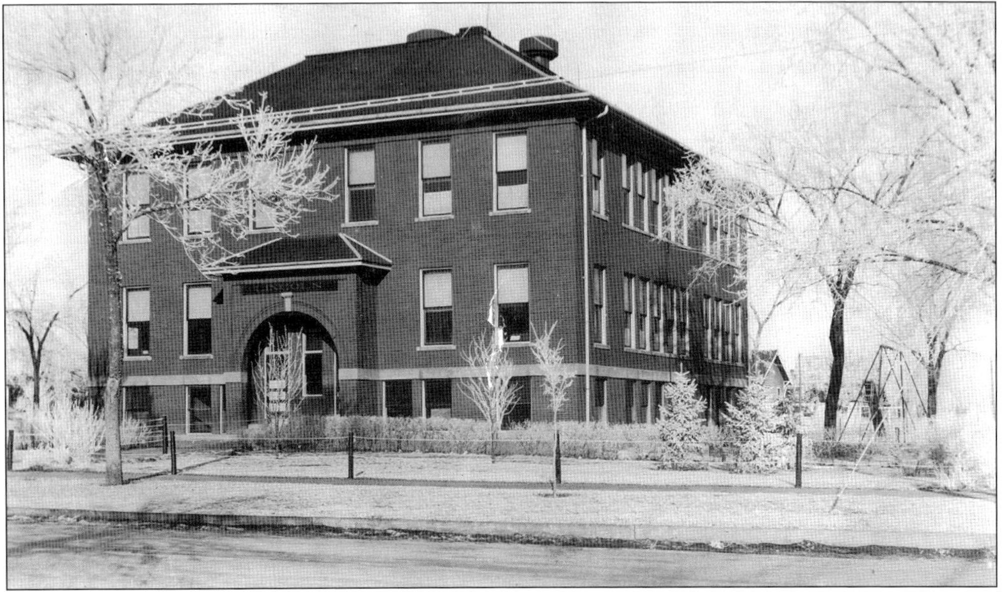

A third elementary building was constructed in 1910 at Illinois Avenue and Tenth Street and was known as the Tenth Street School. It was later renamed Lincoln Elementary School when the district decided to switch from street names, which were getting confusing, to presidents' names for the elementary schools. This building was in use until 1975, when it was sold and razed.

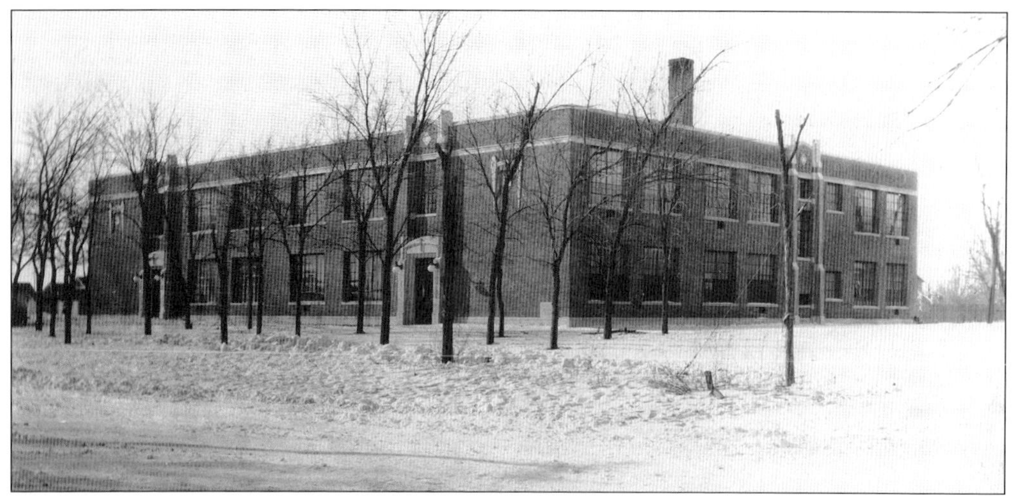

The Utah School stood for 41 years before being torn down and replaced by Jefferson School on the same site in 1927. Jefferson School was in service for 88 years. Due to the cost of renovations to make it accessible, its lack of space for additions, and its small playground area with no grass field, it closed in May 2015 and was sold.

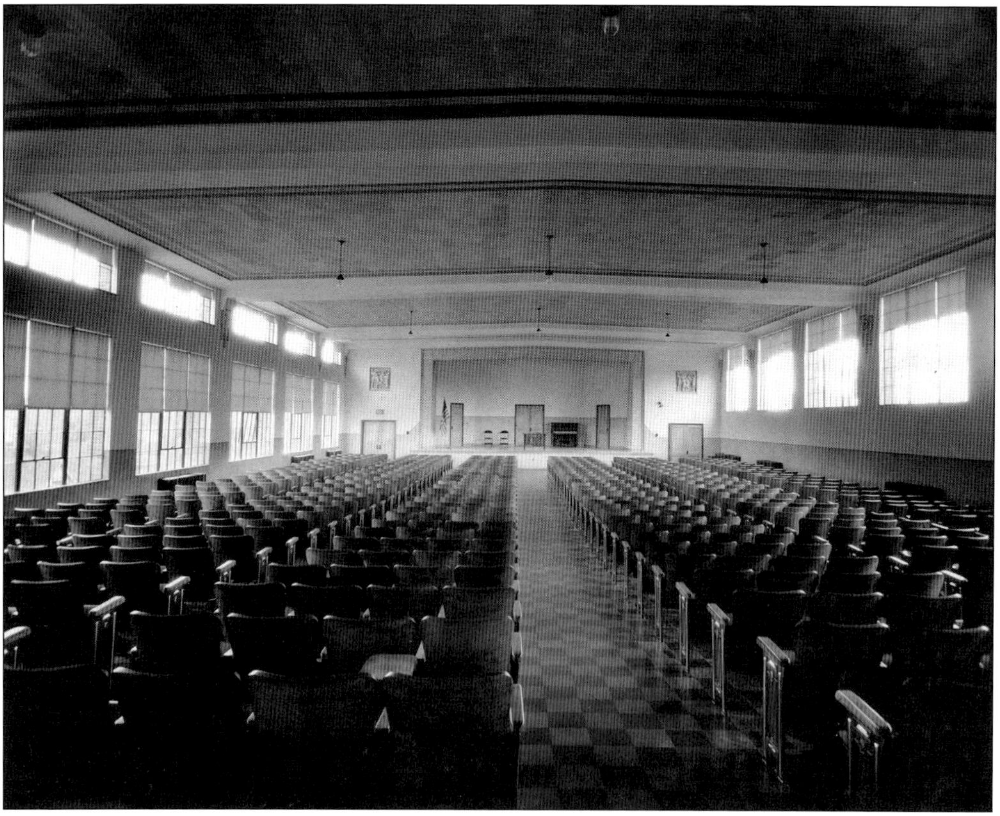

Due to the need for expansion of the junior/senior high school, the Ohio Avenue Annex was added to the west side of the building in 1937. The auditorium on the third floor was used for school dramatics and civic concerts for many years. Until this addition, school events had been held at Huron College.

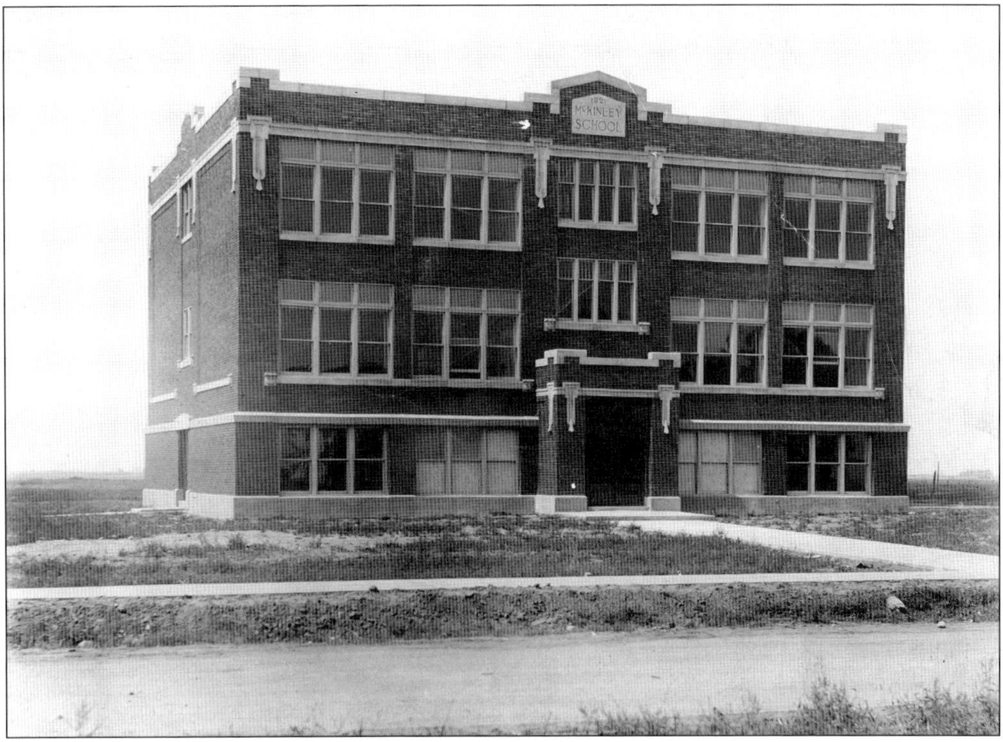

The district added two more elementary schools. McKinley School, above, at 705 Dakota Avenue North, opened in 1921, followed by Wilson School, below, in 1925 at Montana Avenue and Seventh Street. A one-story wing was added to McKinley, but later, as the district moved toward single-story buildings, the original structure was removed, and eventually McKinley was closed. It was home to the Northeast South Dakota Head Start program for many years. It is now McKinley Learning Center and houses the Huron School District Preschool Program. Wilson was closed in 1984 and housed the Wilson Center for the Arts before being converted into the Wilson Apartments.

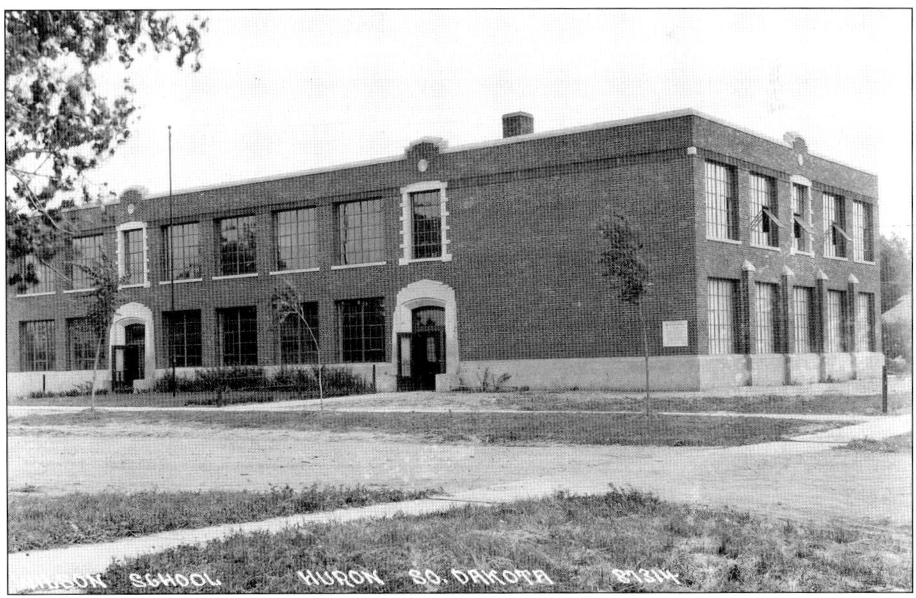

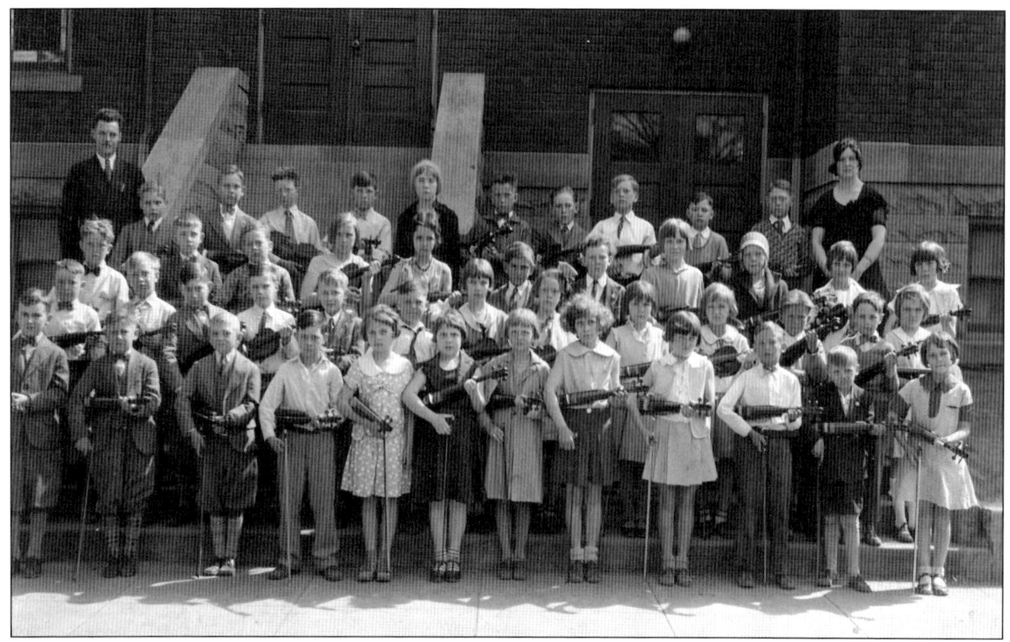

With the turn of the century, special teachers were hired to lead music programs, such as the elementary violin class seen above. Below is the 1916 high school sextet vocal group. From left to right are Lester Brock, Clarence Coop, Roy Daum, Lester Randall, James Baudy, Ross Matsen, and director Ralph Jones; pianist Blanche Pennington is at center. Music was always an important part of the community. The students helped raise money to buy a reed organ for the school in 1882. This was the first organ in Huron and was used for community entertainment as well as school functions. The school concentrated on public performances held in the Grand Opera House, with the students providing recitations, declarations, essays, and singing. One event held in December 1885 had 700–800 people in attendance.

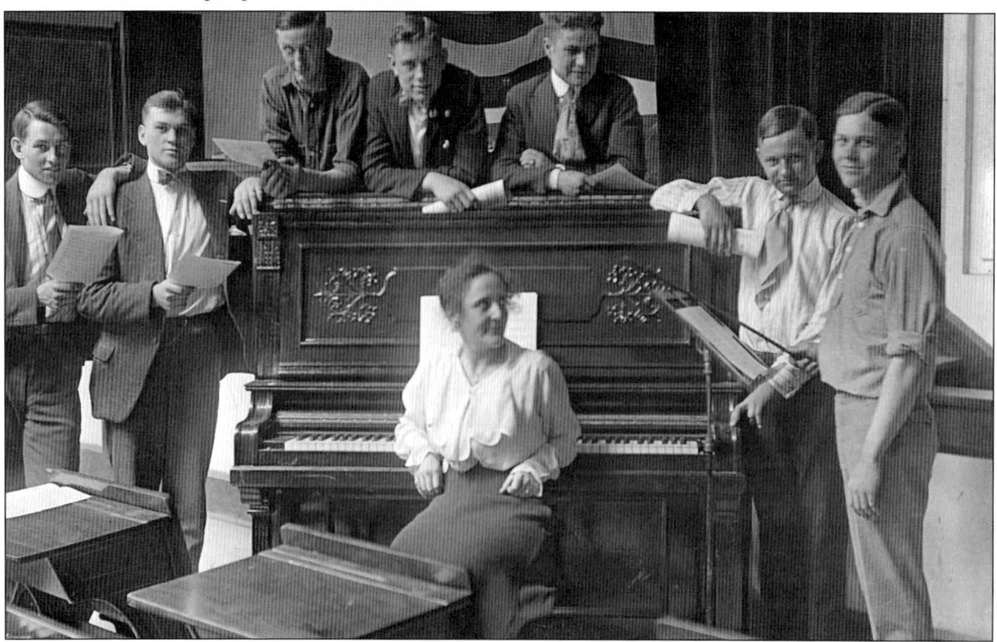

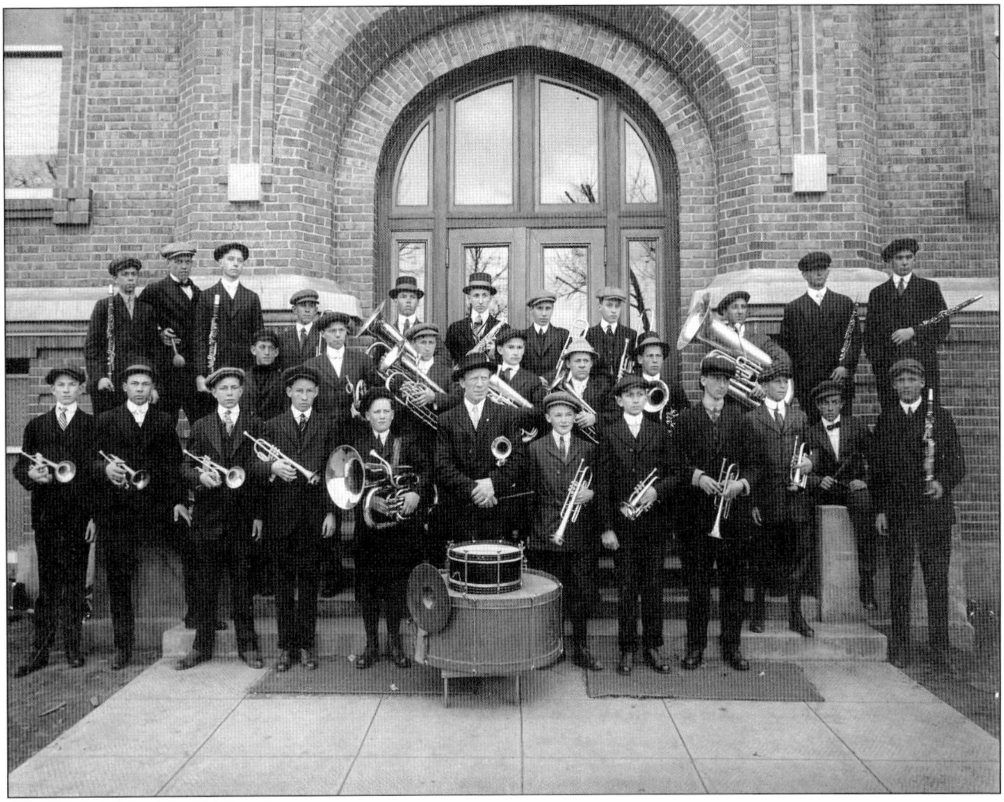

The first Huron High School band was formed in 1915. Bands, both school and municipal, were an important part of community life, performing in parades and in the parks. In 1912, gramophones were added to the schools to introduce students to opera music. The first musical revue was given in 1936 with orchestra and vocalists. Art instructors were also added to the staff at this time.

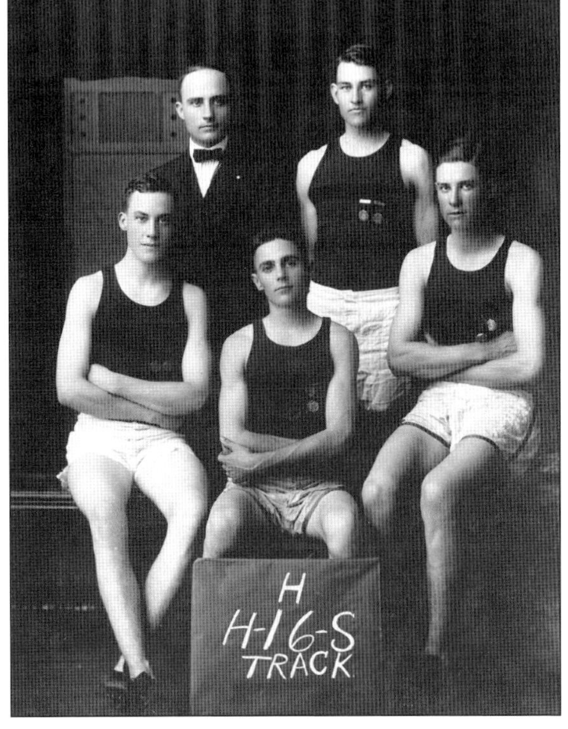

Athletics became a part of the district early on with Huron fielding basketball and track teams. The members of the 1916 track team are, from left to right, (first row) Max Price, Dewey Gascoigne, and Ed Licht; (second row) Coach Bouden and Lester Brock. Girls' basketball was added in 1915. The district used the college facilities for indoor sports until the Huron Arena was built in 1950.

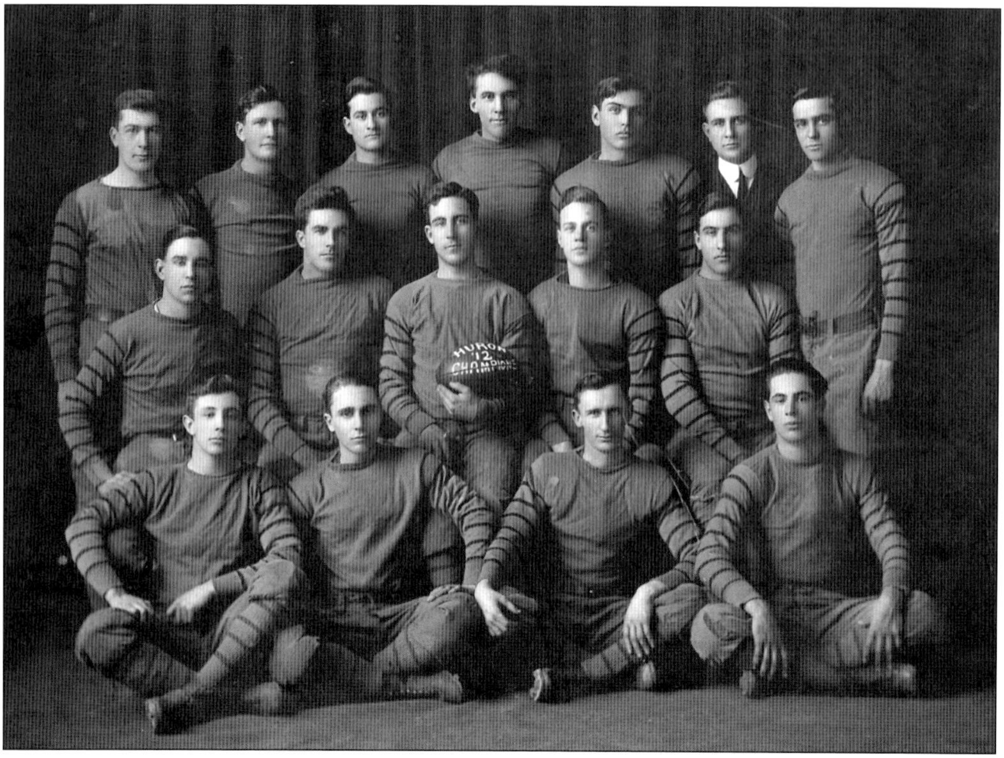

Football began soon after the turn of the century. The team in 1912 was the state champions. The football uniforms did not offer any padding or protection. The first football field was on the state fairgrounds and did not include stands or bleachers, as no one came to watch the games except a few parents.

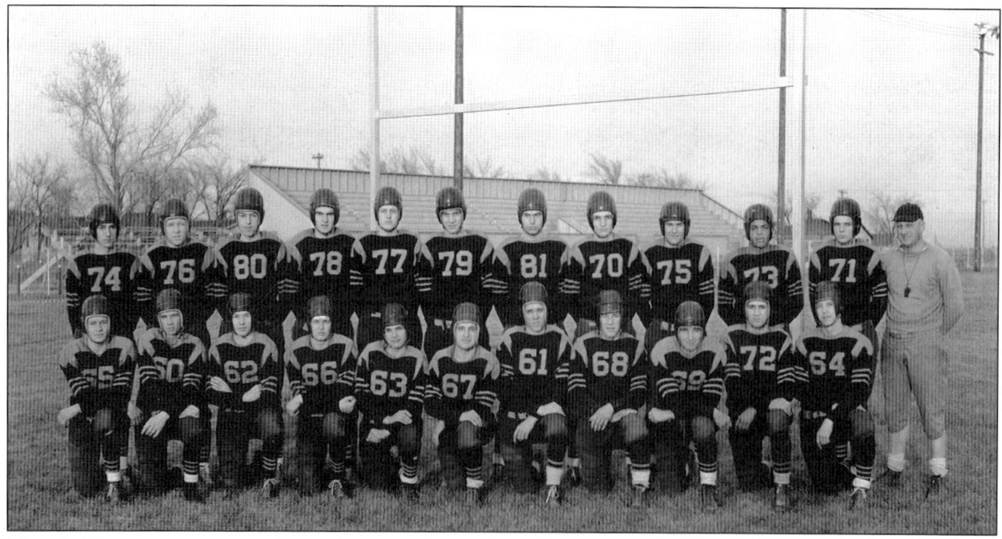

The 1937 runners-up are shown here in the athletic stadium built in the 1930s. They were one of the first teams to use the new football field located at Fifteenth Street and Illinois Avenue, which is now Quarterback Court and Gridiron Place. As football's popularity grew, the team began using the college field until Tiger Stadium was built in 1974.

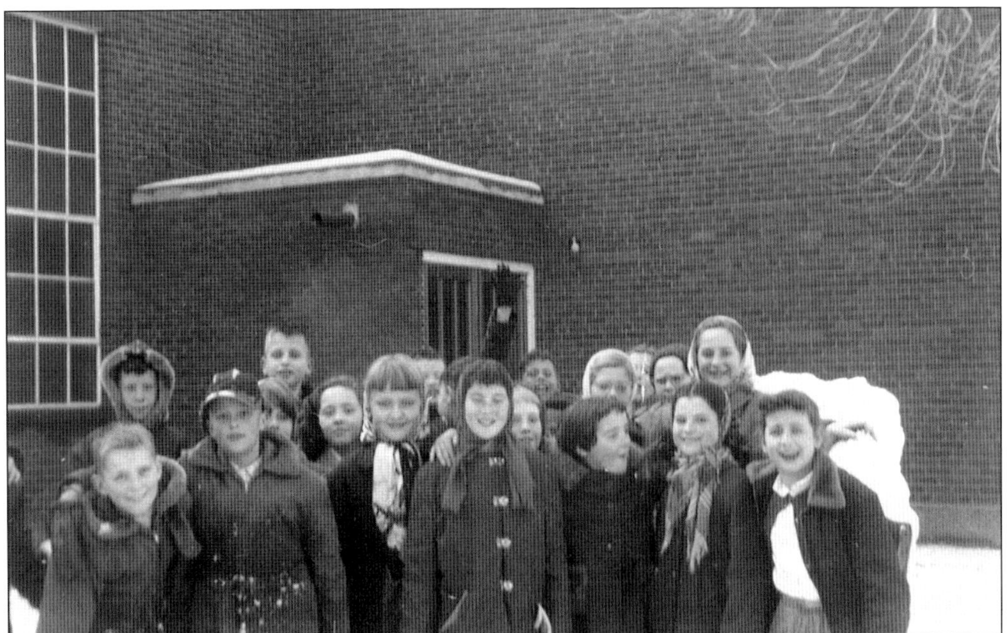

On November 12, 1929, the Catholic church opened St. Theresa School. Classes were taught by Sisters of the Presentation Order in Aberdeen. After a major renovation in 1961, the name was changed to St. Martin School. Holy Trinity Catholic School opened in 2004 after St. Martin was closed and razed. (Courtesy of Holy Trinity Catholic School.)

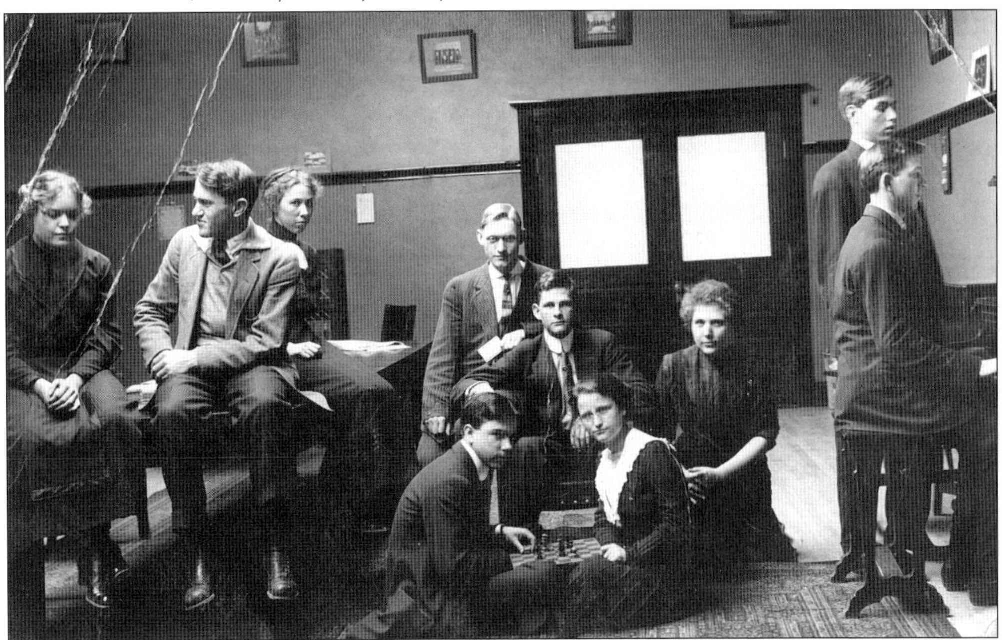

The school district added a college preparatory course called the Academy. Shown here is the senior Academy class of 1912. These students attended classes at Huron College, participated in many college activities, and joined the athletic teams. The Academy ended in 1927. By 1926, Huron boasted the Studio of Music, Le Olde Art Shoppe, and the School of Music offering private classes. (Courtesy of Huron College.)

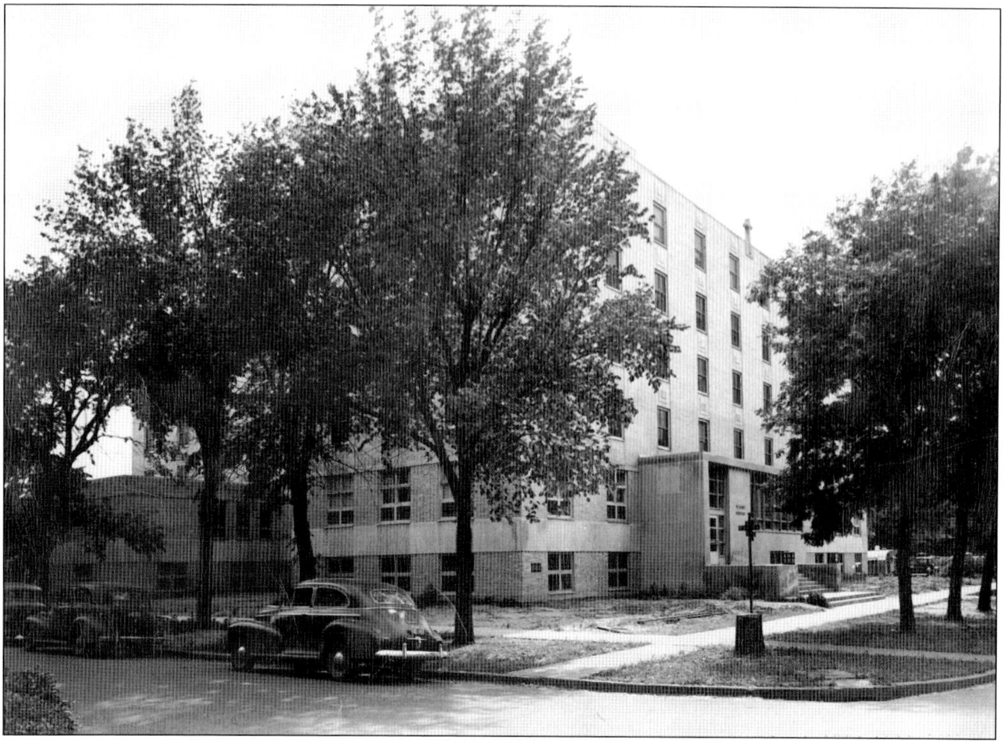

Specialized educational opportunities came along in 1917 with the Sprague School of Nursing, held in the Sprague Hospital at 450 Dakota Avenue. When St. John's Hospital, above, opened in 1947, it operated St. John's School of Nursing. In 1948, during the polio epidemic, the Huron School District added classes for the physically handicapped that were held in the hospital.

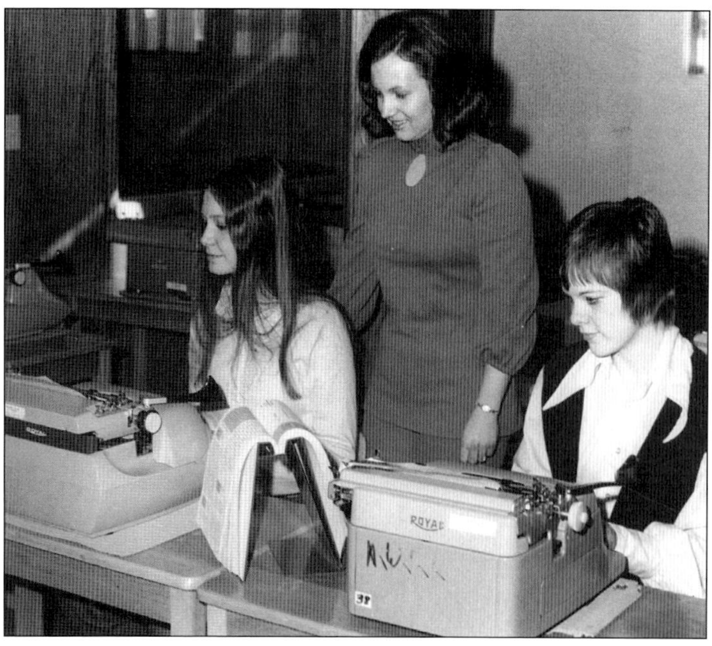

Northwest College of Commerce operated from 1933 to 1989, training men and women for careers in business and civil service. It included fields of study in secretarial, accounting, and business management. In 1949, Rev. Walter Stram started Dakota Bible College south of the Huron Airport. It offered bachelor of arts and bachelor of theology degrees. It closed in 1987, and the grounds were developed into an apartment complex in 2009.

Five

Huron Was a College Town

Pierre University was established in 1883 by the Presbyterian church in Pierre. Growth of the college was slow, and financial backing was difficult to obtain. When Pierre was designated the state's temporary capital in 1889, the community shifted its focus to the capital instead of the college. By 1897, college president William Blackburn announced that the school no longer had the means to continue and would close.

Hearing the plight of the college, members of the Huron Presbyterian Church, led by John and Mamie Pyle, convinced administrators to move the college to Huron. Members of the community collected money to purchase the Royal Hotel for classrooms and housing. Soon the college outgrew the hotel and began looking for land to build a campus. In 1906, the Chicago & Northwestern Railroad gifted four blocks on the edge of town for that purpose. Generous donations from New Jersey philanthropists Ralph and Elizabeth Voorhees paid for the construction of the first two buildings. The university's name was changed to Huron College.

The first school year held on campus was in 1907. As a private, four-year liberal arts college, students could obtain bachelor's degrees in art, science, and music. Certificates could also be obtained in music, education, and secretarial work. There was a wide variety of extracurricular activities, many of which received statewide recognition, such as speech and debate. The men's football and basketball teams also excelled, winning numerous championships.

Huron as a whole benefited from being a college town. Local students who could not afford to travel to larger universities could attend college locally. Sporting events, speakers, and music performances on campus provided cultural and educational opportunities for students and residents.

Facing severe debt, the college was sold to a for-profit business school in the 1980s. After succeeding owners tried and failed to keep the educational institution going, the campus was officially closed in 2005. The city purchased the property in 2011 and created Central Park, which includes Splash Central Water Park, the Huron Fine Arts Center, and the Huron Campus Center.

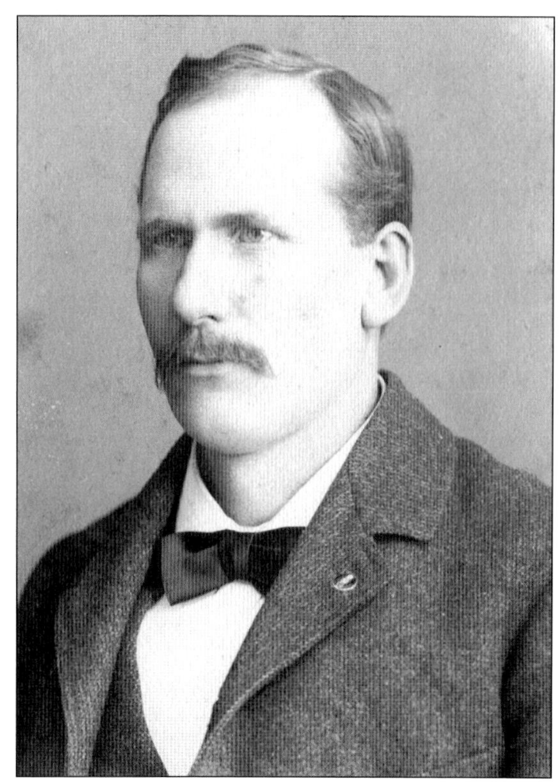

John and Mamie Pyle were married in Miller in 1886. John was a successful South Dakota lawyer and state's attorney for many years. Mamie was a leader in the women's suffrage movement in South Dakota. The Pyles were also members of the Huron Presbyterian Church and were instrumental in bringing the college to Huron. John served as a trustee until he passed away in 1902. Mamie continued his position as trustee for the next 46 years. She led fundraising campaigns to build the girl's dormitory by writing letters to Presbyterian Women's groups across the state asking for donations. (Both, courtesy of Huron College Archives.)

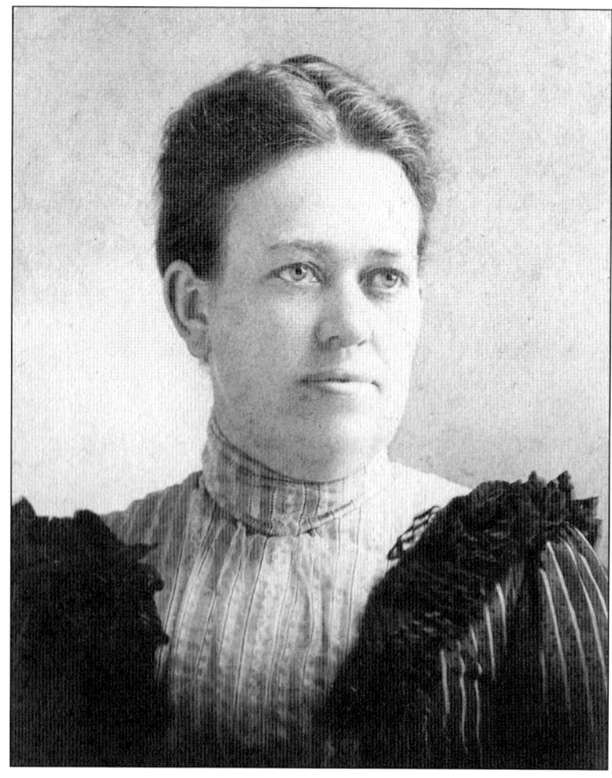

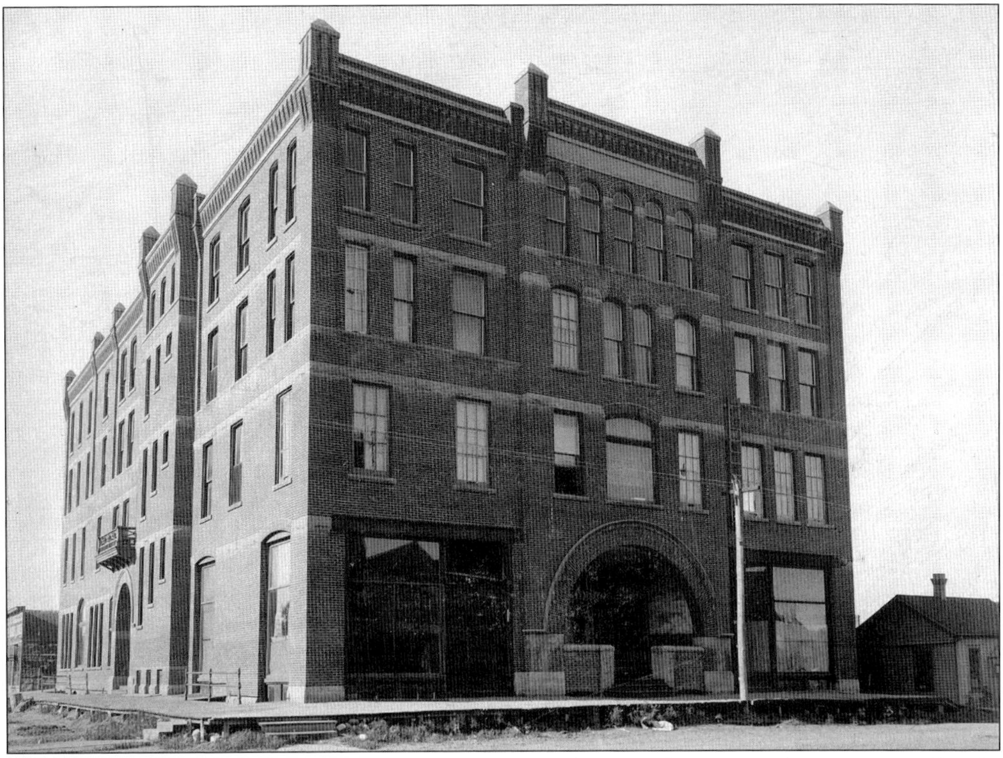

The Royal Hotel was built in 1888 in anticipation of Huron becoming the state capital. The hotel was abandoned when Pierre was chosen for the capital. When news of the closure of Pierre University reached Huron, local citizens purchased the building and donated it to the Presbyterian Synod to house the college. The photograph above is of the hotel, which was located on the corner of Third Street and Wisconsin Avenue. There was enough room for classes, dining, lodging, and extracurricular activities. Enrollment numbers were small in the beginning. The photograph below is the entire college student body from 1901 in front of the hotel. (Both, courtesy of Huron College Archives.)

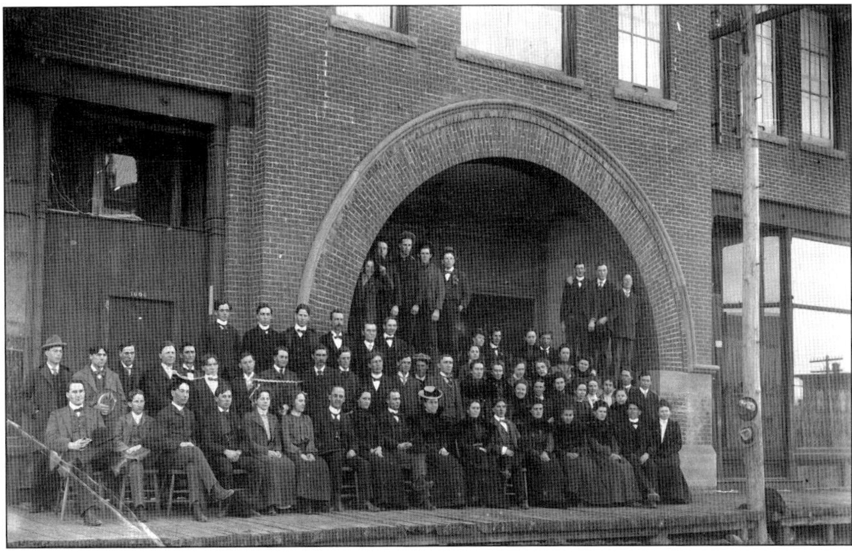

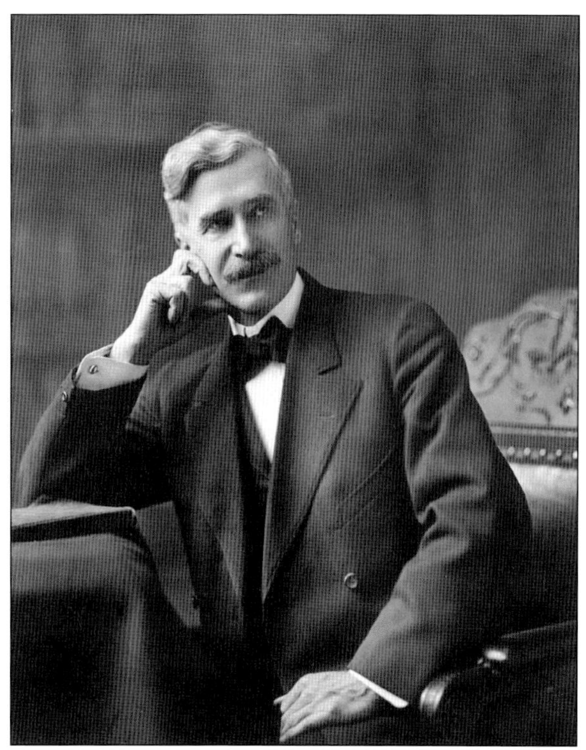

Dr. Calvin French was the first president of Huron College. When he started in 1898, the college was in the process of moving from Pierre to Huron. There were four students, and the facilities were located in the Royal Hotel. By the time he resigned in 1913, the college had acquired land for a campus, built several buildings, and had 100 students enrolled.

The girl's dormitory was the first building constructed on the new campus. Donations from Presbyterian Women's groups throughout the state helped fund the project. The four-story building was dedicated in 1904. Notable features included a large dining room, steam heat, electric lights, and outdoor balconies like the one seen here. (Courtesy of Huron College Archives.)

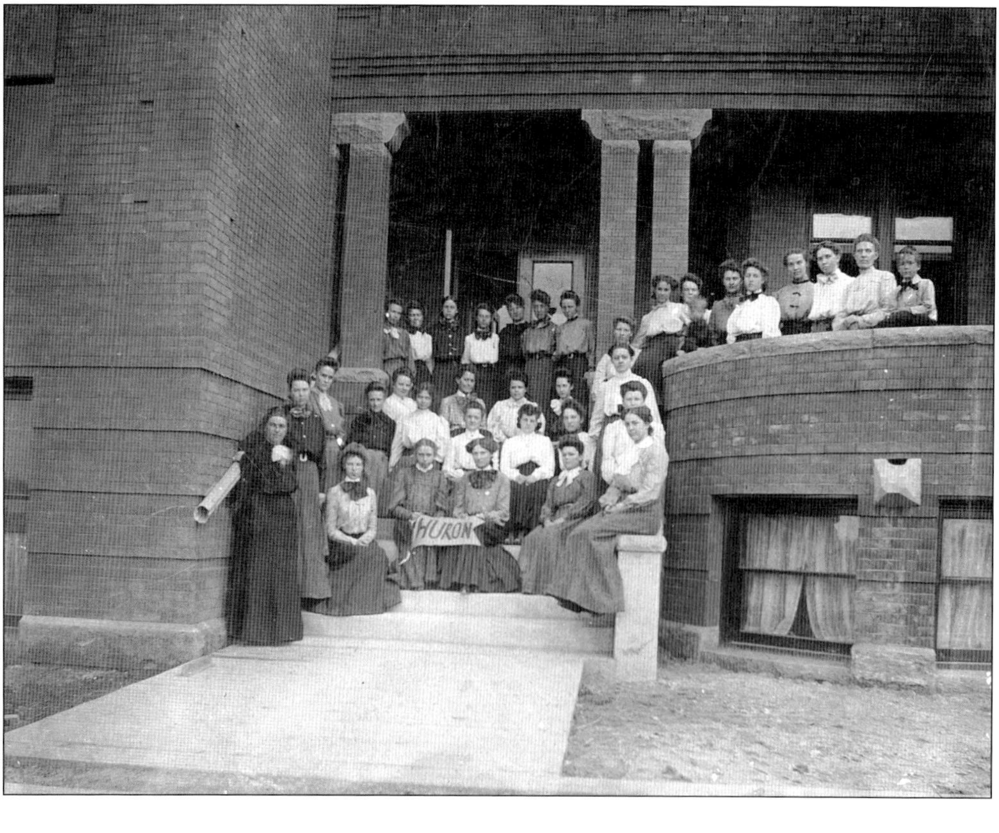

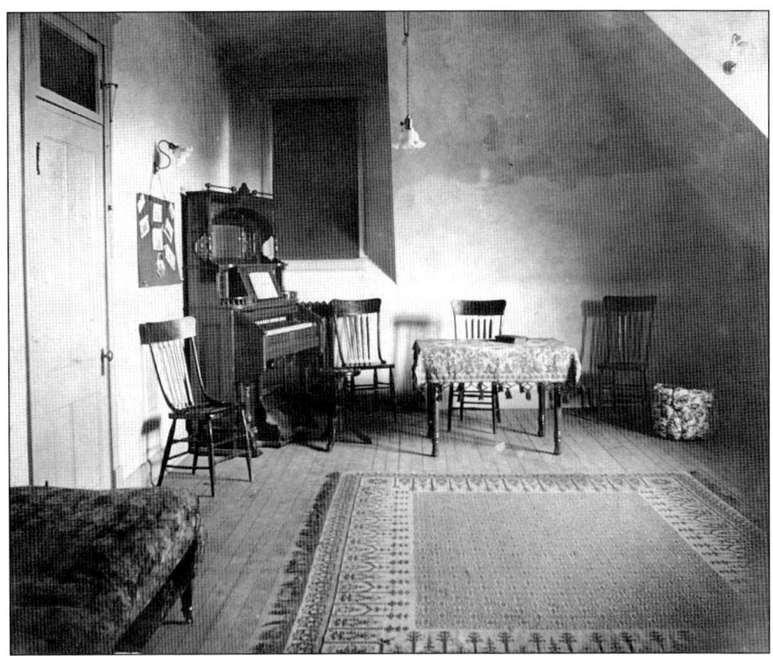

Female students paid 90¢ per week for a room in the dormitory. Students were required to supply their own bedding and pay their laundry bills. Each floor had a reception room and a society room, like the one seen here, for socializing with other students. Male students rented apartments or rooms in private homes. (Courtesy of Huron College Archives.)

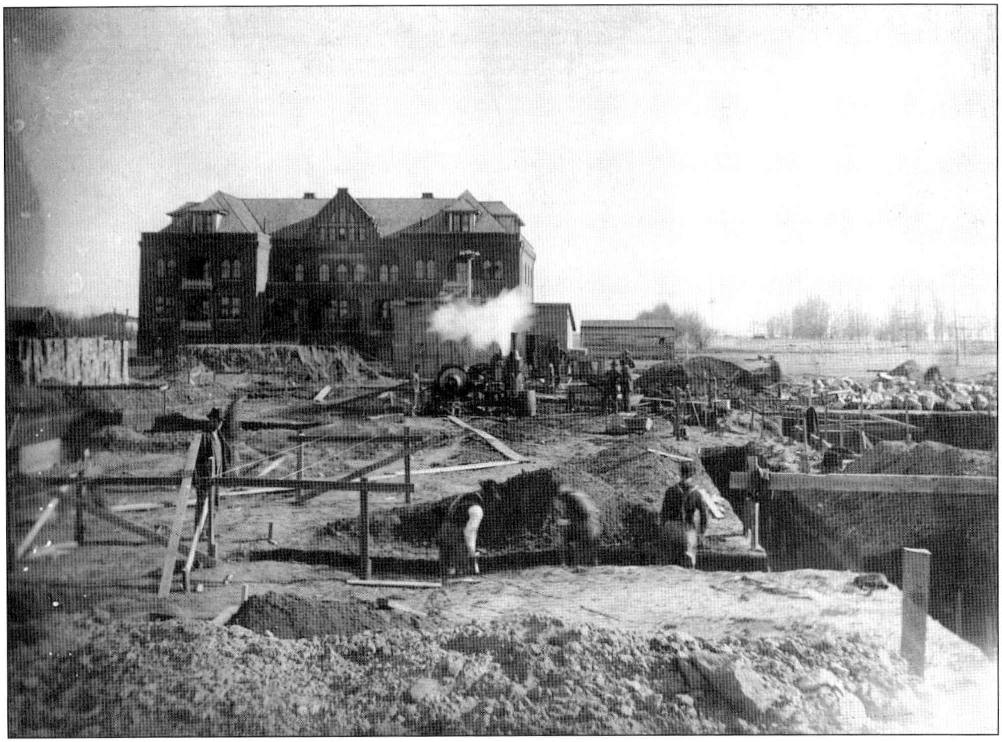

Generous donations from New Jersey philanthropist Ralph Voorhees aided in the construction of several buildings on the Huron campus. The workers seen here in 1907 were digging the foundation for the main academic building on campus, Voorhees Hall. Elizabeth Voorhees Girl's Dormitory can be seen in the background. (Courtesy of Huron College Archives.)

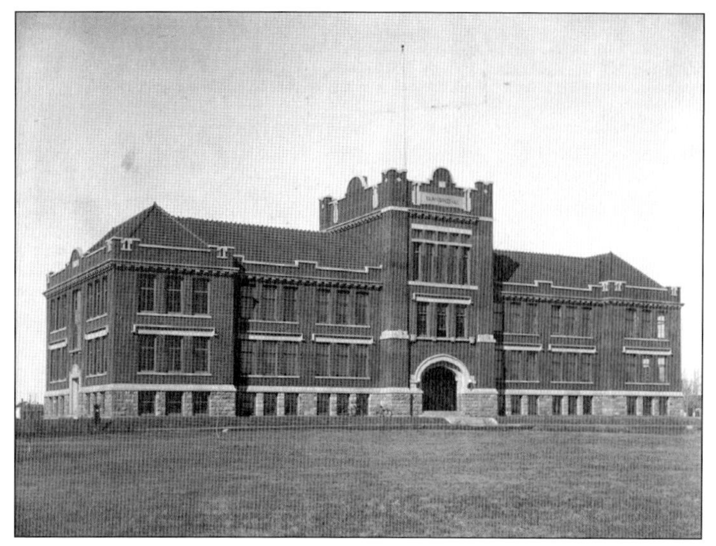

The most recognizable building on campus was Voorhees Hall. The imposing three-story building included a gymnasium and the commercial department on the lower level. Classrooms, offices, a library, and a chapel occupied the first floor. The second floor held the science department and an auditorium. Art and music rooms were located on the third floor. (Courtesy of Huron College Archives.)

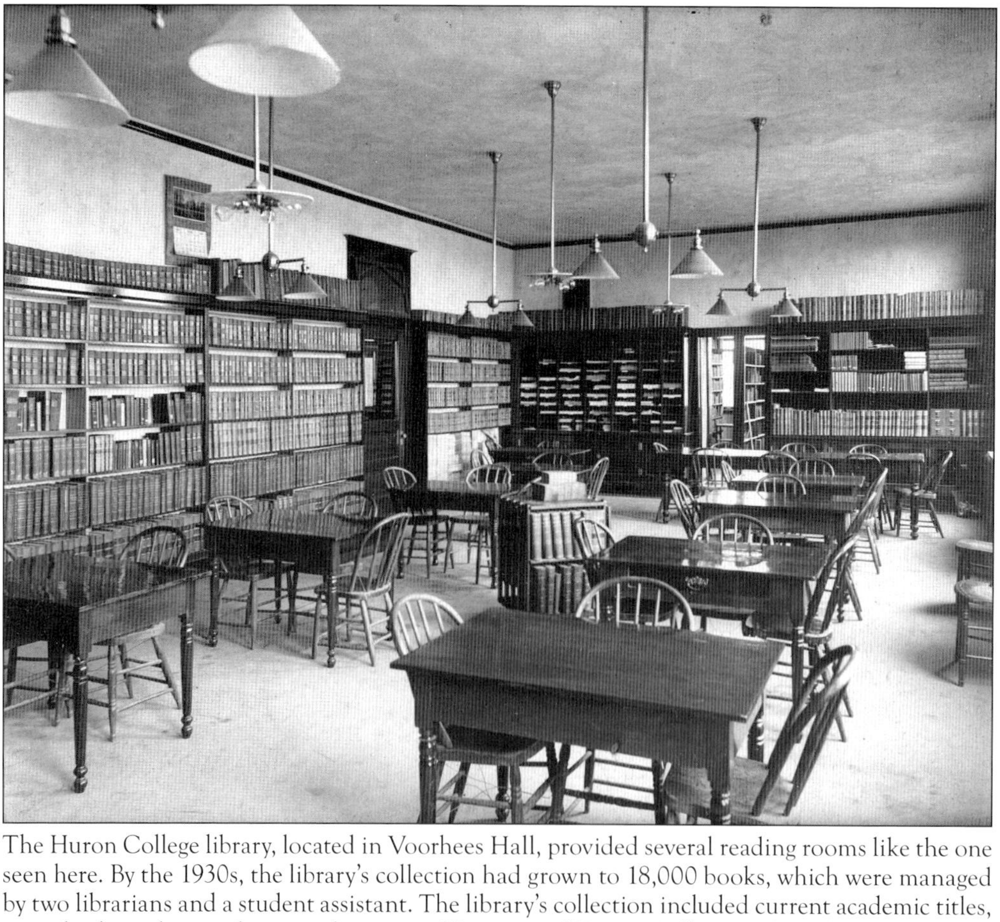

The Huron College library, located in Voorhees Hall, provided several reading rooms like the one seen here. By the 1930s, the library's collection had grown to 18,000 books, which were managed by two librarians and a student assistant. The library's collection included current academic titles, periodicals, and general interest literature. (Courtesy of Huron College Archives.)

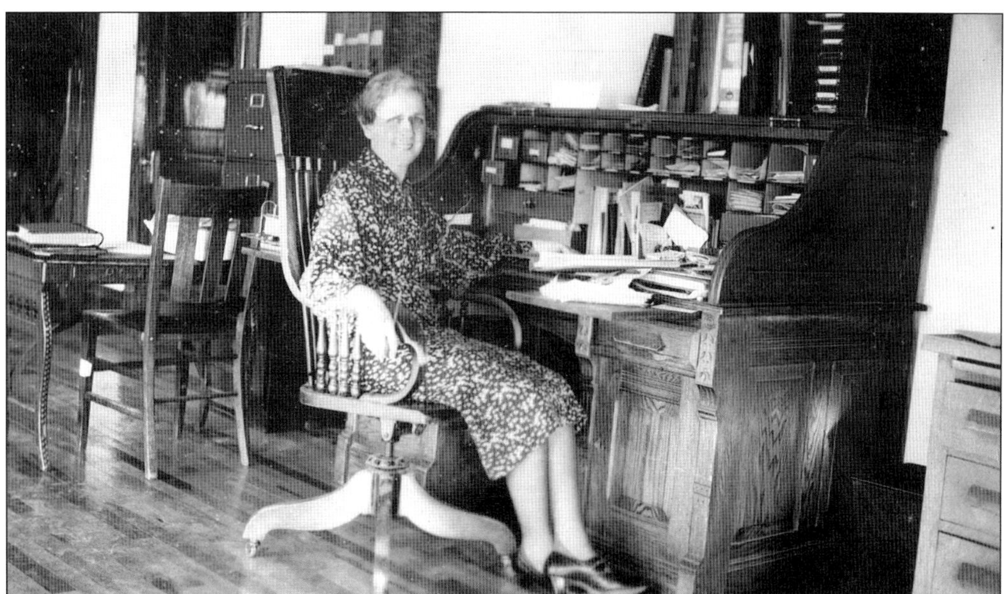

Ella McIntire was the college librarian from 1909 to 1956. In addition to operating the library, she was also the registrar, helping students select classes. When Dean Herbert Titt unexpectedly passed away in 1941, McIntire became acting dean. The new library was built in 1963 and named in her honor. (Courtesy of Huron College Archives.)

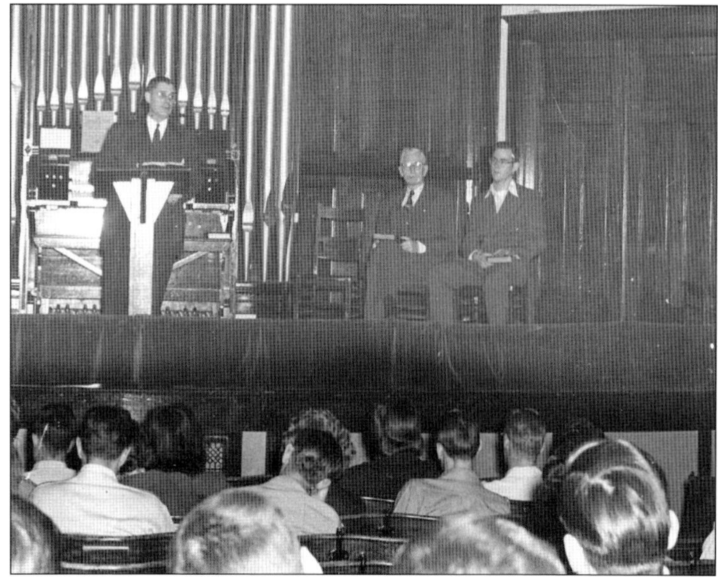

The chapel was the heart of the college. Located in Voorhees Hall, the chapel provided space for church services, concerts, and programs. The pipe organ in the background was used in the Presbyterian church and was donated to the college in 1928. Bess Stackpole, pipe organ instructor in the music department, played during the weekly chapel services. (Courtesy of Huron College Archives.)

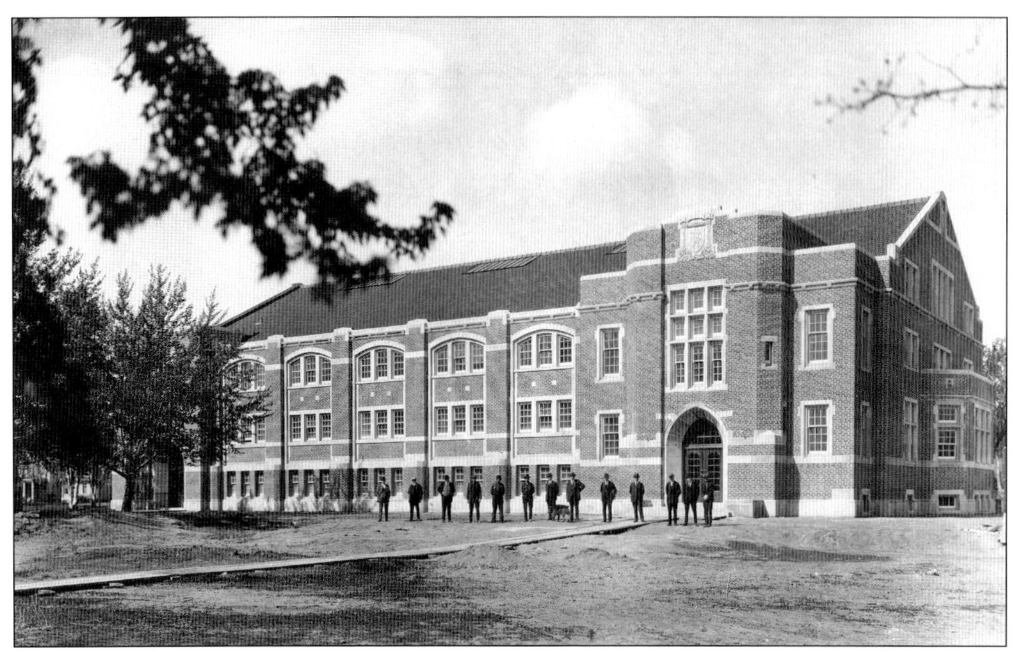

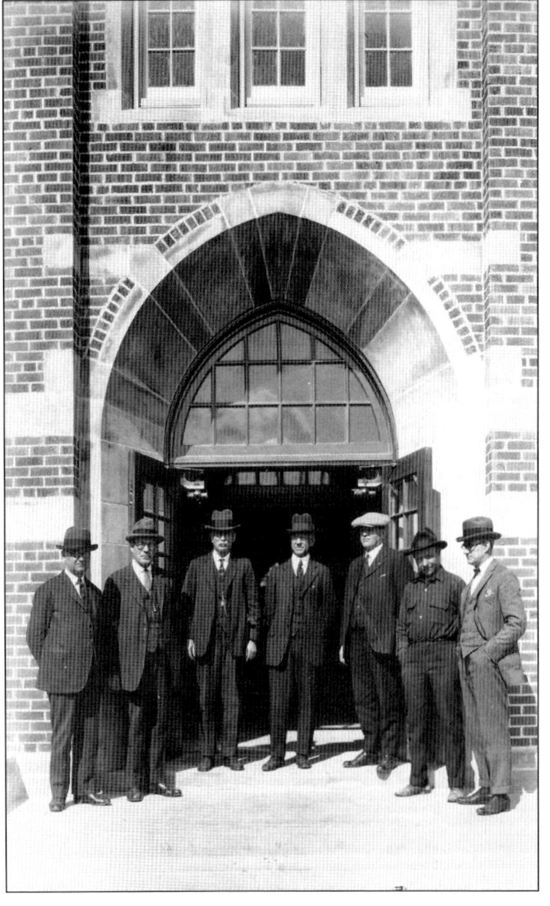

A campaign was launched in 1923 to build a combination auditorium and gymnasium. The building was completed in 1925 for a final cost of $145,000. College, high school, and city organizations frequently used the facility. The photograph above shows the building contractors standing in front of the completed building. To the left are members of the college's building committee, which included, from left to right, John Pasek (college business manager), Ben Olson, Frank Brumwell (chairman), George Fullenweider (treasurer), S.W. Jonason (general contractor), Ole Telste (general foreman), and George McCune (Huron College president). One of the first public events held in the building was a performance by John Philip Sousa and his 100-piece band. (Both, courtesy of Huron College Archives.)

The Huron College men's basketball team defeated Yankton College to become the 1916 state champions. Team members included, from left to right, (first row) Alfred Schroeder and N.H. McKay; (second row) Earl Louder, J.E. Schoof, and coach E.O. Williams; (third row) Edward Richter, George Longstaff, William Pinch, Donald McMurchie, and Carl Voight.

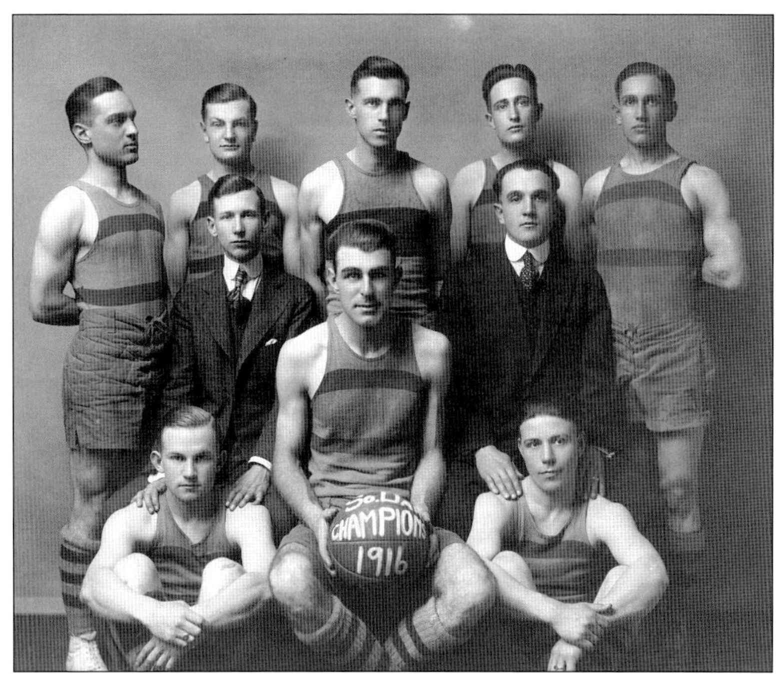

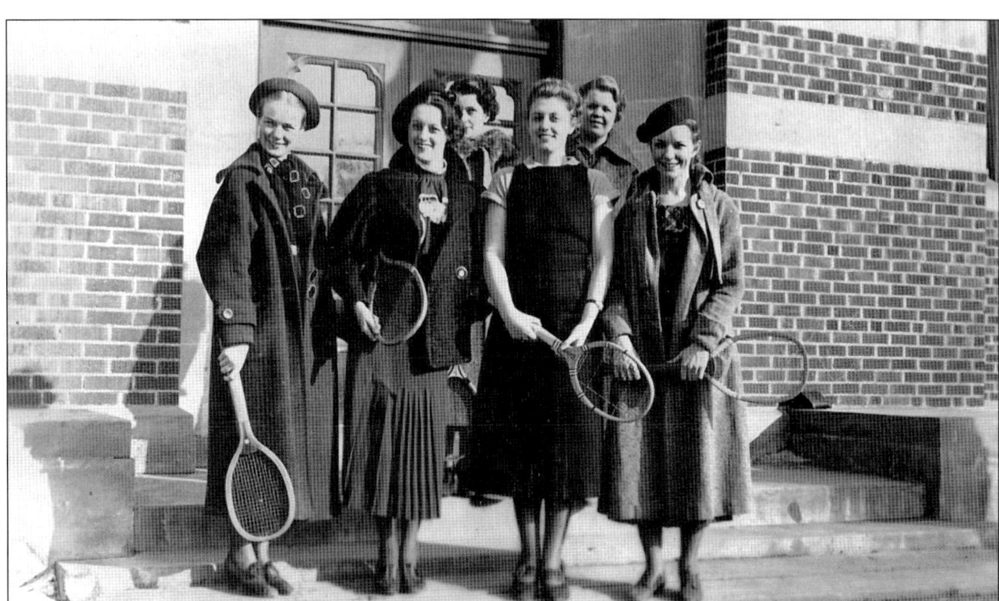

Sports for women on campus began in the early 1930s. Women were chosen for class teams based on their athletic ability, faithfulness, and scholarship. The classes competed against each other in tournaments. Members of the 1937 tennis team included, from left to right, Esther Serr, Margaret Noel, Velma Johnson, Gladys Brown, unidentified, and Joyce Anderson. (Courtesy of Huron College Archives.)

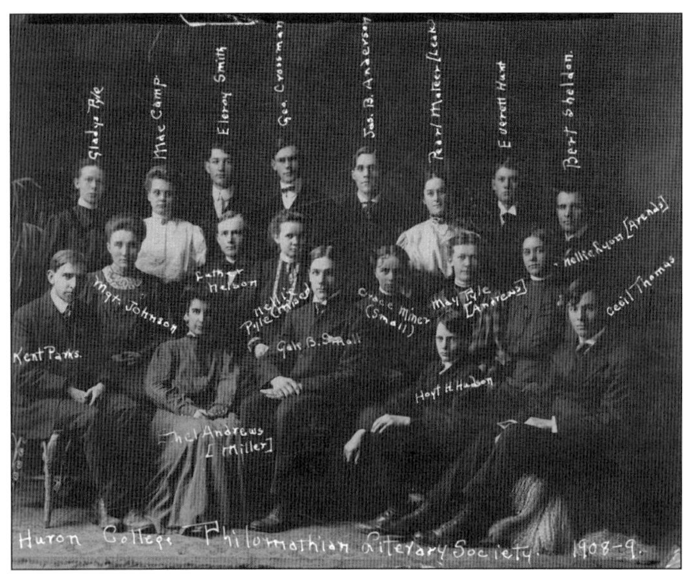

Members of the Philomathian Literary Society participated in orations, debates, mock trials, and short plays. Members included, from left to right, (first row) Kent Parks, Margaret Johnson, Ethel Andrews, Luther Nelson, Nellie Pyle, Gale B. Small, Grace Miner, May Pyle, Hoyt Hudson, Nellie Lyon, and Cecil Thomas; (second row) Gladys Pyle, Mae Camp, Eleroy Smith, George Crossman, James B. Anderson, Pearl Mateer, Everett Hunt, and Bert Sheldon.

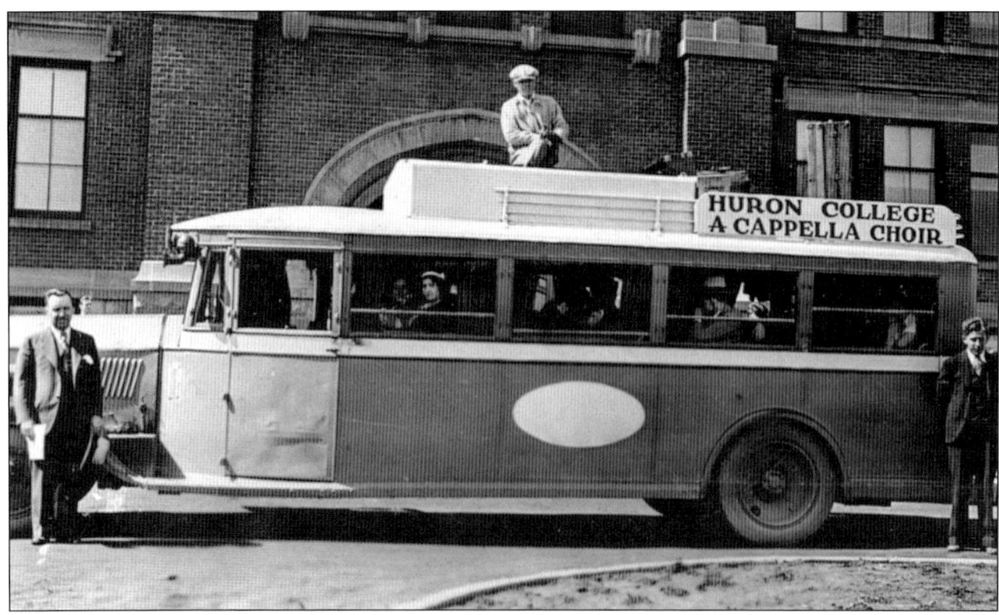

The Huron College A Capella Choir was an active group on campus. The men and women sang for chapel and church services in Huron. They traveled by bus, like the one seen here from 1933, to perform in churches or schools throughout the state. The choir's repertoire consisted of hymns, secular numbers, and songs in foreign languages. (Courtesy of Huron College Archives.)

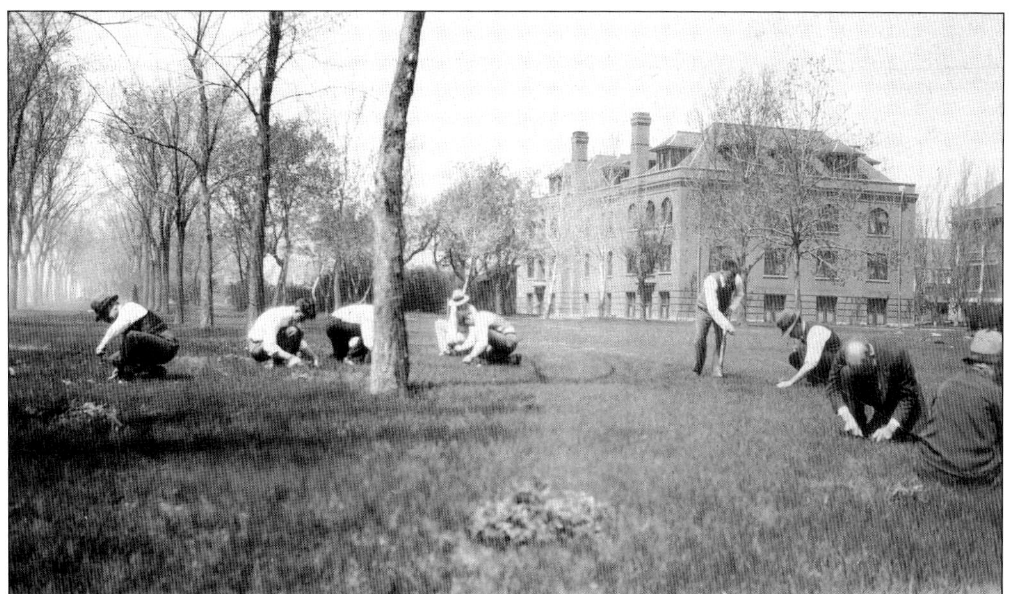

Each year in mid-May, Huron College participated in Dandelion Days. Students and faculty were assigned sections of campus to pull dandelions to make the campus look nice. In 1932, the freshmen, seen here, were assigned the worst corner of campus. They persevered, however, and in the end, accumulated the largest pile of dandelions. (Courtesy of Huron College Archives.)

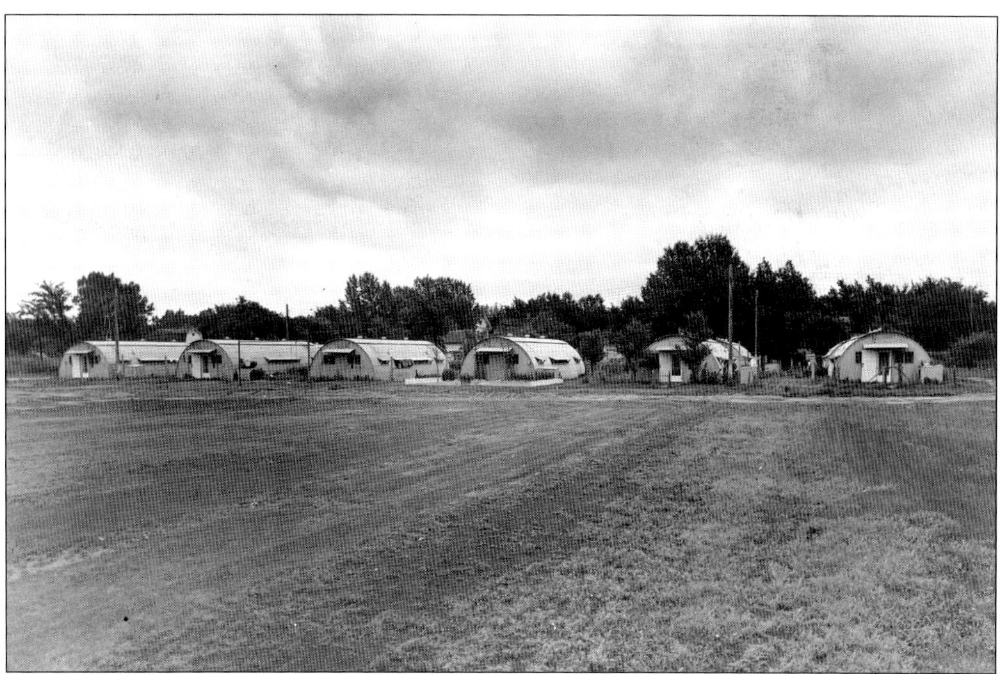

Huron College erected 12 Quonset huts on an unused portion of the football field to accommodate the influx of married servicemen returning to college after World War II. Ten of the semicircular metal buildings were divided in half to house two families each. The remaining two huts contained laundry services and a communal lavatory. (Courtesy of Huron College Archives.)

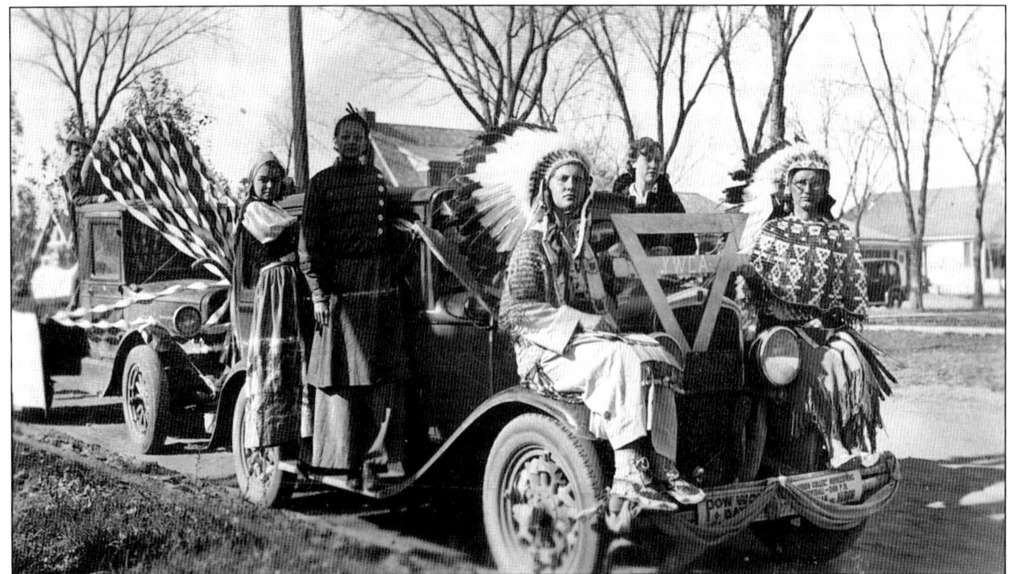

Pow Wow Days was a yearly tradition on campus. The idea of an Indian theme was introduced in 1923 and replaced the traditional homecoming activities. The day of celebration was a way to promote the college and generate community support. This photograph from the 1930s shows a parade car carrying the students chosen as Chief Warrior and Pow Wow Princess. (Courtesy of Huron College Archives.)

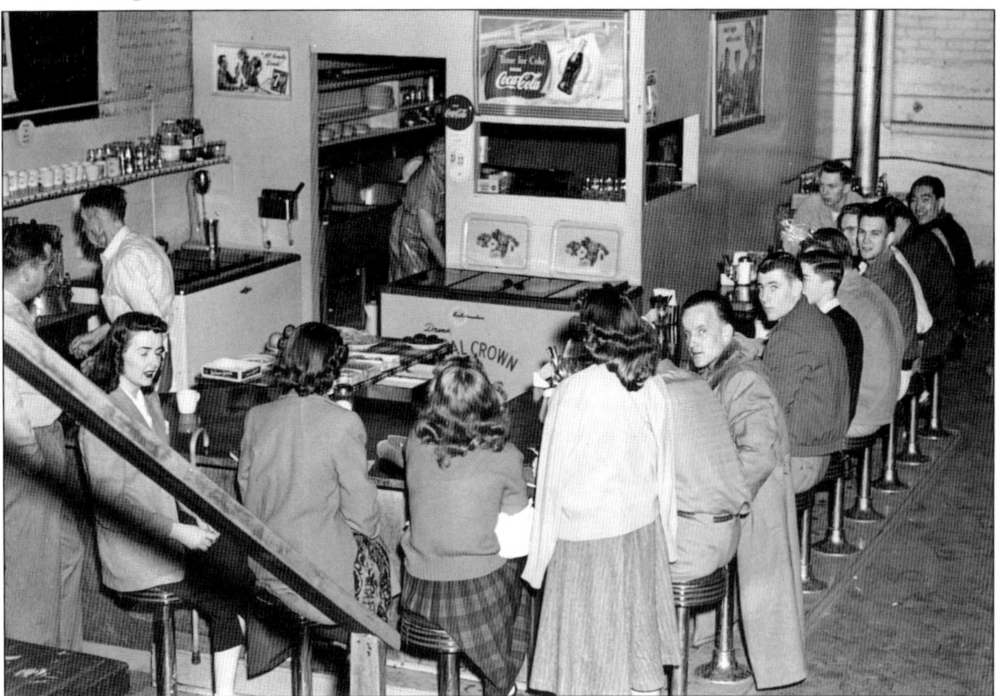

The Wigwam, or student union, was located in the basement of the college gymnasium. It was the most popular meeting place on campus. Students could gather to chat, play Ping-Pong, or drink a cup of coffee between classes. These students are enjoying a bite to eat from the café. (Courtesy of Huron College Archives.)

Six

Founded in Faith

Early Huron pioneers brought strong European religious beliefs and cultural traditions. People who shared the same language, customs, and beliefs tended to settle in the same towns, which helped foster a sense of belonging and fellowship. Congregations were formed, and finding a place to worship became a priority. Due to limited funds, it was common for different congregations to worship together at a common location. In Huron, congregations met at places like the schoolhouse, train depot, courthouse, and the Dakota House Hotel.

Clergymen were few and far between during Huron's early history. Ministers often followed the construction of the railroad, serving new communities as they were established. Traveling pastors came to Huron on horseback or by buggy in the summer and by train in the winter. They often spoke to crowds of people from many different denominations.

Railroads were eager to help the new congregations. Having a physical church building indicated that the town was permanently established. This in turn encouraged more people to move to town, which ultimately benefitted the railroad. In Huron, the Chicago & Northwestern Railroad donated one lot to each of the five established congregations to build a church. Raising funds for construction became the next priority at the turn of the century.

During World War I, ethnic-oriented churches became more integrated and often changed their name to avoid discrimination toward Eastern European countries. During the Great Depression, people relied heavily upon the church to provide emotional and spiritual strength, as well as food, temporary shelter, and clothing to endure the hard times.

Churches continued to grow and change to meet the needs of their congregations and the community. As new cultures moved to the area, new places of worship were erected. In 2023, the Huron Chamber of Commerce business directory listed 35 places of worship, reflecting the wide variety of cultures and religious beliefs of the people who now call Huron home.

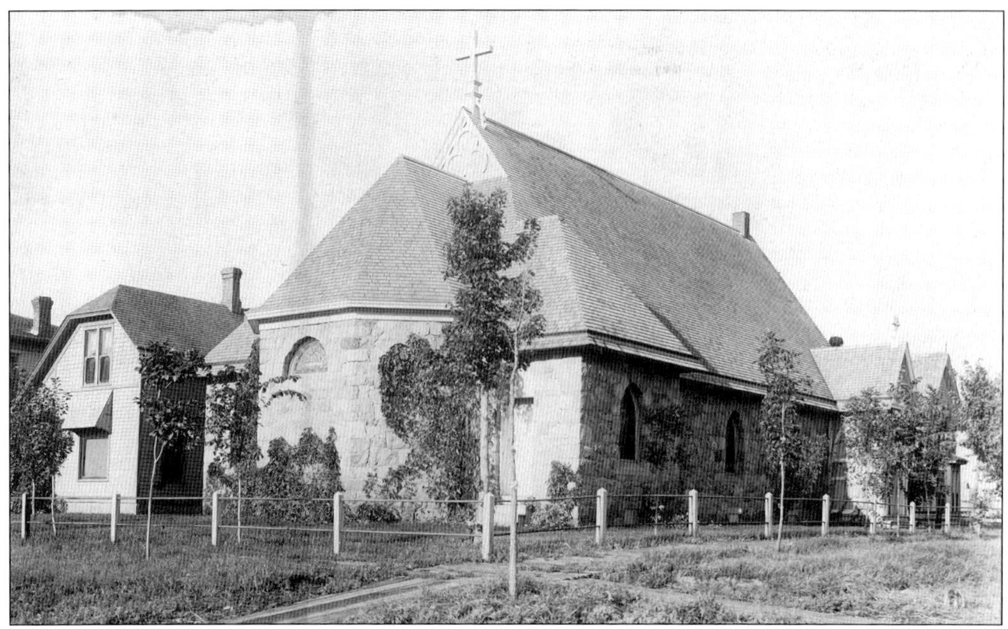

Grace Episcopal Church had its beginnings in 1881. It was not until 1887 that a permanent building was constructed. The thick rock walls were made of native fieldstone from the Charles May farm northeast of Huron. The building served the congregation until 1964. It is now the Centennial Stone Church Center and houses part of the Dakotaland Museum's collection. It is listed in the National Register of Historic Places.

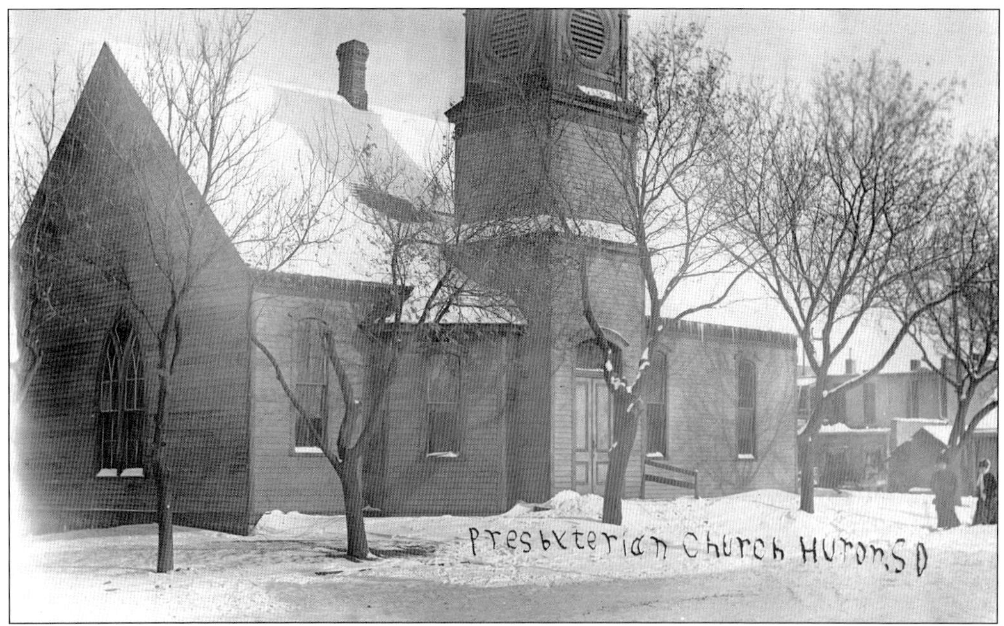

The First Presbyterian Church in Huron was organized on August 29, 1880. Ten members met at the Chicago & Northwestern Railroad depot. The following year, the congregation voted to construct a church. The building was located at the corner of Wisconsin Avenue and Fourth Street. Some of the first church members included Fred Kent, proprietor of the Depot Hotel, and Mamie and John Pyle. (Courtesy of Jennifer Littlefield.)

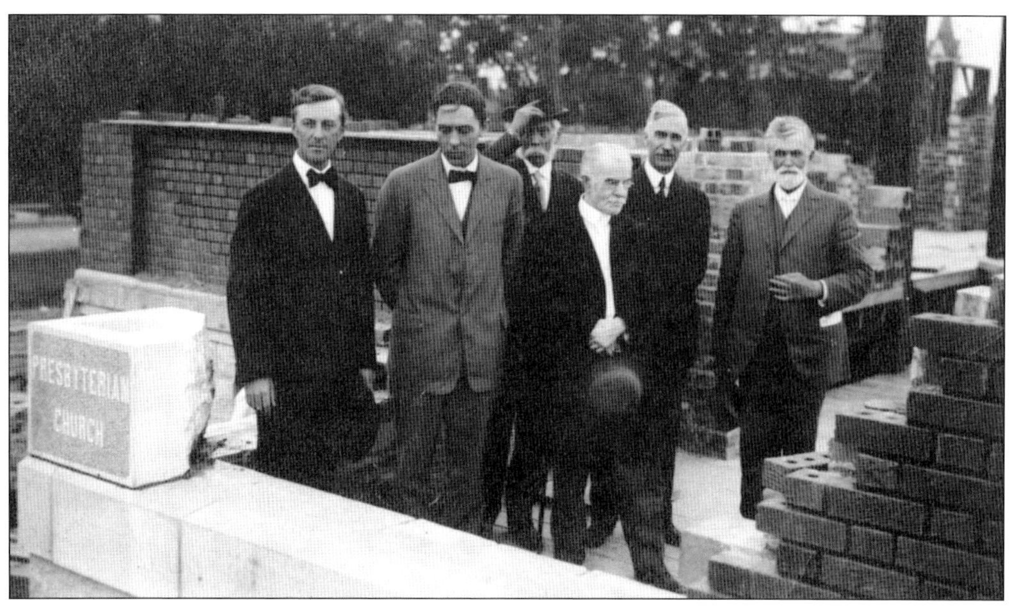

Within four years, the Presbyterian congregation had outgrown the original building. A new church was constructed on the corner of Dakota Avenue and Fifth Street. The church was dedicated in September 1915. The photograph above shows prominent members of the church during the cornerstone dedication. They are, from left to right, Rev. Hubert Ketelle (pastor), Dr. H.M. Gage (Huron College president), unidentified, E.H. Grant (elder), Dr. Calvin H. French (former Huron College president), and Rev. H.P. Carson (stated clerk of the Presbytery of South Dakota). The photograph below is of the completed church. (Above, courtesy of First Presbyterian Church; below, courtesy of Huron Public Library.)

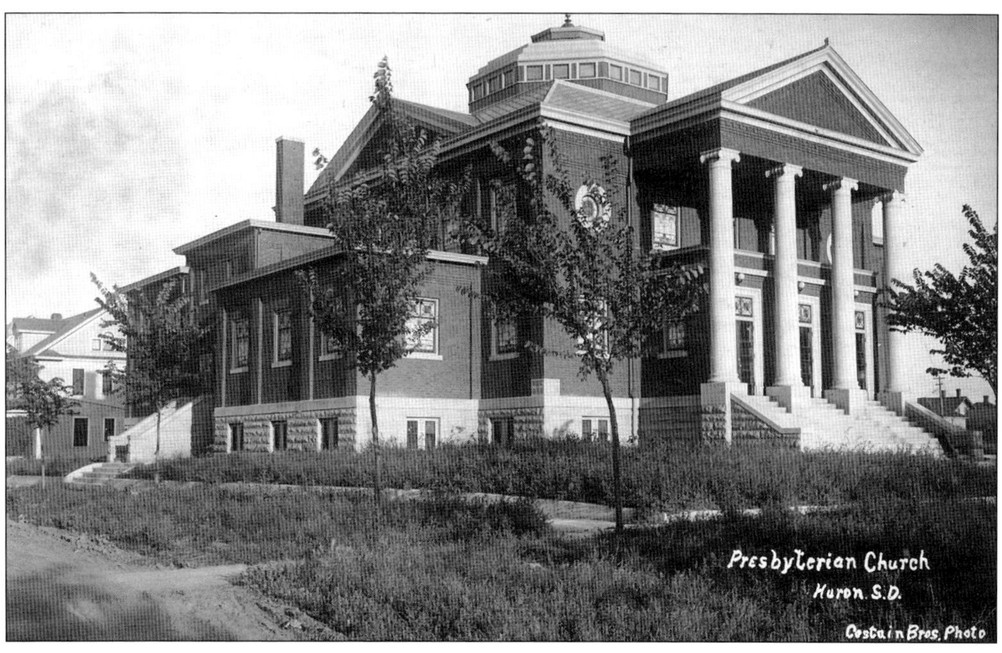

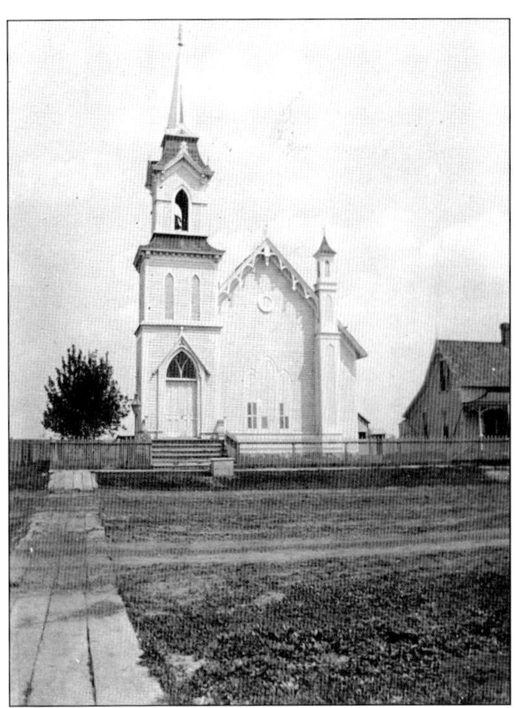

Fr. Robert Haire traveled from Aberdeen on horseback in the spring of 1881 to conduct the first Catholic mass. Services were held at the Dakota House Hotel. By 1882, a church building had been completed on land donated by T.J. Nichol, superintendent of the Chicago & Northwestern Railroad. This photograph shows the church in 1903 with the addition of an ornate vestibule and spire.

St. Martin's Catholic Church was completed in 1914 on the corner of Kansas Avenue and Fifth Street. The crowd seen here is gathered at the building site for the blessing of the cornerstone, led by Father Desmond. The cornerstone was contributed by J.T. Breen. The original church, seen in the background, was moved to Cavour. (Courtesy of Holy Trinity Catholic Church.)

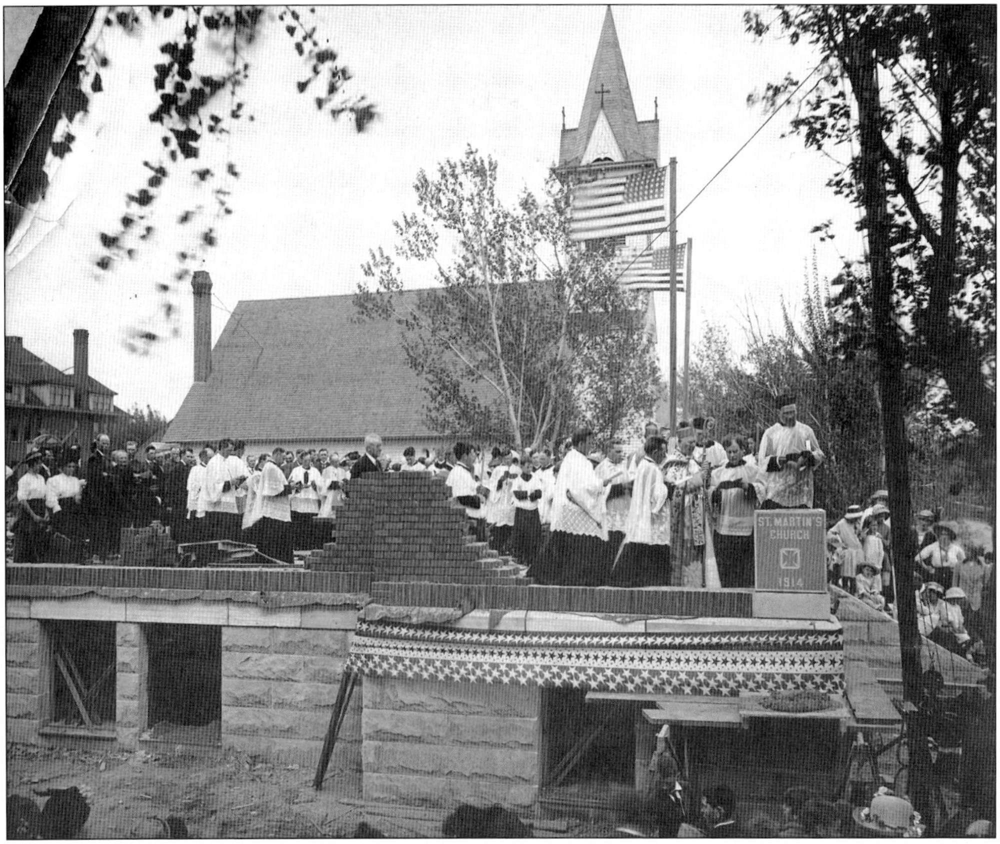

In 1952, large stained-glass windows were installed in St. Martin's Catholic Church. Andre Rault, an artist from Rennes, France, created the stained glass using a formula known only to his family. He added color to the molten glass instead of painting it on the surface. This resulted in more vibrant colors and allowed sunlight to shine through the glass. (Courtesy of Holy Trinity Catholic Church.)

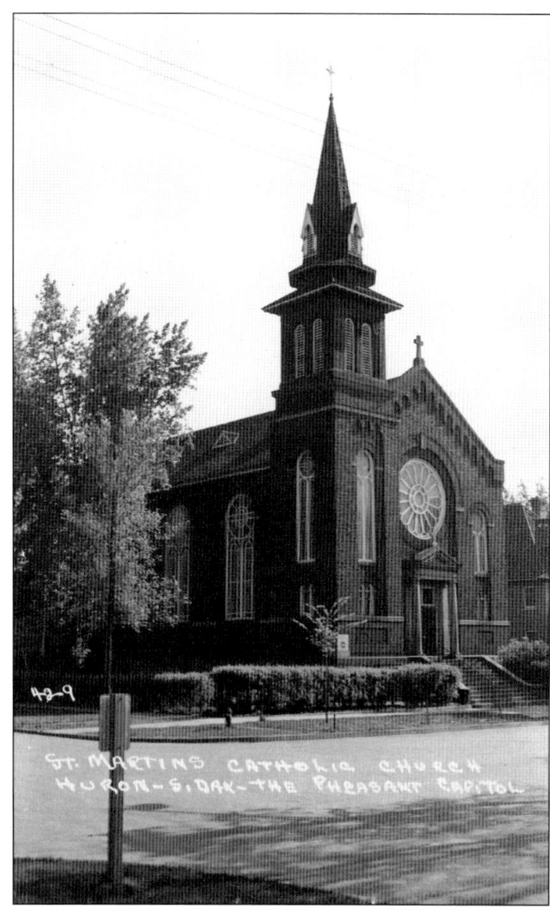

The Congregational church was organized in 1884. Services were held in a building owned by John Campbell, president of the First National Bank. The following year, a church was built on a lot donated by the Chicago & Northwestern Railroad at California Avenue and Fifth Street. This photograph shows the original church after it was enlarged in 1903.

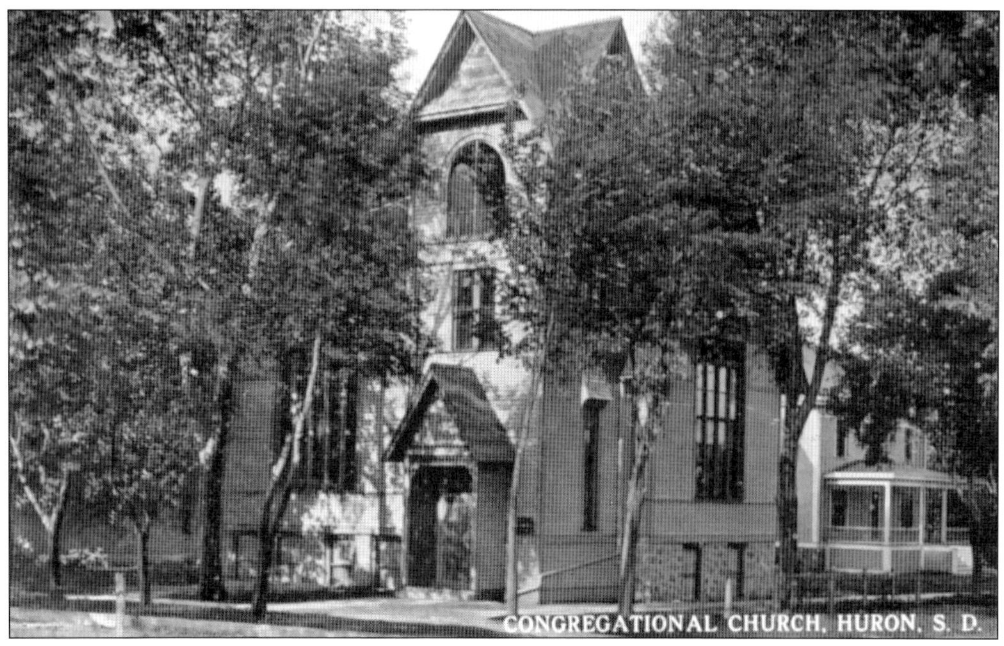

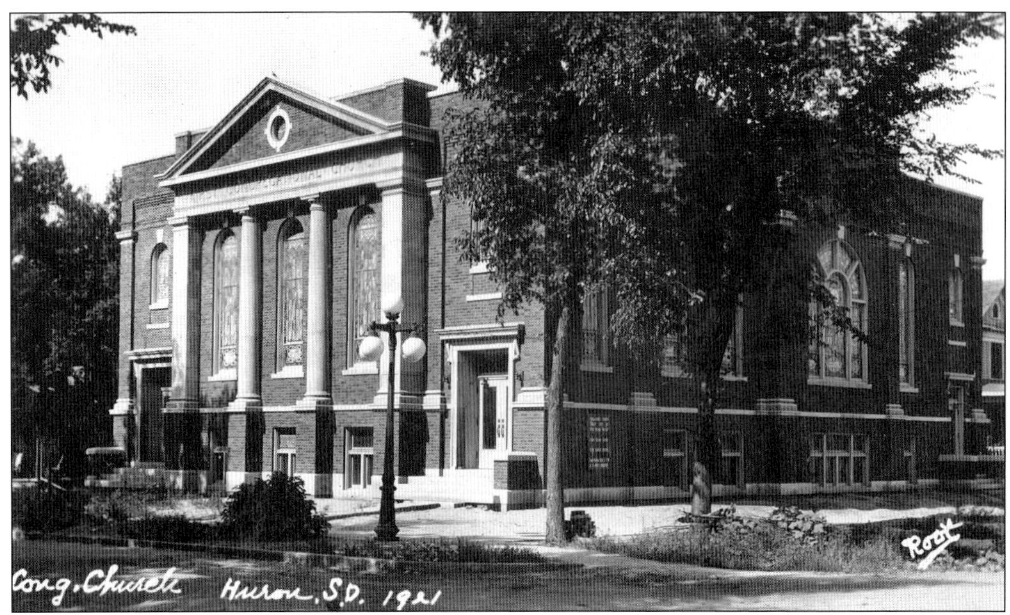

In 1919, the Congregational church was replaced with a brick building at the same location. During construction, a fire started, damaging the inner walls of the building. This delayed the dedication of the building by a year. This photograph shows the completed structure in 1922 before its dedication. (Courtesy of Jennifer Littlefield.)

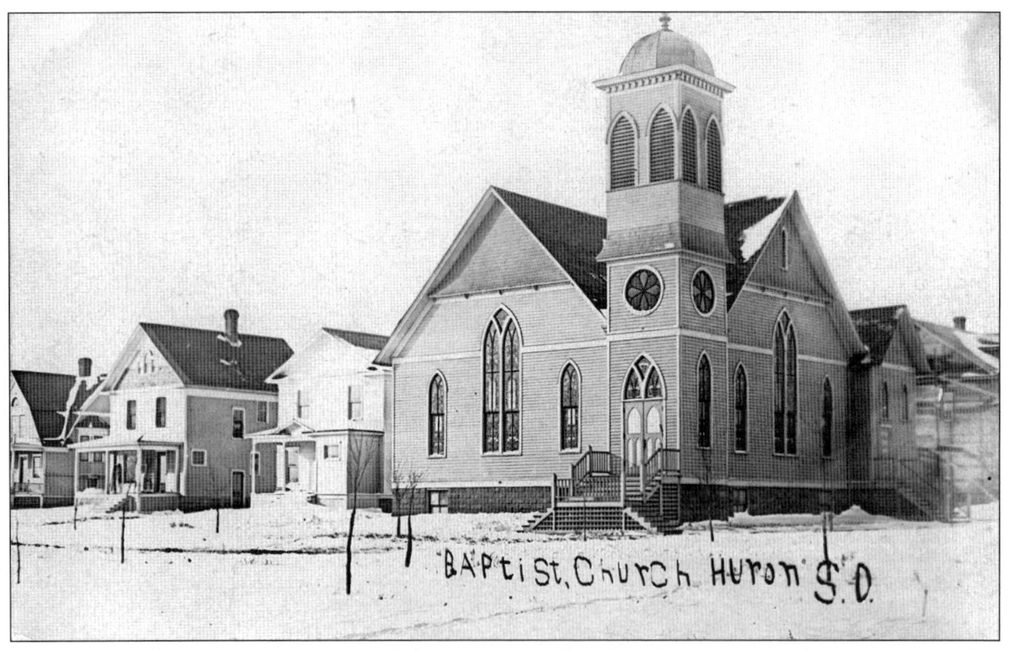

Rev. George Cressey, a missionary of the American Baptist Home Mission Society, arrived in Huron in July 1880. He gave the first sermon by a Baptist minister in Beadle County to a group gathered at the Chicago & Northwestern Railroad depot. This photograph is of the second Baptist church, completed in 1908. Six hundred people attended the dedication of the church on January 23, 1908. (Courtesy of Jennifer Littlefield.)

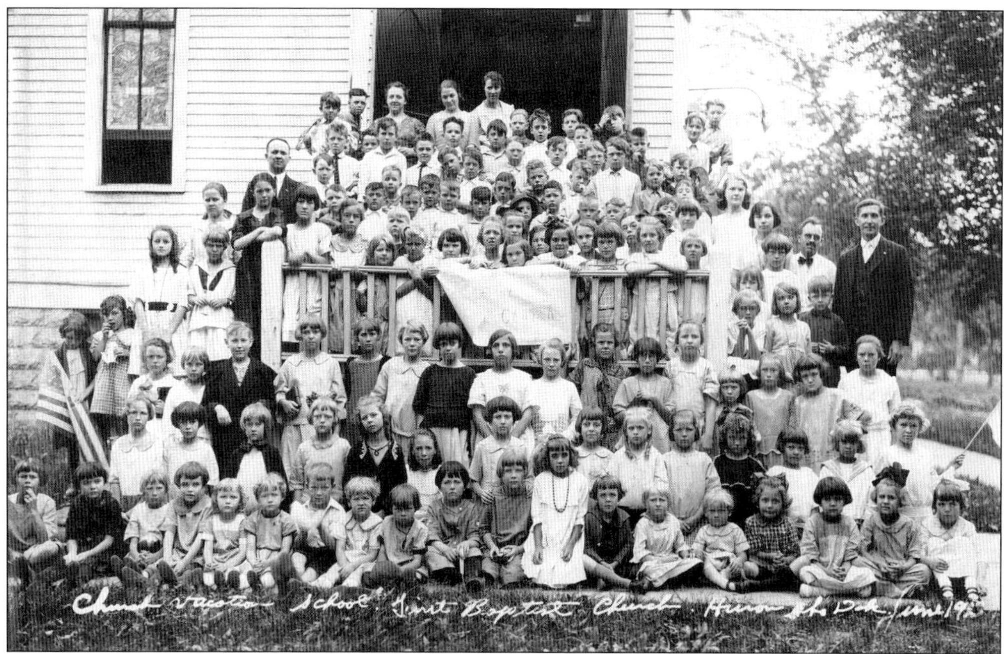

The Baptist church offered vacation church school during the summer. This group attended in June 1923. All children ages 5 to 13 were invited to attend. In addition to songs and stories, children also learned the Pledge of Allegiance and about good citizenship. Activities for older boys included making knotted hammocks and woven baskets. Girls learned sewing and raffia work.

Like many other denominations in Huron, the first meeting of Methodists was held in the Chicago & Northwestern Railroad depot. The church building was completed in 1884 and was described as the finest church in the Dakota Territory. The congregation is standing in front of the Gothic-style structure located at the corner of Kansas Avenue and Fourth Street.

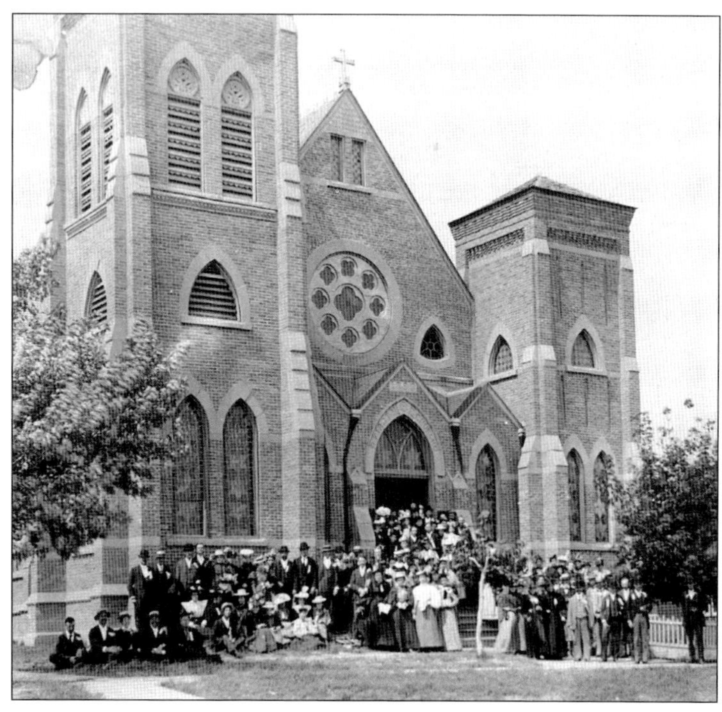

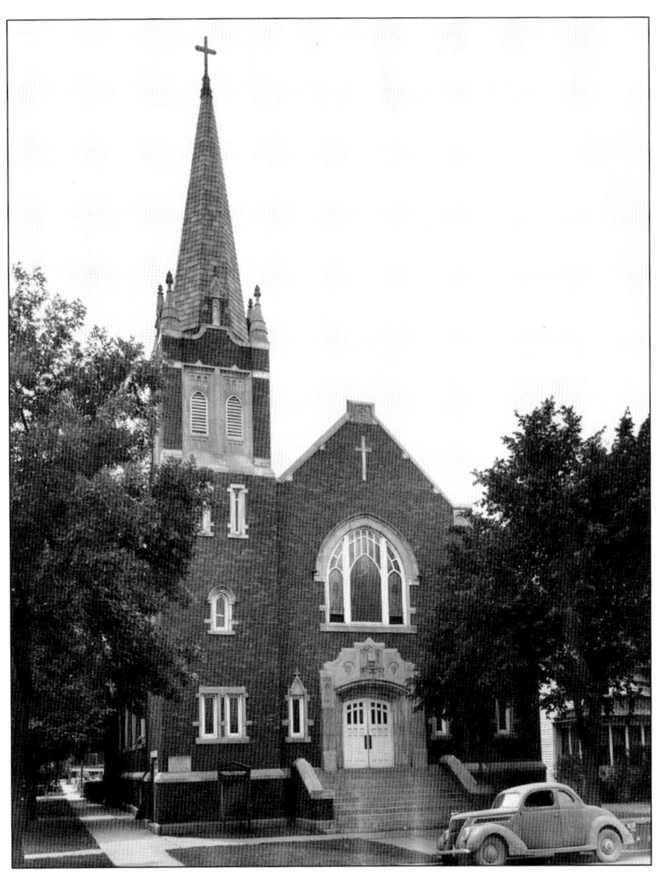

In 1923, plans were underway to construct a larger Lutheran church. The basement was completed that year, and services were held there until construction was complete in 1926. Architect F.C.W. Kuehn designed the building in a Gothic style with high open beams and extensive windows. This photograph shows the church as it looked in 1949. (Courtesy of American Lutheran Church.)

Ruby Matson became the American Lutheran Church's organist and choir director in 1932. She held that position for 32 years. She is seen here at the piano with the church choir during a Christmas service. Christmas Eve concerts were so heavily attended that the concert had to be repeated the following Sunday evening. (Courtesy of American Lutheran Church.)

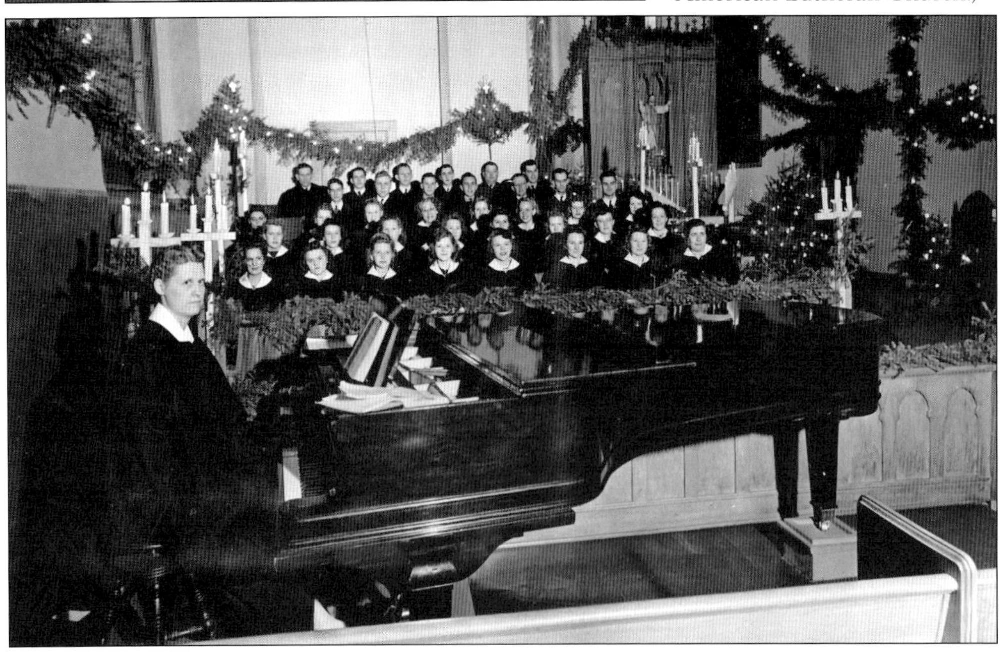

Seven

The Fair City

The Annual Territory Fair began as a promotional tool to entice settlers and businesses to move to the Dakota Territory. Huron was chosen as the site of the first fair in 1885 because of its accessibility to the populated sections of the territory. The fair was extremely successful with total receipts reaching nearly $7,500.

Huron was again chosen for the 1886 fair, which was even more successful, but in 1887, it was decided to move the fair to different locations every two years. The South Dakota State Fair Board continued this policy after the division of the territory in 1889.

The fair was losing money due to the expense of moving every two years. Visitors and vendors also decreased because of the inconvenience and confusion caused by the change of venue. It was determined that the state fair needed a permanent location at a central point, on its own grounds, that could be enlarged and improved upon to accommodate a growing state. In 1905, the legislature authorized Huron to be the permanent location of the state fair, and Huron quickly became known as "the Fair City."

The decision was validated when income jumped from $8,700 in 1904 to $12,200 the next year, along with a record-breaking 10,000 people in attendance. Entries and exhibits across the board doubled and, in many cases, quadrupled within the first three years. By 1913, the fair hosted 40,000 to 50,000 guests.

Buildings and land were added over the years, and buildings were razed and rebuilt as needed. The fairgrounds now encompass 190 acres with buildings to accommodate livestock, displays, trade shows, and special events year-round; 1,200 campsites; a grandstand seating capacity of 6,000 plus a large standing room section; and a new Dakota Event Complex, known as the DEX, which was completed in 2023 to replace the beef complex that burned down in 2021. The fair averages 200,000 visitors, exhibitors, vendors, and 4-H participants annually.

The South Dakota State Fair is the largest agricultural fair in the nation and continues to be the pride of the Fair City.

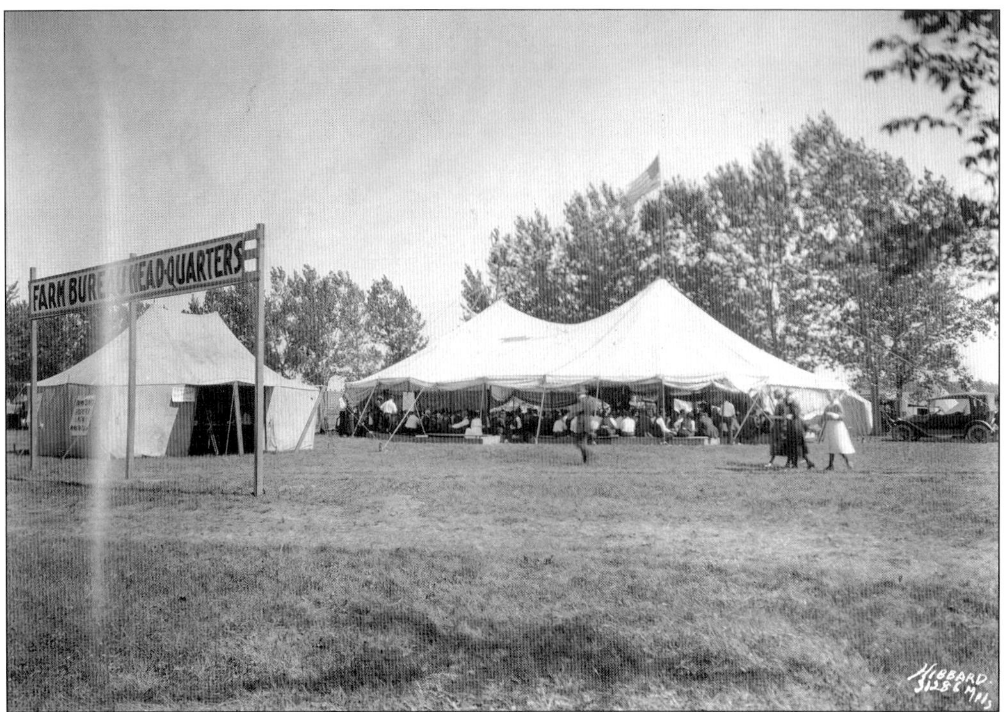

The Territorial Fair was conceived to promote the agriculture, horticulture, manufacturing, animal husbandry, and domestic arts of the settlers in the Dakota Territory to attract people to move to the area. Many exhibits and vendors were housed in large tents scattered across the fairgrounds, such as these Farm Bureau tents. The Farm Bureau has been an integral part of the agricultural community in South Dakota since 1917.

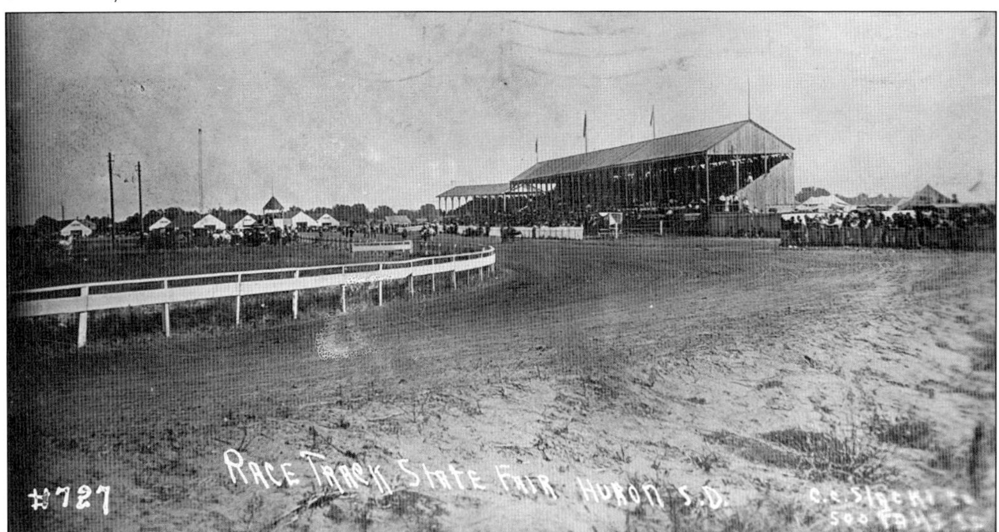

Huron was chosen as the location for the first fair because it had an established fairground with a few buildings and a racetrack. The fair ran from September 29 to October 2, 1885. In 1886, more than $600 was spent improving the track and doubling the grandstand, increasing the seating capacity to 1,500. In 1905, a grandstand was purchased from the Yankton Fair Association and moved to Huron.

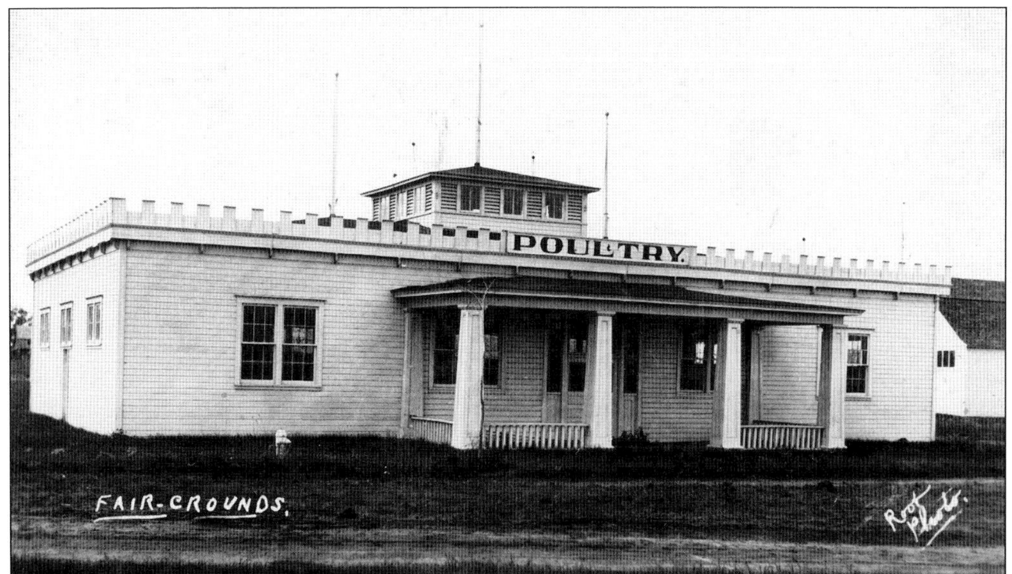

In January 1903, the Chicago & Northwestern Railroad deeded 85 acres within the city of Huron to the state fair board. This parcel contained the racetrack and a few buildings like the Poultry Building above acquired from the Central South Dakota Fair Association. The legislature authorized Huron as the permanent location for the state fair in 1905 and appropriated $15,000 for the improvement of the grounds.

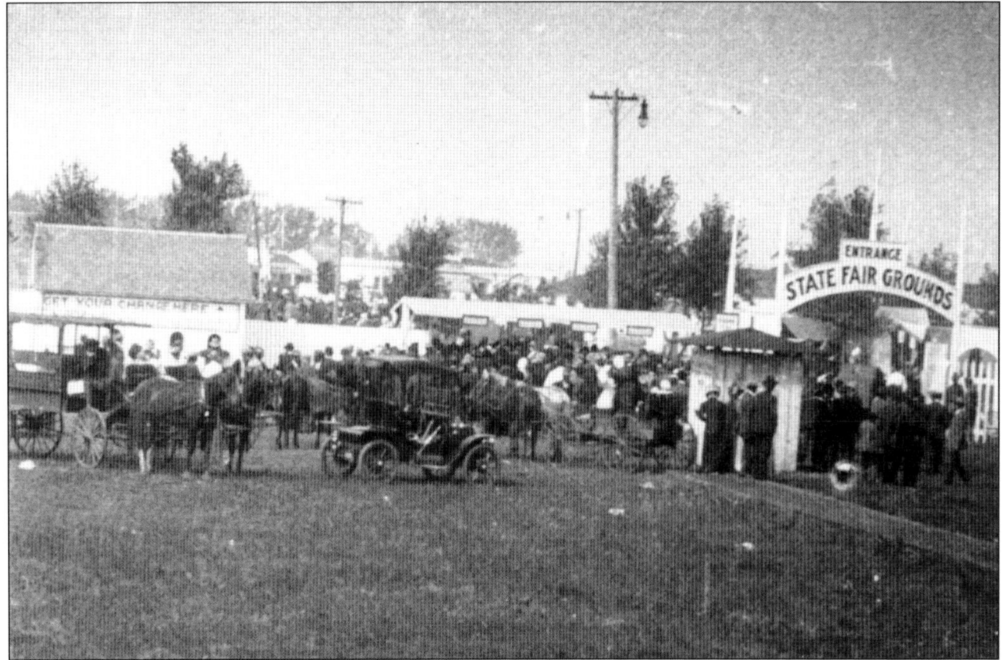

Many fairgoers and exhibitors arrived by train. There were special excursion routes and schedules planned with a designated stop at the main gate on Second Street. The Chicago & Northwestern Railroad sold more than 3,000 tickets to Huron on September 20, 1905. Both the Chicago & Northwestern and the Great Northern Railroads had dedicated tracks for unloading livestock, equipment, and other cargo for the exhibitors.

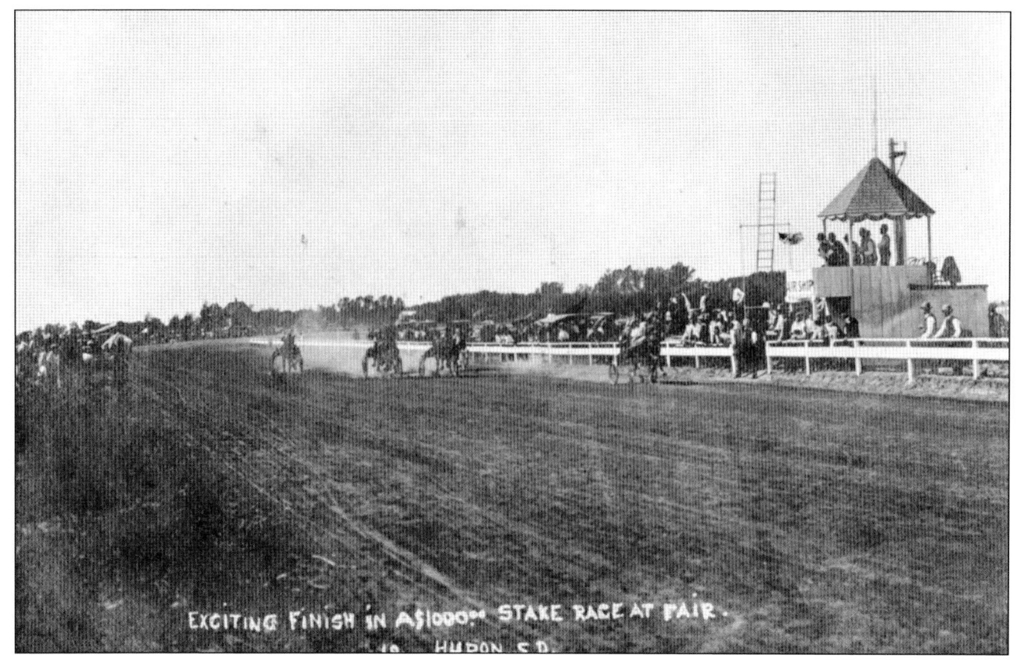

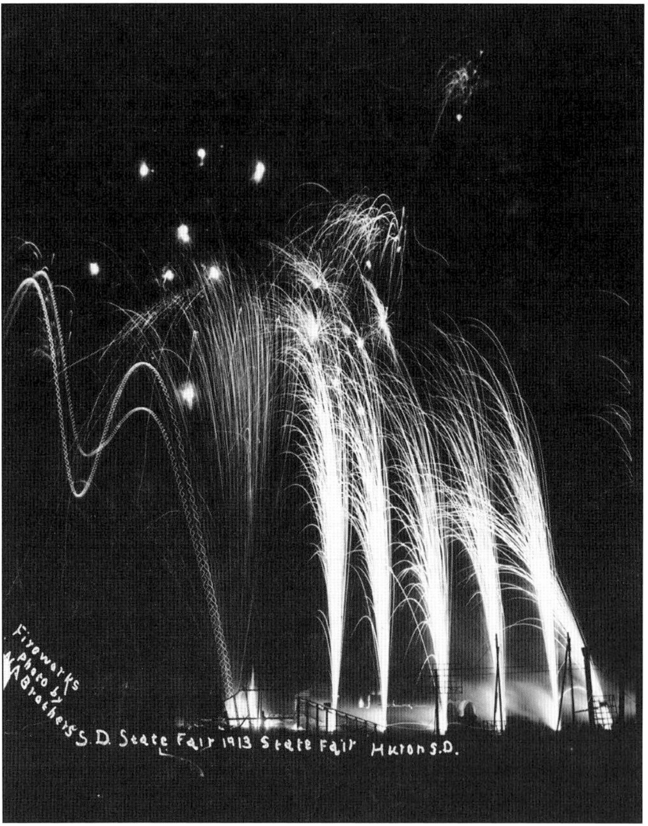

Daytime grandstand entertainment at the state fair included horse and mule races—and even ostrich races at one time. Due to the large purses offered, the fair attracted many of the fastest horses in the country. The photograph above shows the finish line of a race in 1910 with a $1,000 purse. By 1910, the fairgrounds included six barns to house 500 horses competing in the various events, and the grandstand seating capacity had increased to 6,000. According to the September 21, 1905, edition of the *Dakota Huronite*, "Long before the races began the two large grandstands and bleachers were filled to overflowing." Evening entertainment included pageants, circuses, musical revues, vaudeville productions, sacred concerts on Sunday, and lavish fireworks displays such as the one shown at left from 1913.

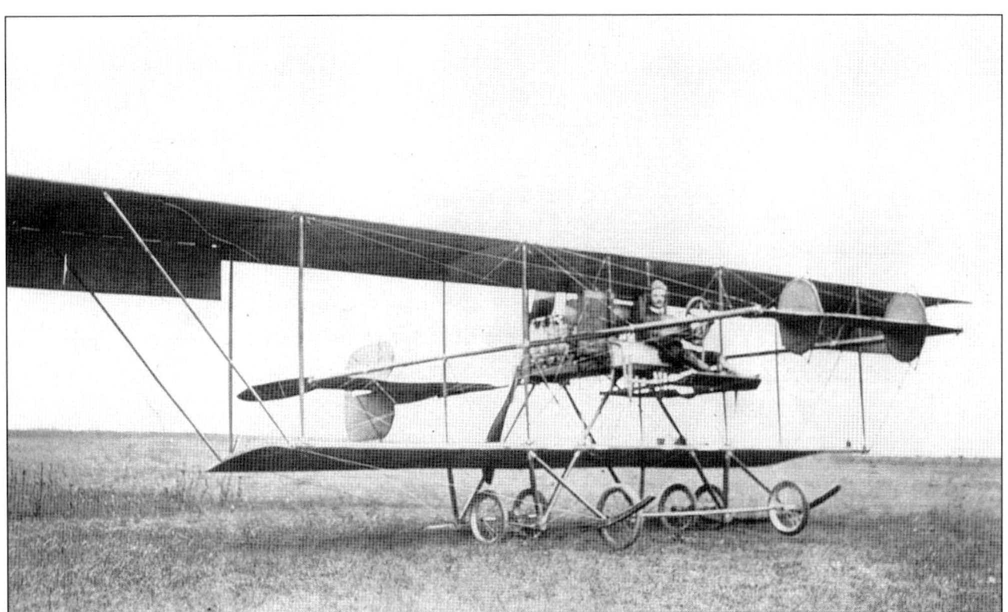

In 1911, the fair added air shows to the grandstand entertainment. Glenn Curtiss, above, was the first daredevil stunt pilot. He performed aeronautic acrobatics in his flimsy airplane, brought to Huron by train. Curtiss died the following year at a county fair in Spokane, Washington, when he crashed his airplane. Auto racing joined the grandstand lineup in 1916. A new steel and cement grandstand was completed in 1918 at a cost of $50,000 and included the three-story stand for officials pictured below and two tracks: one for racecars and one for horses. An addition to the grandstand was built in 1929. Horse racing continued into the 1950s but was limited to only two afternoons.

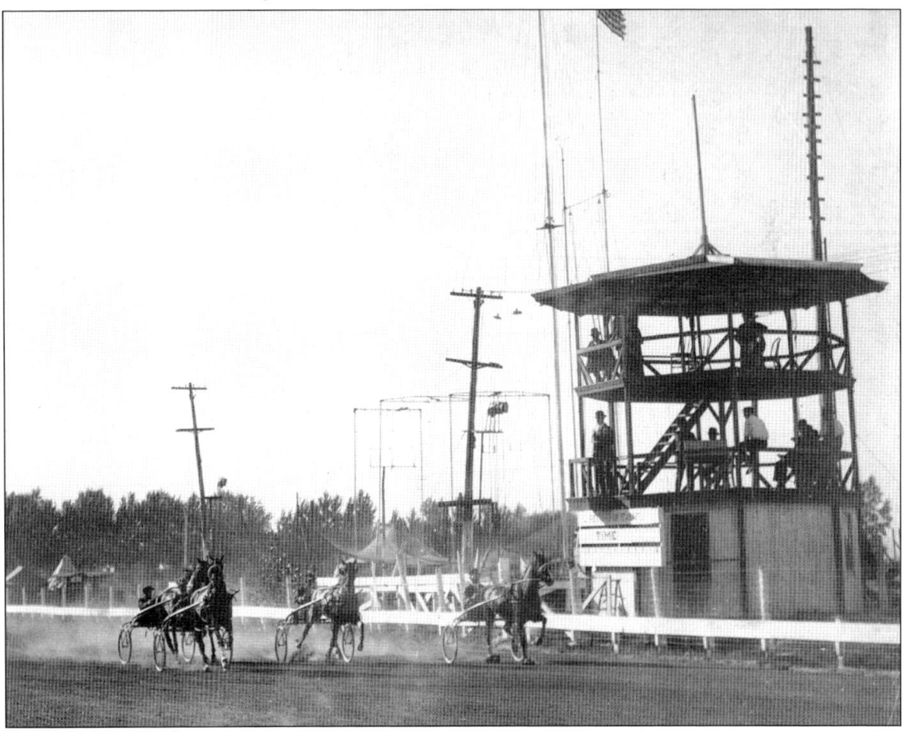

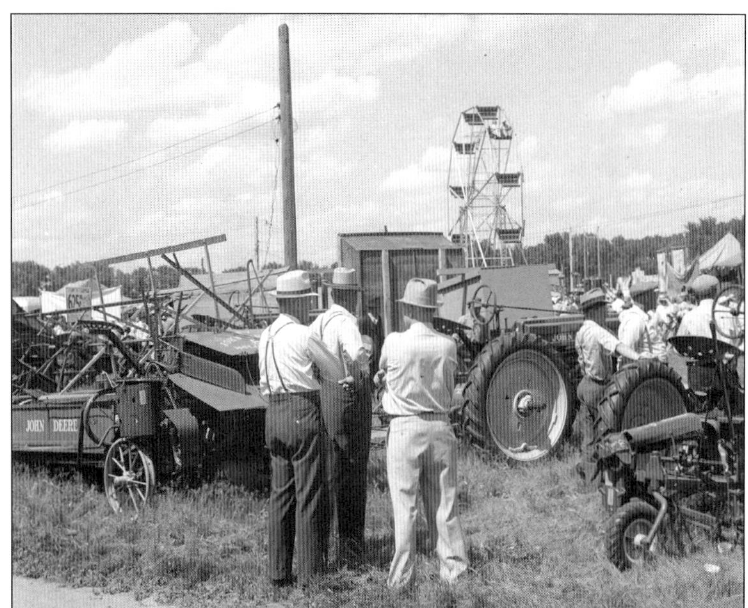

Machinery Row and Machinery Avenue have been a meeting place for farmers to gather and inspect the latest innovations in farm equipment and purchase new implements and tools. The John Deere Company, Moline Plow Company, and Monitor Drill Company all exhibited at the first fair in 1885, and they continue to be annual participants.

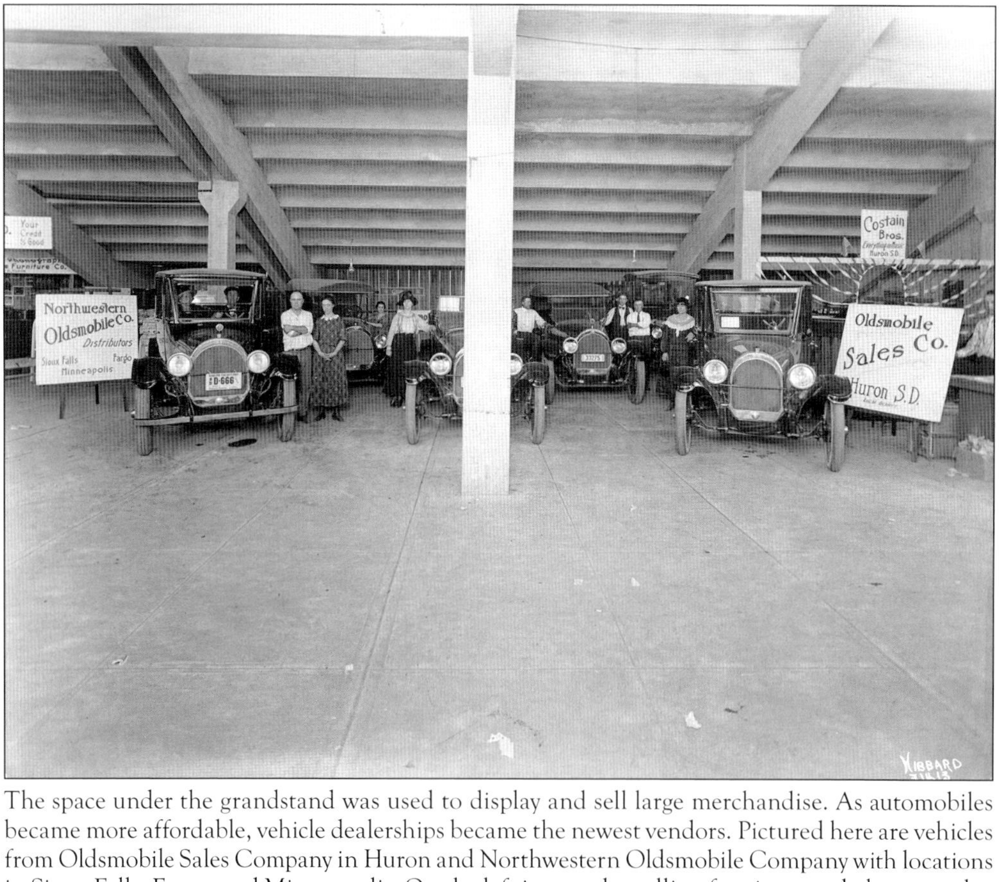

The space under the grandstand was used to display and sell large merchandise. As automobiles became more affordable, vehicle dealerships became the newest vendors. Pictured here are vehicles from Oldsmobile Sales Company in Huron and Northwestern Oldsmobile Company with locations in Sioux Falls, Fargo, and Minneapolis. On the left is a vendor selling furniture and phonographs. At far right is Costain Bros. of Huron advertising "Everything in music."

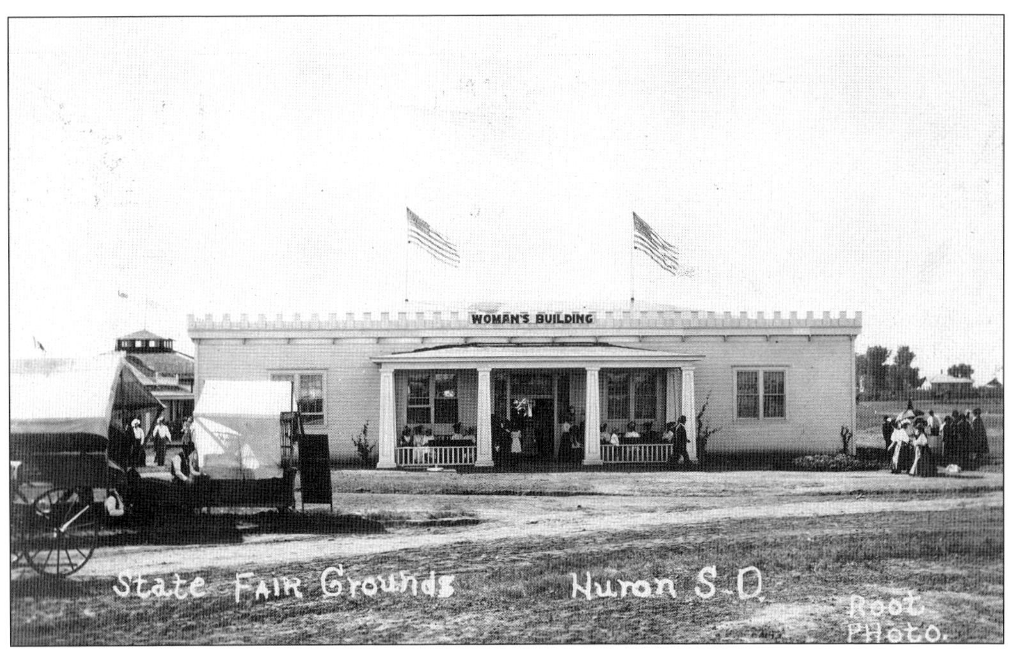

The Women's Building was housed in one of the original buildings on the fairgrounds and was always a favorite spot for folks to gather. It housed displays of domestic arts and offered programs on cooking, homemaking, and other skills. It was replaced by a two-story cement building in 1909. The building was also used for social gatherings and musical and literary events. The 1909 Women's Building was named Civic Hall in 1958 when a new Women's Building was completed. Plans began in the 1970s to have it preserved as a historic building, but instead, it was razed in 1974 to make room for the Food Court.

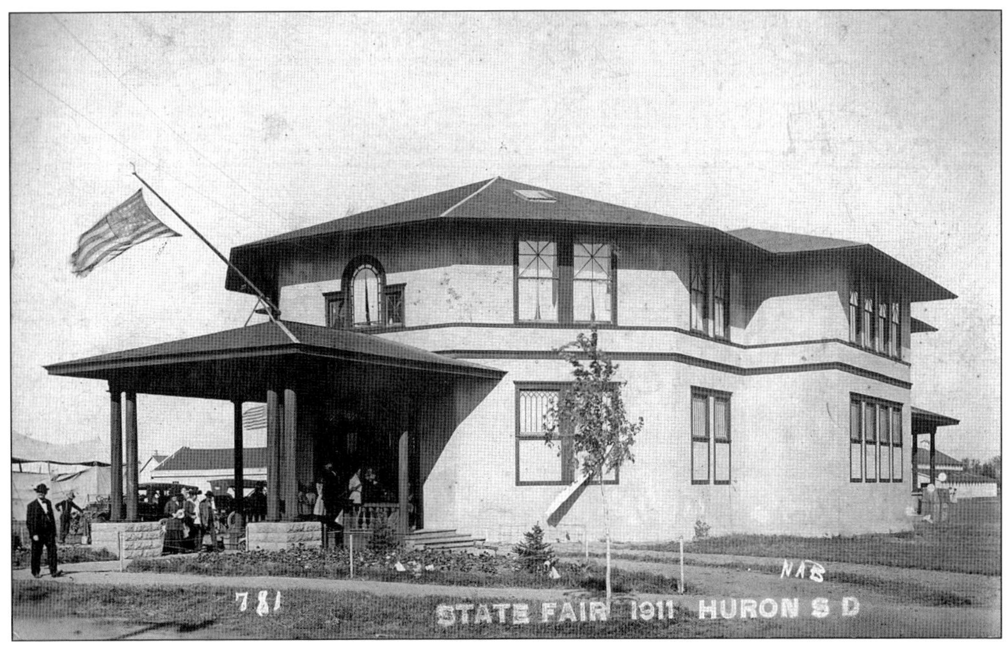

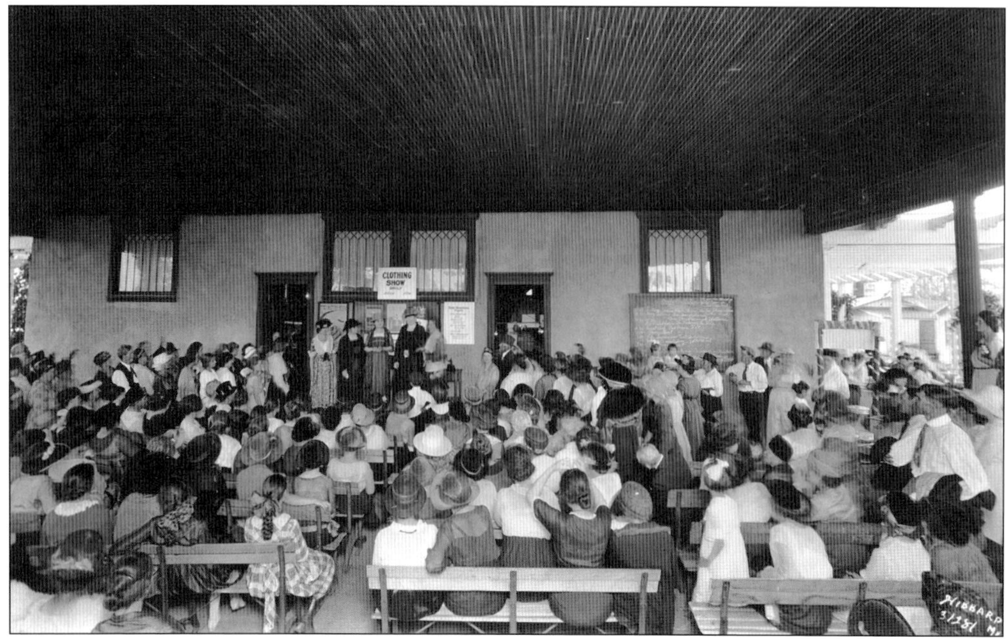

In a time without air-conditioning, the 1909 Women's Building was designed with wide porches and verandas that would provide a shaded resting spot for everyone. It was also the location for many of the programs, such as this clothing show. Static displays of needlework, sewing, and canning were showcased inside.

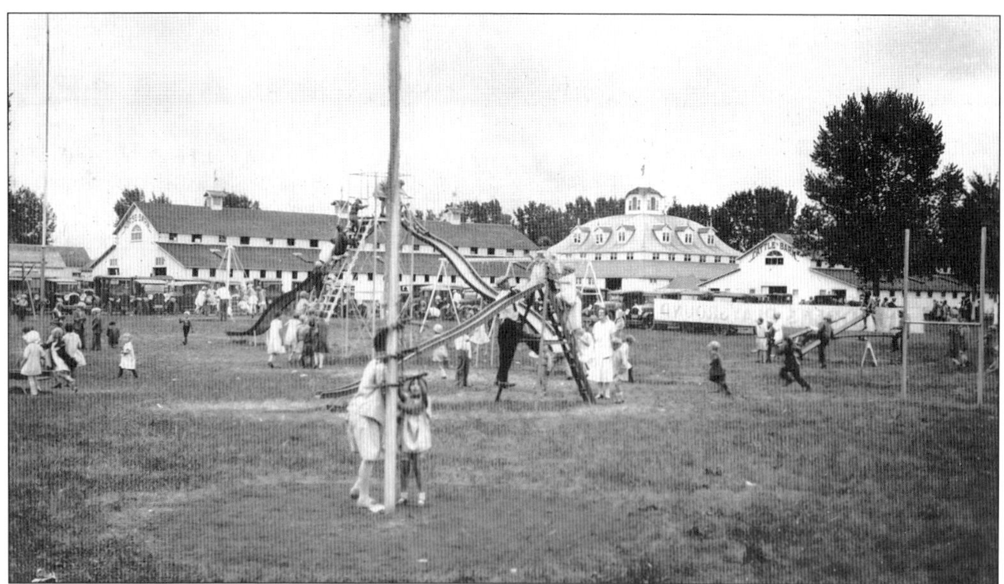

In 1926, a children's playground was added. It was fenced and staffed by paid attendants so mothers could enjoy the fair without their children, and this led to a sharp decrease in the number of lost children. This 1938 photograph shows the variety of playground equipment available. (Courtesy of Huron College.)

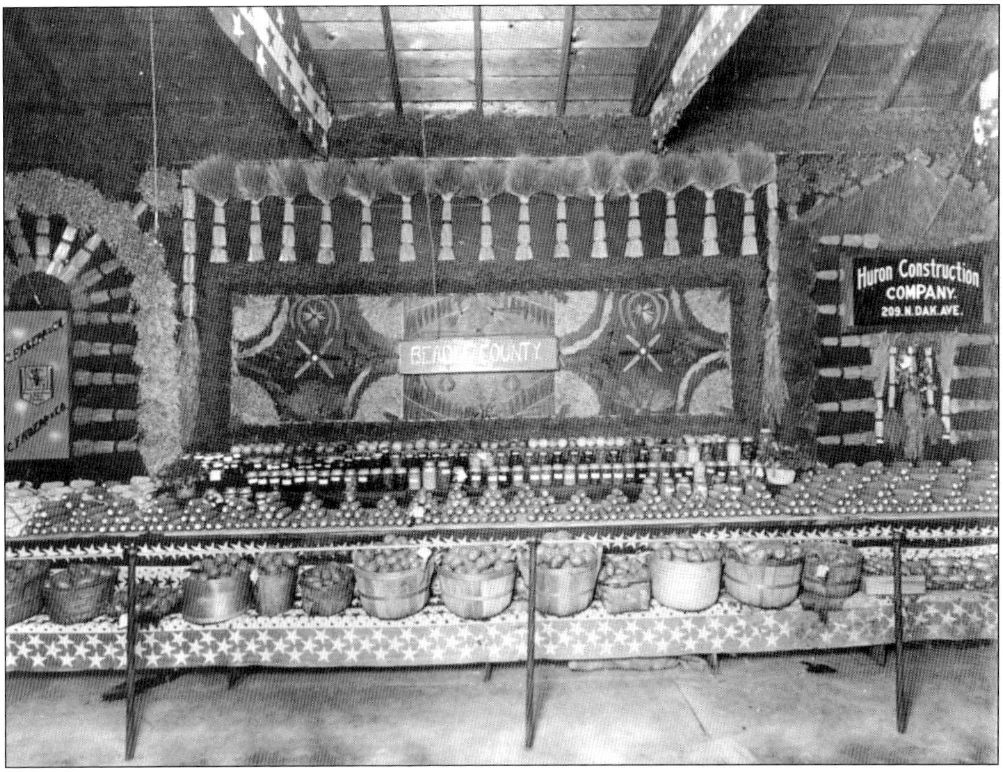

From the beginning, the fair board encouraged each county to display its produce and resources. Beadle County erected a spacious and elegant building in 1907 at a cost of $4,500. This building had more space to accommodate the county's displays than could be allotted to it in Agriculture Hall. It showcased elaborate and artistic grain displays, newly designed and constructed each year, as can be seen in this 1908 photograph above. From a glass-enclosed walkway on the second story, people could enjoy a panoramic view of the fairgrounds. Below, seen behind the Midway, are the Beadle County Building on the right and the Women's Building on the left.

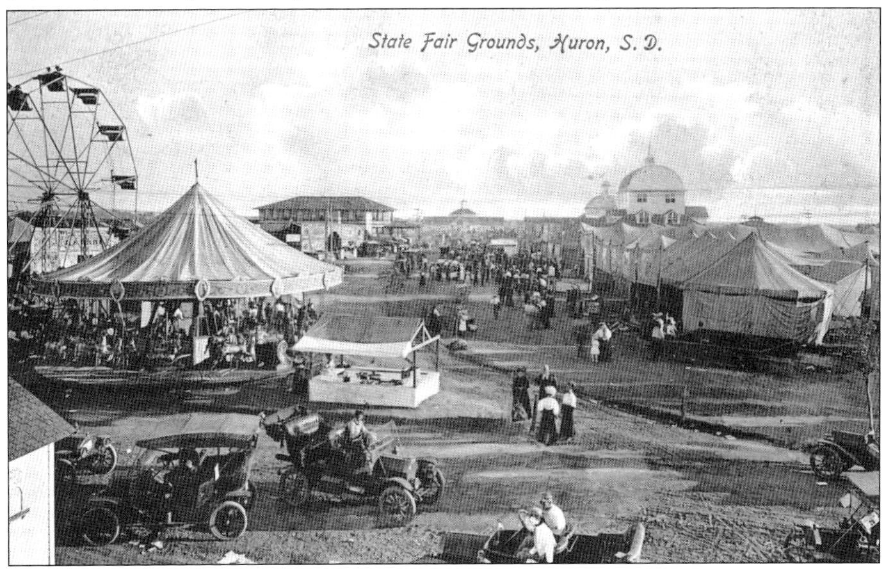

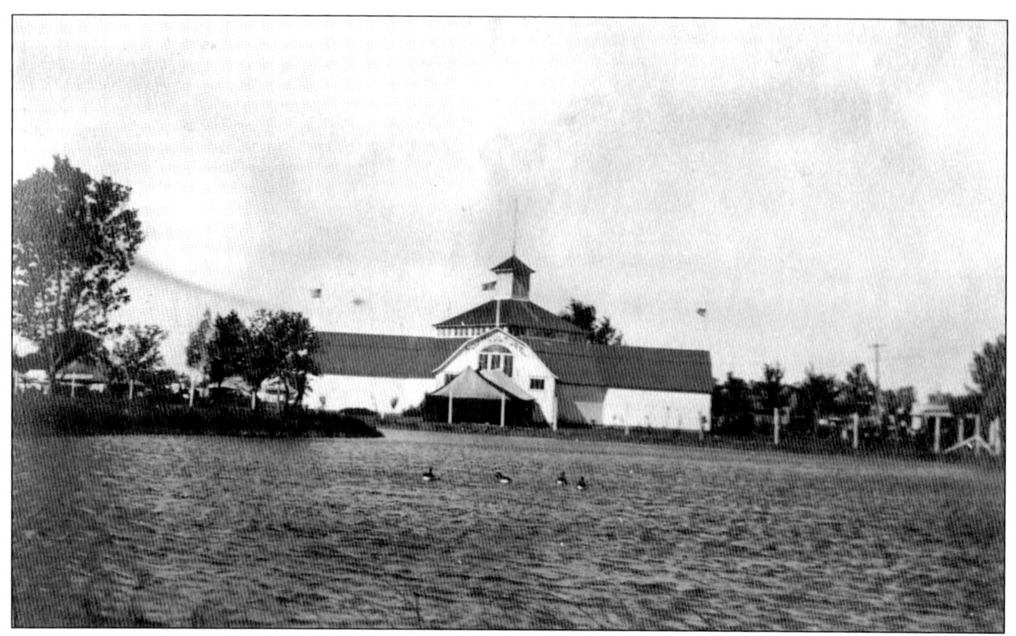

In 1907, Horticulture Hall, above, and Agriculture Hall, below, were both built in a cross design. Agriculture Hall had a large dome in the center and cost $5,750 to build. It burned down in 1967. The smaller, $4,000 Horticulture Hall was replaced on the same site in 1965 for $83,542. The Mirror Room was added in 1976. By 1910, permanent buildings on the fairgrounds included the Poultry Building, still housed in one of the original buildings, Agriculture Hall, Horticulture Hall, the Beadle County Building, the Women's Building, the Dairy Building, several barns for horses, cattle, swine, and sheep, and speed barns for the racehorses. The effect of having a permanent location and better facilities soon became apparent when the total receipts jumped 300 percent in three years, from $15,978 in 1906 to $43,217 in 1909.

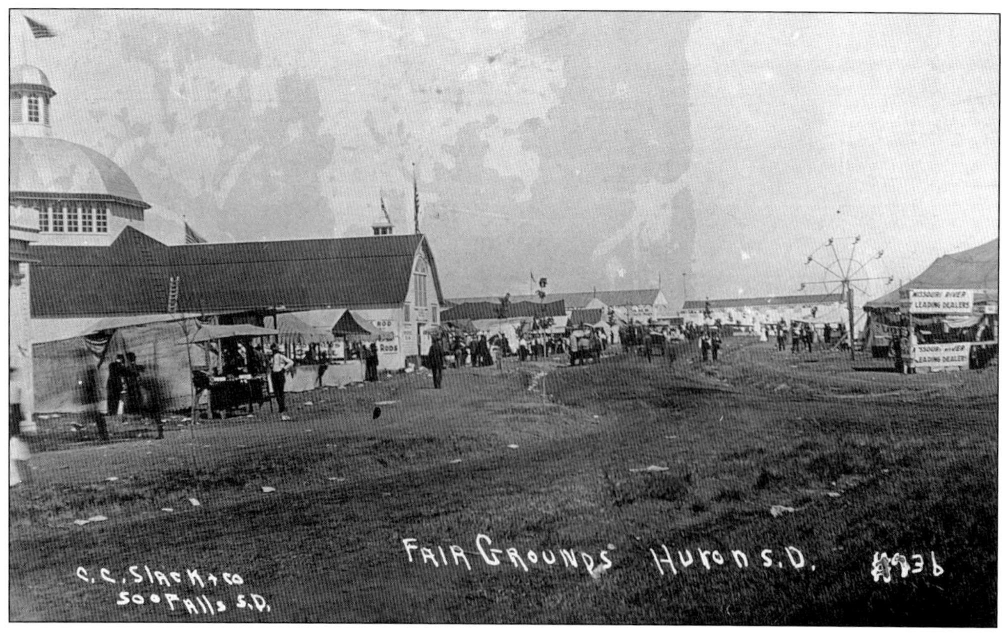

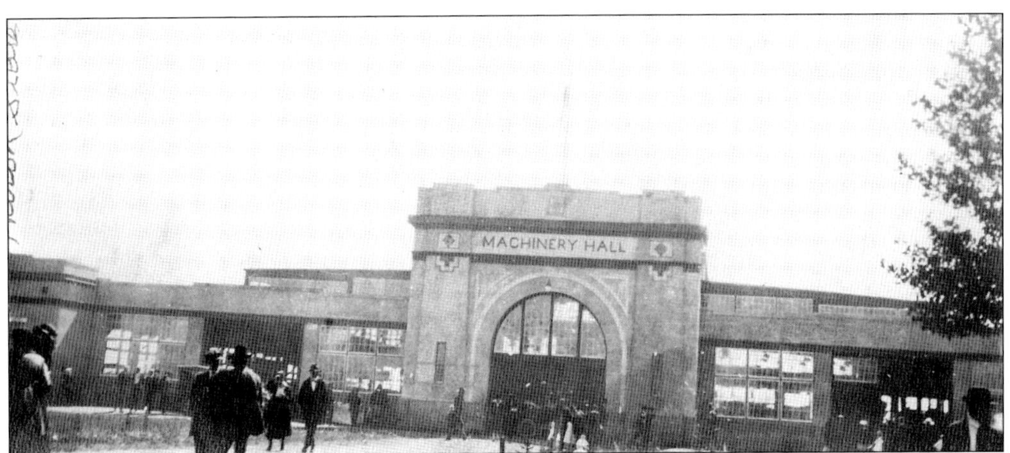

The state fair acquired the land south of Third Street in 1911. In 1912, a larger Dairy Building was completed, and the massive Machinery Hall, above, was finished in 1913. Machinery Hall was equipped with a modern electric power plant for running the dynamos to light the fairgrounds and power the waterworks. The Dairy Building had a glassed-in, refrigerated case in the center used to showcase various dairy products. In 1960, it became the home of the Pioneer Museum, now known as the Dakotaland Museum. The Dairy Building is the oldest building on the fairgrounds and is listed in the National Register of Historic Places. In the photograph below, Machinery Hall is the large building on the left, and the Dairy Building is two buildings to the right. (Below, courtesy of NorthWestern Energy.)

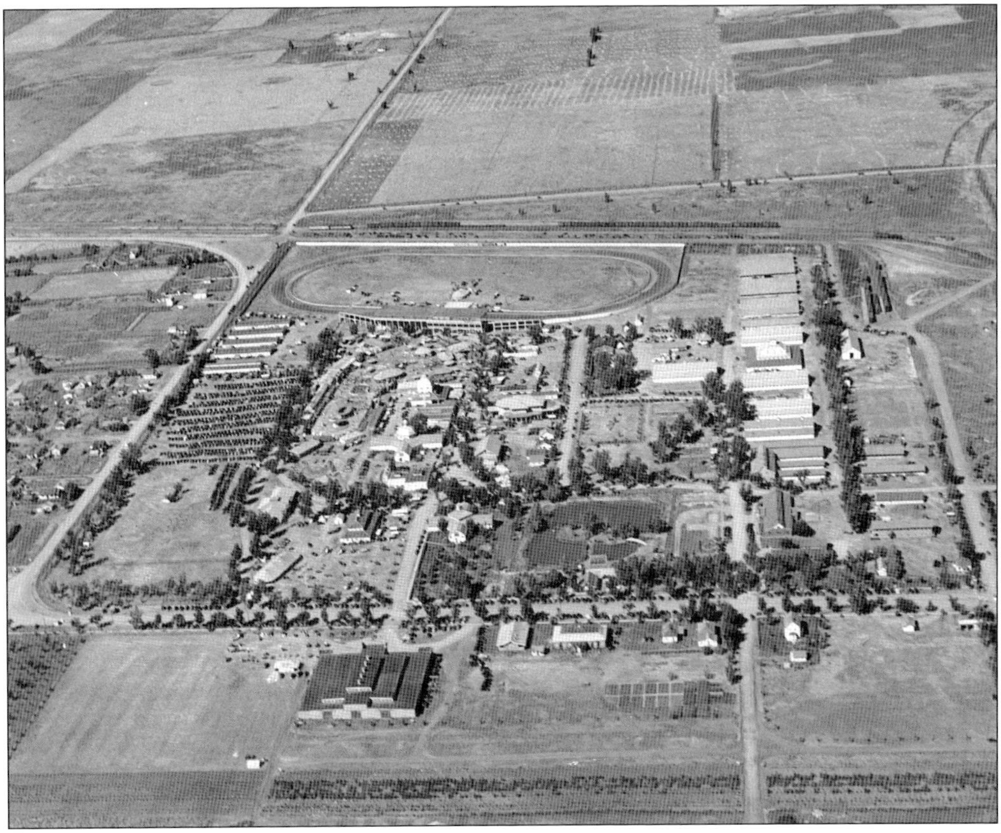

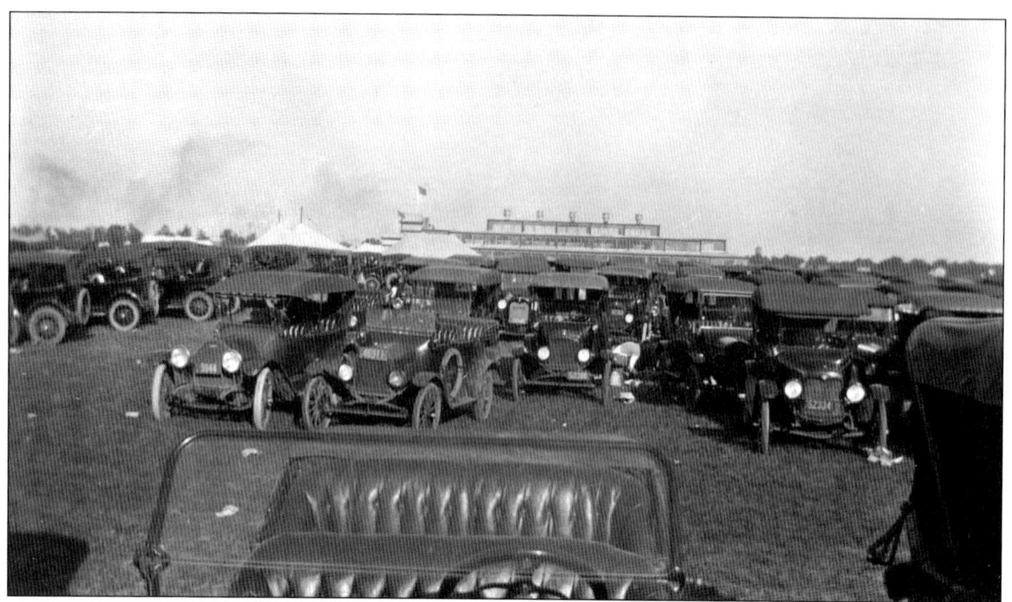

The main gate was moved to Third Street in 1913 to accommodate vehicles. Jack Rabbit Transportation Company scheduled round-trip state fair bus routes from Pierre, Aberdeen, and Sioux Falls. This 1913 photograph shows the parking lot on the south side of the fairgrounds looking east. The large structure in the background is Machinery Hall. The main gate was moved to Sixth Street in 1953. This area is now a campground.

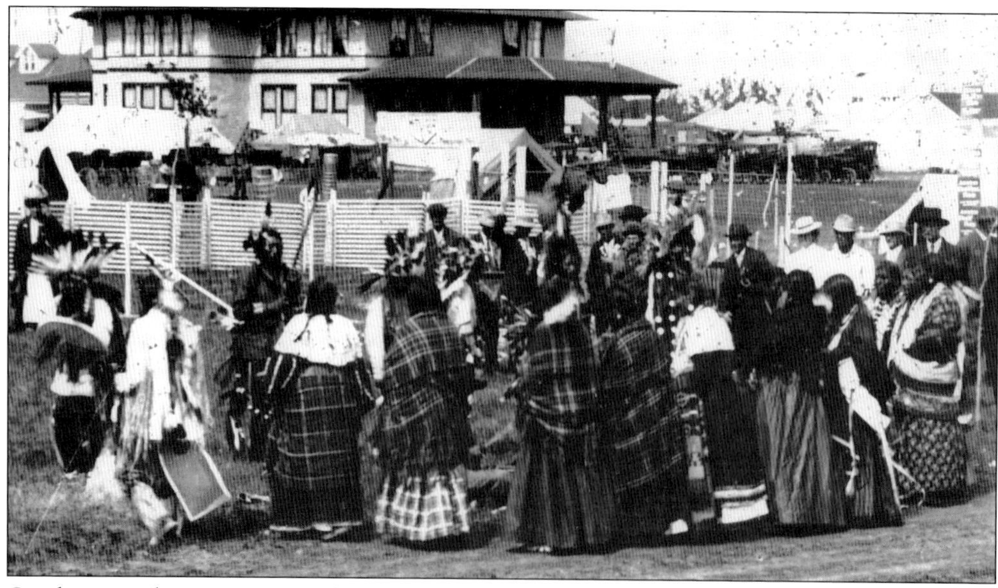

One long-standing attraction at the fair was a traditional Native American camp on the fairgrounds complete with indigenous cooking, singing, and dancing. The photograph here shows Crow dancers in 1912 with the Women's Building in the background.

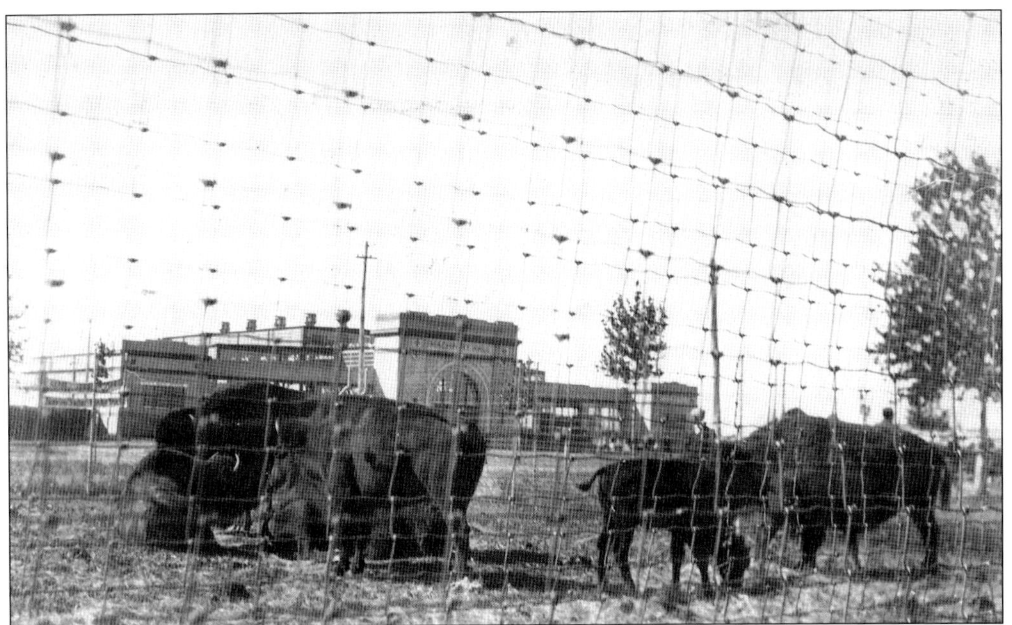

The state fair had a bison herd on display for several years. In 1905, the herd of 15 animals was in the northeast corner of the fairgrounds, near the main gate. This photograph, taken after 1913, shows them on Third Street, across from Machinery Hall and near the lake, which was a popular attraction.

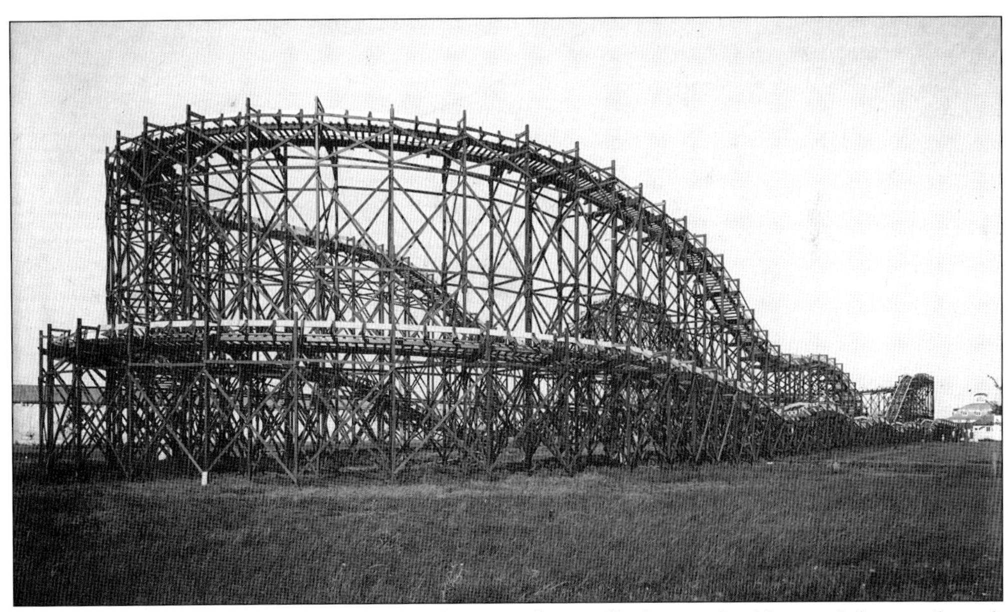

The wooden roller coaster was built in 1912 between the Beadle County Building and the grandstand. It was enjoyed by adults and children alike. Unfortunately, it was continually being damaged by wind and storms, which caused it to be repaired annually at a considerable expense. Although it was a popular attraction, it was consequently dismantled prior to 1920.

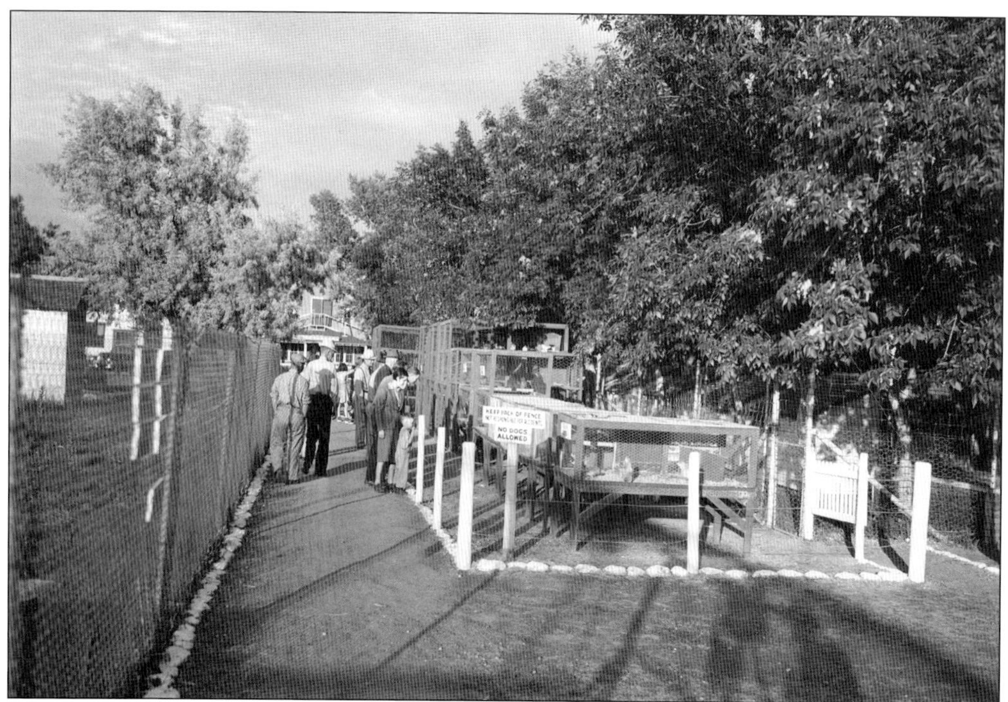

Another short-lived attraction, which opened in 1941, was the State Fair Zoo. Housed next to what is now the Game, Fish, and Parks Department, it was open year-round and included a variety of animals, including bears. It was closed after several animal escapes scared children and neighbors alike. (Courtesy of NorthWestern Energy.)

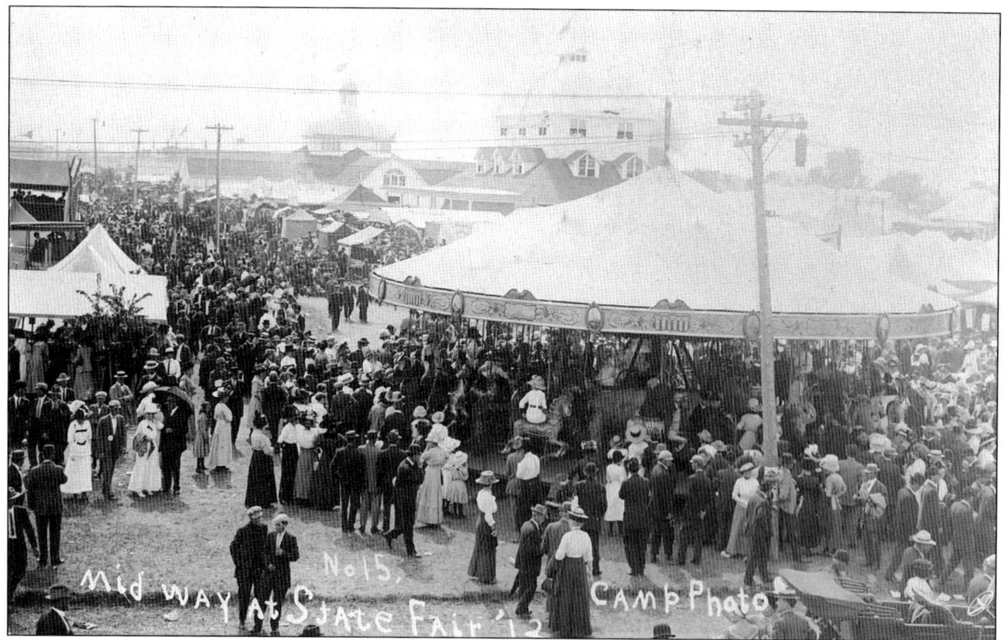

The Midway has always been a popular area at the fair, as this photograph from 1912 shows. That year, it featured food vendors, carnival rides, arcade games, and even a palm reader. The Midway continues to be a busy spot with many of the same attractions, except maybe the palm reader.

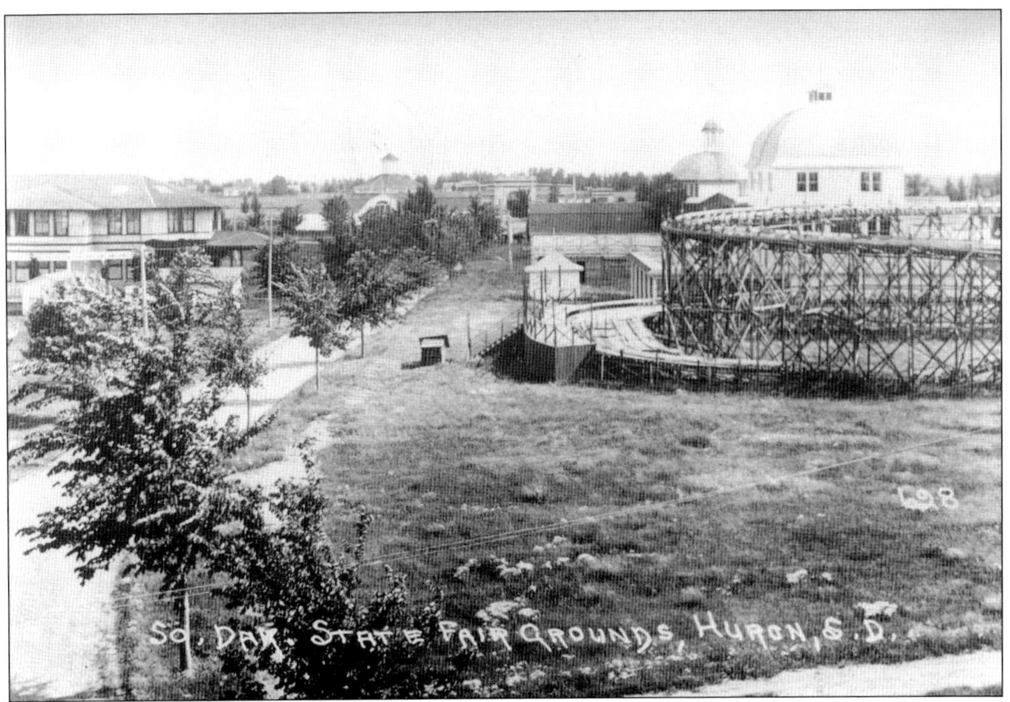

This 1918 photograph looks south from the grandstand. On the left are the Women's Building, the Industrial Building, and just visible, the cupola on Horticulture Hall. Anchoring the end of the street is Machinery Hall. On the right are the roller coaster, Beadle County Building, and Agriculture Hall. The Industrial Building was erected in 1918. It was the Senior Citizens Building for many years and is currently a taproom. (Courtesy of Lynn Green.)

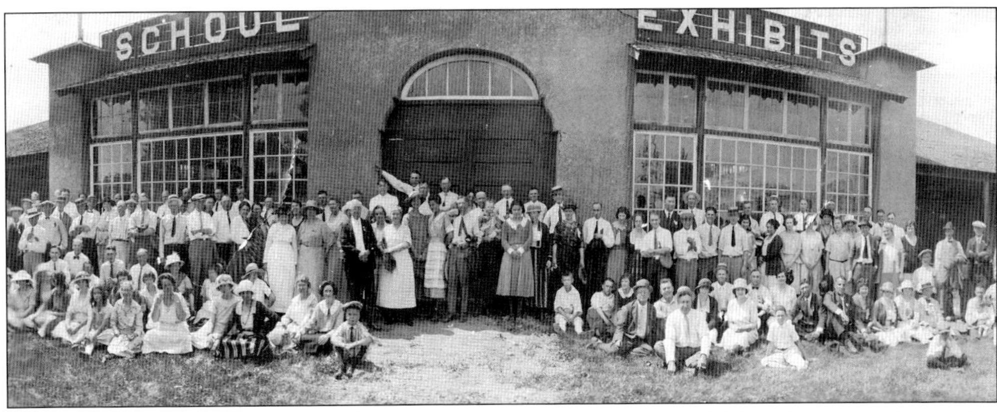

A large building simply named School Exhibits was constructed in 1915 to house the increasing number of entries arriving from schools and classrooms throughout the state. These exhibits included essays, poetry, artwork, and woodworking projects. Displays from schoolchildren are still an important part of the state fair and can now be seen in the Education Building.

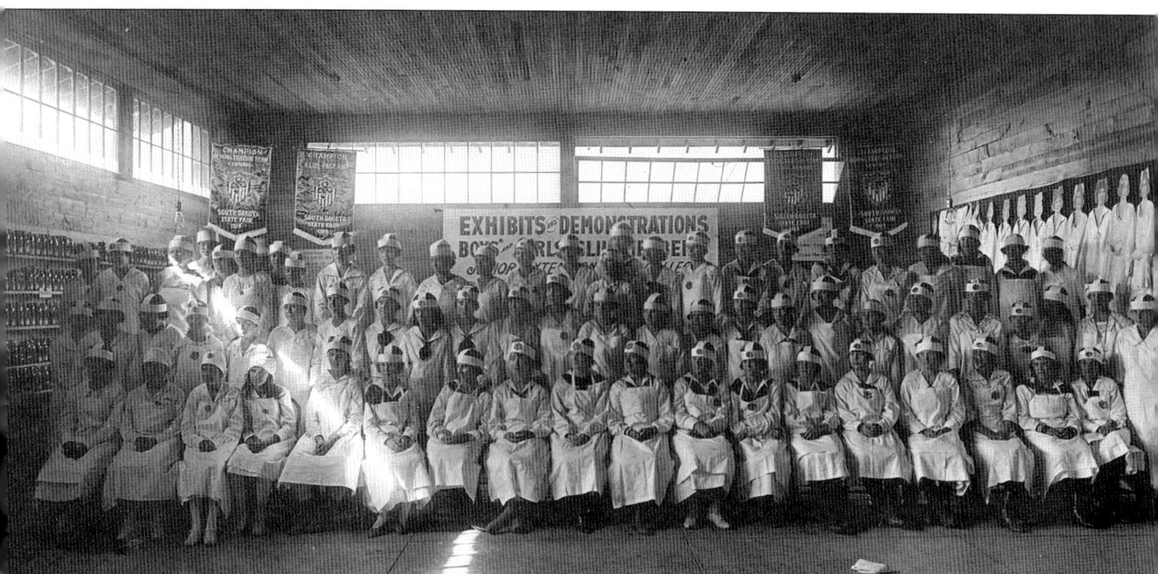

A Boys State Fair Camp was established in 1915 and included one delegate from each county selected by each county's superintendent of schools based on their skill in growing potatoes and corn and their ability to judge crops and livestock. A Girls State Fair Camp was added in 1918 with food-canning and sewing demonstrations. Each county now sent teams of three participants to each camp. This photograph shows the Girls Camp in 1919. That year saw 86 girls and 90 boys in attendance. It was also in that year that the 4-H program, under the supervision of the State College Extension Service, took over running the camps with 100 exhibits on display. In 1920, premiums totaling $5,000 were paid out in special awards and educational trips. Participation continued to increase dramatically, and currently, in addition to the state fair, annual features on the fairgrounds include 4-H Achievement Days and the State 4-H Horse Show.

Eight

Community Involvement

Although the early pioneers were busy establishing businesses, schools, and churches, they found time to get together to start civic, fraternal, and community organizations. Fraternal organizations like the Masons, Elks, and the Independent Order of Odd Fellows brought like-minded people together, providing them an opportunity to make business connections, socialize, and carry out charitable, educational, and social projects that helped others in the community. Several organizations constructed buildings for meeting space as well as offering space for businesses. Others raised funds for community improvements like the Campbell Park bandshell, swimming pools, baseball fields, and parks.

Social clubs and church groups also brought people with similar interests together. Men and women had the opportunity to connect with others, share ideas, and work toward common goals. Clubs organized and sponsored community events like picnics, theater productions, concerts, and dances. Church groups helped raise funds for church improvements and building projects. Organizations for children like the Boy Scouts, Girl Scouts, and 4-H gave children a place to learn new skills.

There were plenty of social activities available as well. Huron had two opera houses that brought in theater groups, variety acts, talent shows, speeches, debates, local band concerts, and graduation ceremonies. Dances, community picnics, and parades were something everyone could enjoy. Athletic activities were also available, including baseball, basketball, football, bowling, swimming, and roller skating.

Organizations and clubs fostered a sense of community by bringing people together to collaborate toward shared objectives. In return, the members supported each other and helped the community grow.

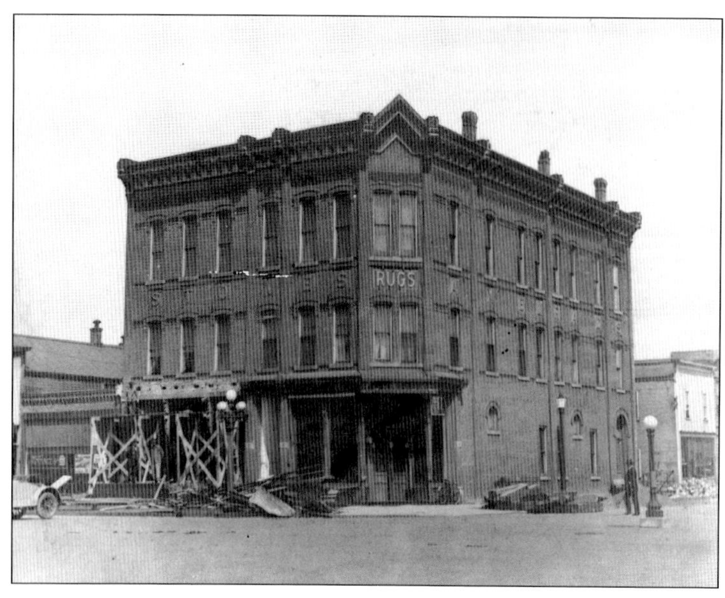

The Independent Order of Odd Fellows (IOOF) James River Lodge No. 32 was organized in 1881. It started Huron's first cemetery, Riverside Cemetery, in 1883. The cemetery is still owned and operated by the lodge today. The building in this photograph was constructed in 1885 on the corner of Third Street and Wisconsin Avenue. The top floor was the IOOF Hall, and Axelrad Furniture occupied the lower level.

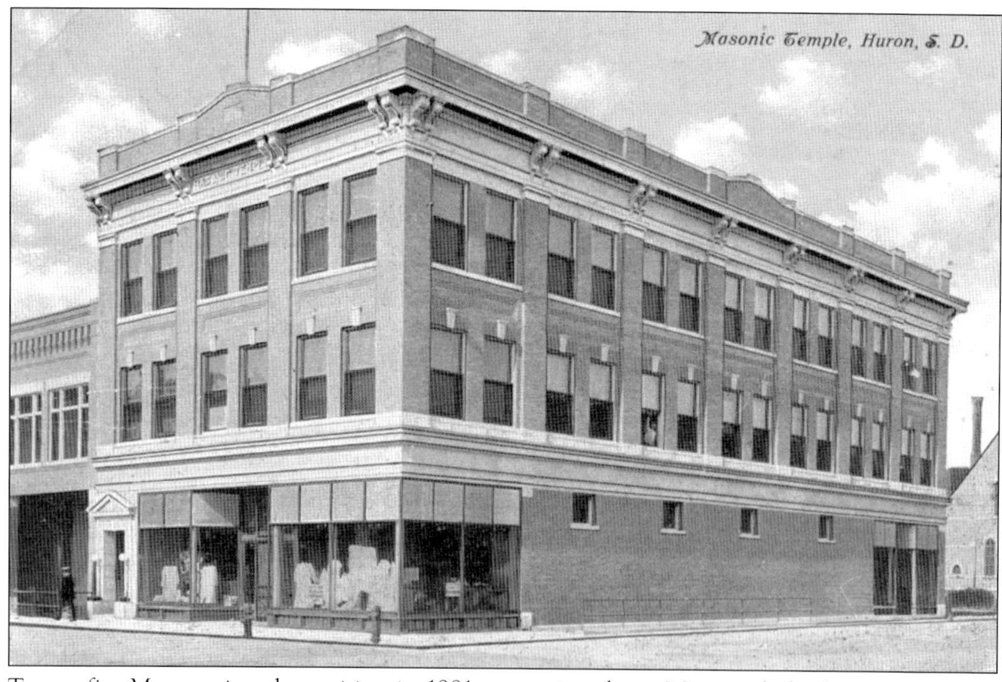

Twenty-five Masons signed a petition in 1881 requesting that a Masonic lodge be established in Huron. The petition was granted, and during the first few years, the Masons met at various buildings downtown. In 1908, the lodge erected this building at the corner of Dakota Avenue and Fourth Street. The Order of Eastern Star was established in 1890 and had 26 charter members. (Courtesy of Huron Public Library.)

Royal Arch Masons Huron Chapter No. 10 has been active in the community since the 1890s. Shown here are the officers in 1894. They are, from left to right, (first row) E.C. Walton, C.L. Whitaker, Bruce Rowley, G. Kerry, Charles Felt, W. Tolmie, and E. Wilson; (second row) J.E. McDowell, J.M. Jarvis, W.J. Vannix, E.J. Miller, and John Banks.

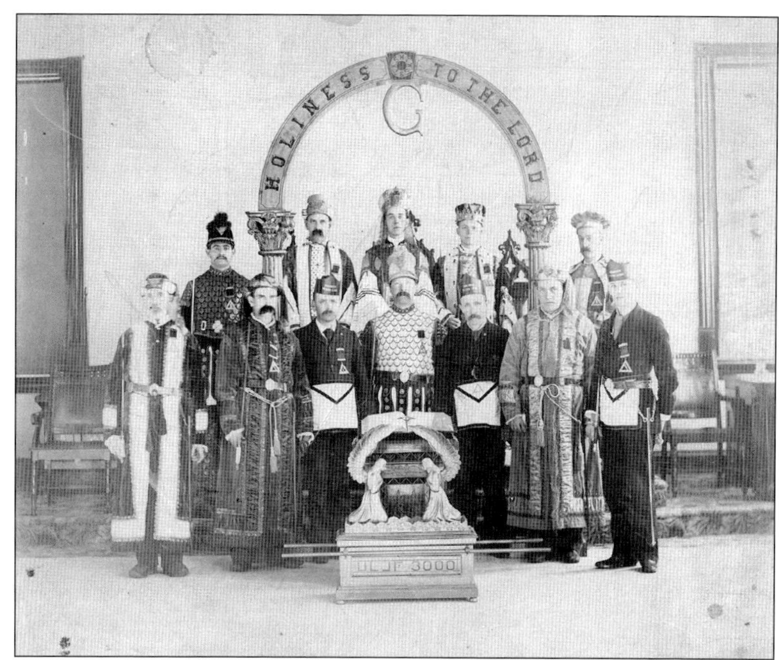

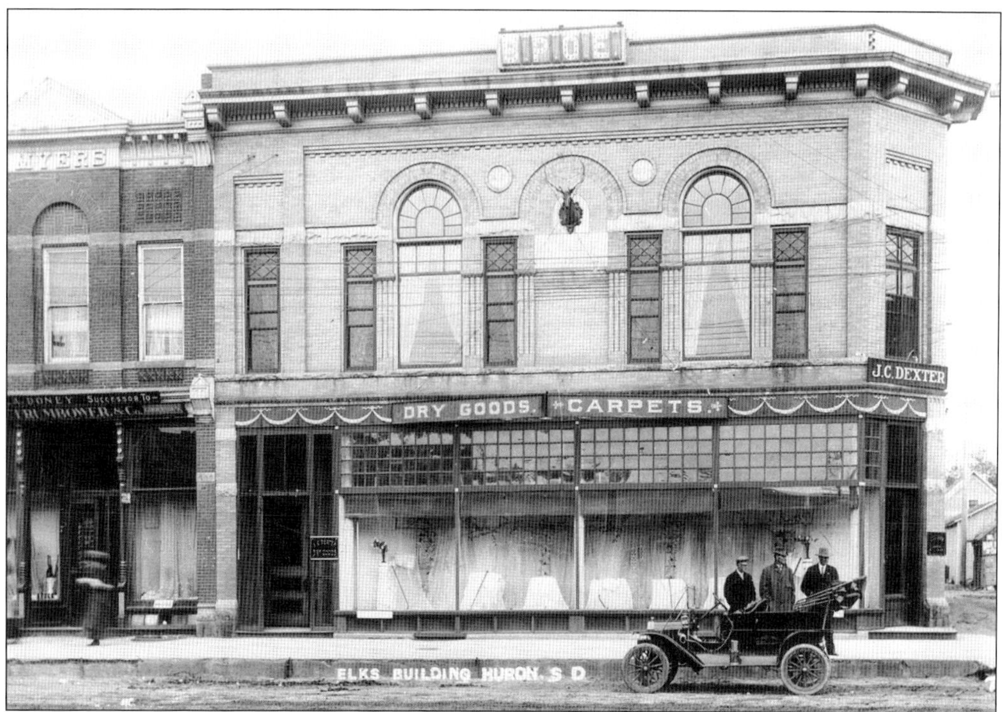

The Huron Benevolent and Protective Order of Elks Lodge No. 444 was chartered in 1898. Their original building, seen here, was located on Third Street. Joseph Dexter owned a dry goods and women's ready-wear store on the first floor. In 1921, the Elks lodge constructed the Marvin Hughitt Hotel on Dakota Avenue. They operated the building until it was sold in 1969. (Courtesy of Huron Public Library.)

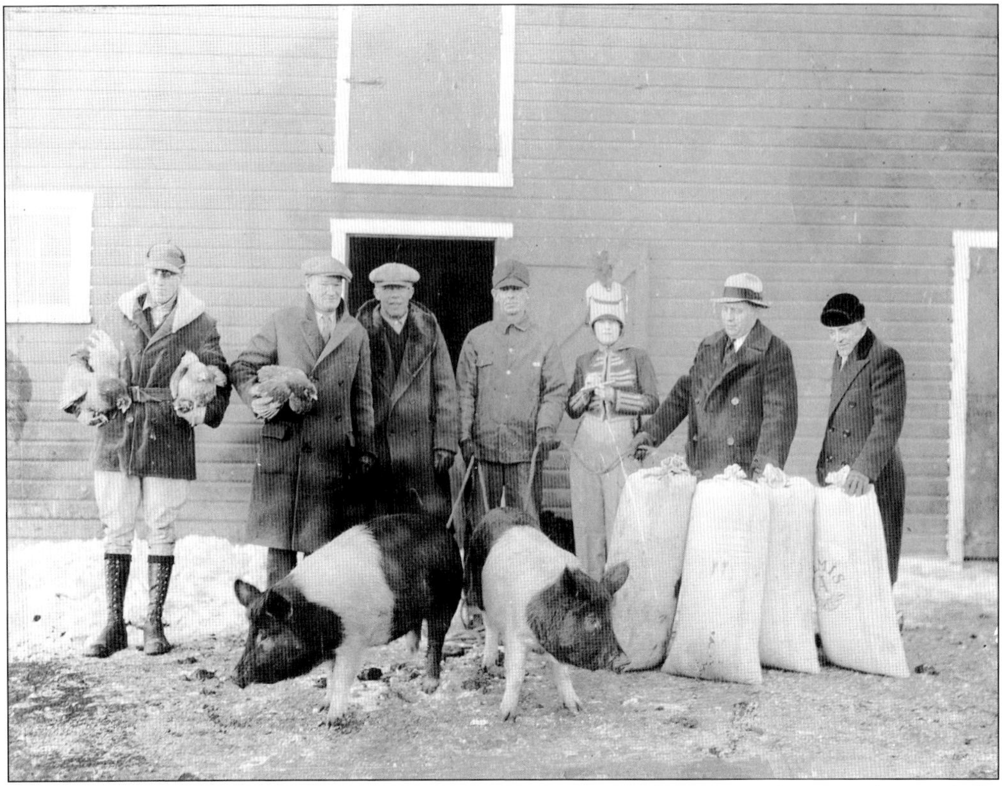

The Huron American Legion was founded in 1919 to aid local veterans, their families, and the community. During the Great Depression, members who were unable to pay dues with cash gave pigs, poultry, and grain instead. Local commander Ernest McKenzie, second on the right, shows the items received from Huron American Legion members, which were then distributed to those in need in Beadle County. Members of the American Legion provided funeral honors to veterans, marched in parades, and held concerts to raise money for special projects. Below, the Huron American Legion Drum and Bugle Corps can be seen marching in a parade past carnival rides on Dakota Avenue. (Both, courtesy of American Legion.)

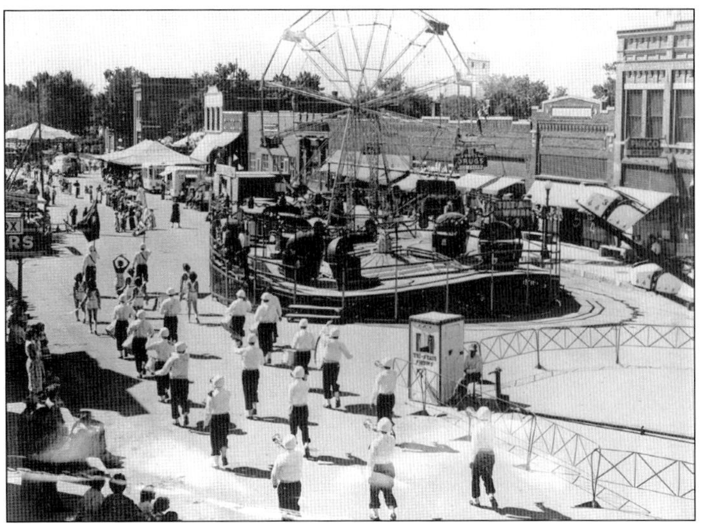

Huron's first entertainment venue was the Grand Opera House, built and operated by O.P. Helm and J. Walters in 1885. Entertainment ranged from professional traveling troupes to local talent shows, concerts, high school graduation, dances, and debates. One interesting program held on July 10, 1888, was the debate on whether to divide the Dakota Territory into North and South Dakota. The Grand Opera House burned down in 1902.

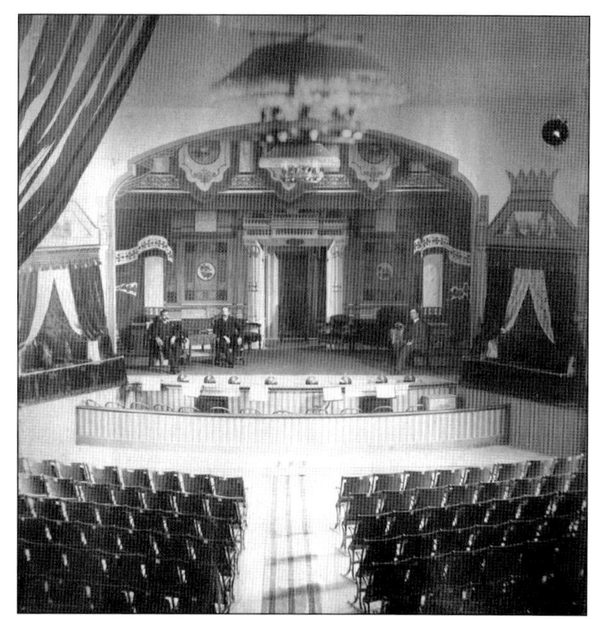

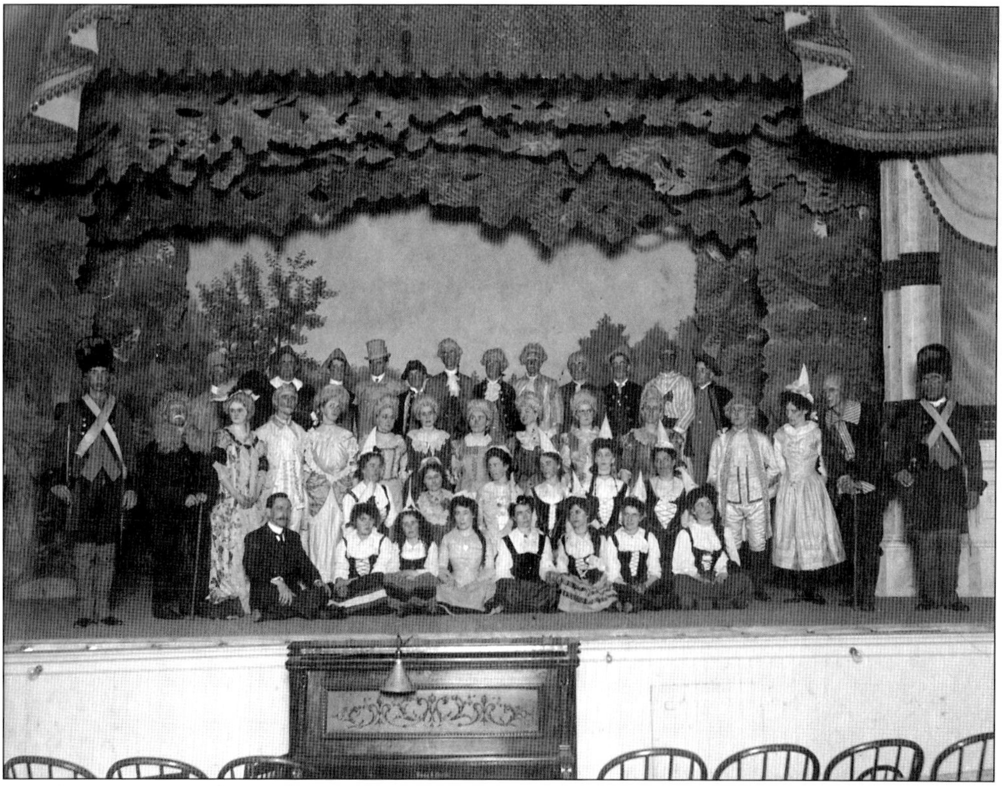

Joseph Daum opened Daum's Opera House on the corner of Illinois Avenue and Second Street in 1890 as a competitor to the Grand Opera House. In 1902, he moved the opera house to Dakota Avenue near Fourth Street. The name was changed to Grand Opera House after the original opera house burned down. The people seen here are cast members in a Gilbert and Sullivan operetta presented in 1900.

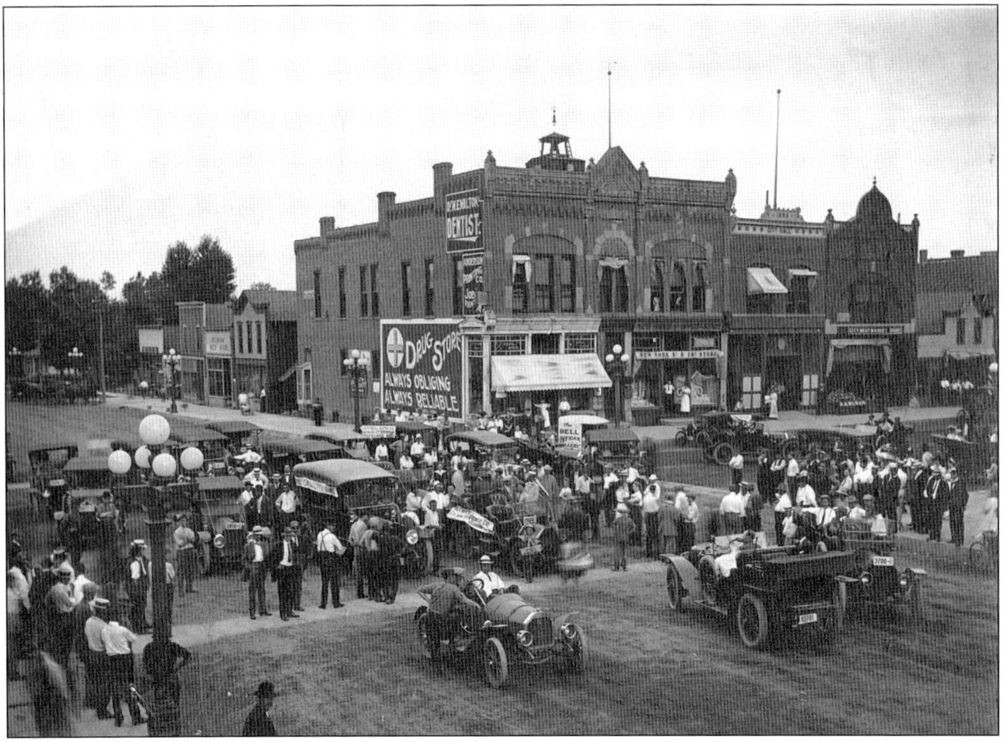

Thirty cars with members of the Huron Booster Club gathered in town on August 4, 1913, for a 110-mile road trip. The boosters carried advertising material promoting the upcoming state fair. Their cars were outfitted with loud horns, banners from various businesses, and members of the city band. The group stopped at 10 communities on its trip. Huron's mayor gave a speech after the band performed.

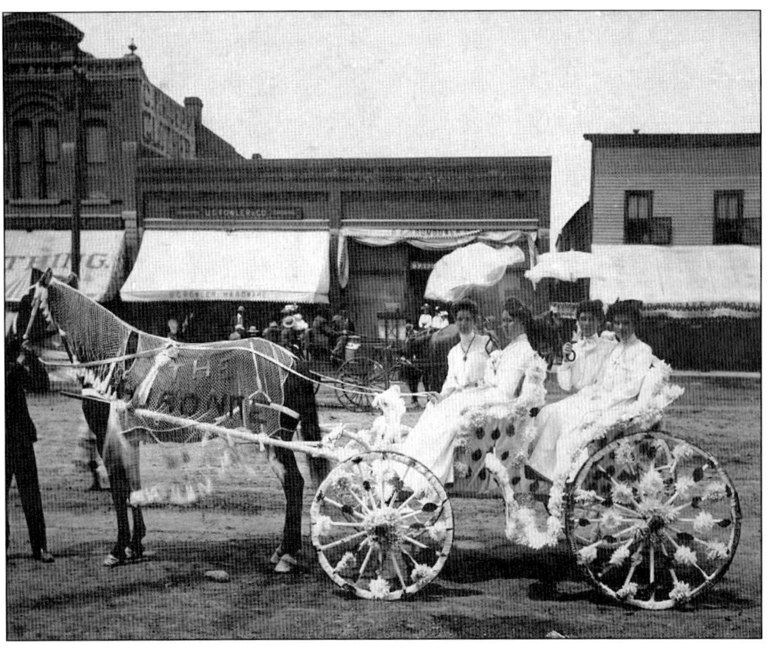

Local parades were a common occurrence to celebrate holidays, special events, and the state fair. Pictured here from left to right are Anna Payson, Lillian Thompson, Lydia Ritchslag, and Mary Ormond in a decorated wagon advertising the *Huronite* newspaper. Payson was an employee in the newspaper office.

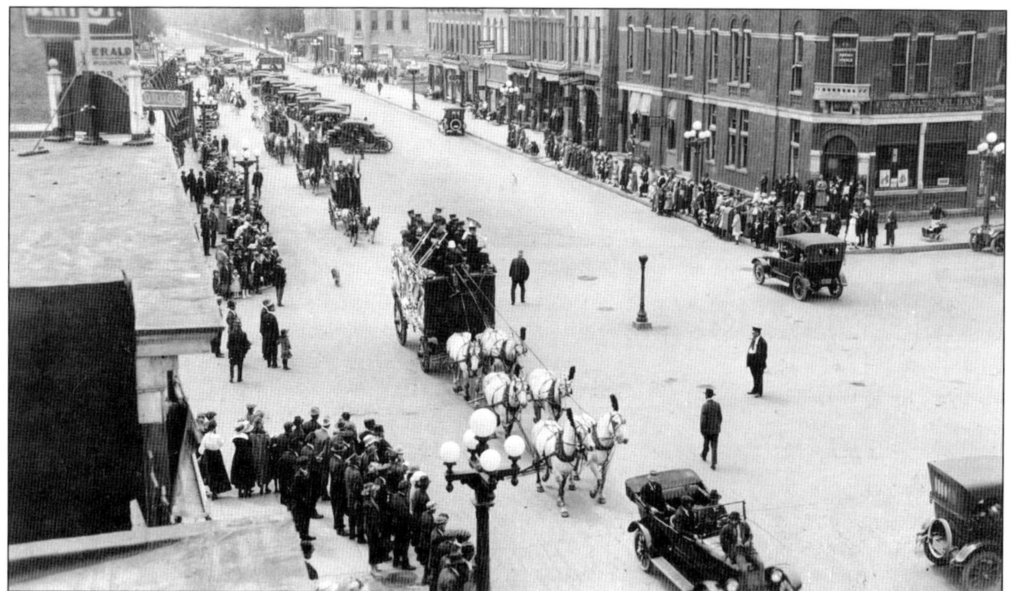

The Ringling Brothers Circus arrived on August 3, 1914, to give several performances. To generate excitement and advertise the show, the circus wagons paraded along Dakota Avenue. The newspaper mentioned that 89 train cars were needed to haul the tents, animals, sideshow acts, and crew. Circus acts included elephants, boxing kangaroos, trained seals, trapeze and tightrope artists, and a chariot race on the fairgrounds.

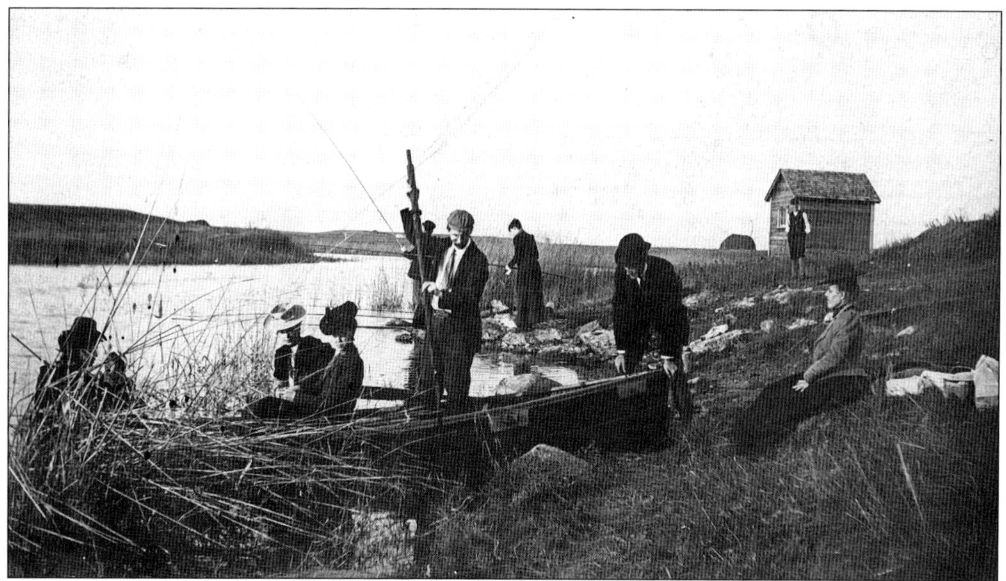

The James River was a popular location during the hot summer months. People spent time swimming, fishing, and boating. There were also several picnic locations north of town. These individuals were faculty for the college's first summer school session in 1901. They spent an afternoon picnicking and boating along the river.

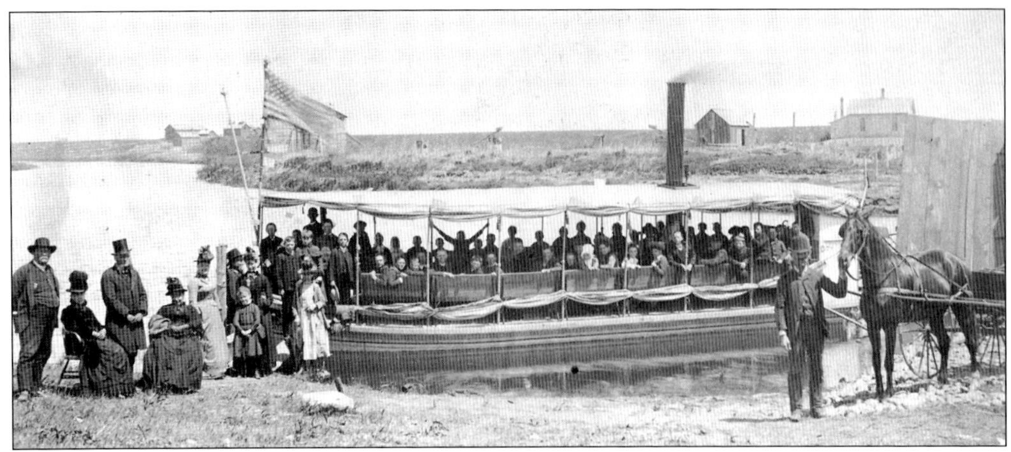

In 1887, S.A. Bowe and his two sons built an excursion steamboat called the *City of Huron*. The boat held 50 people, and tickets were 30¢ for a round trip. The boat traveled up the James River, where people could disembark at various picnic areas. The boat was in use until 1900.

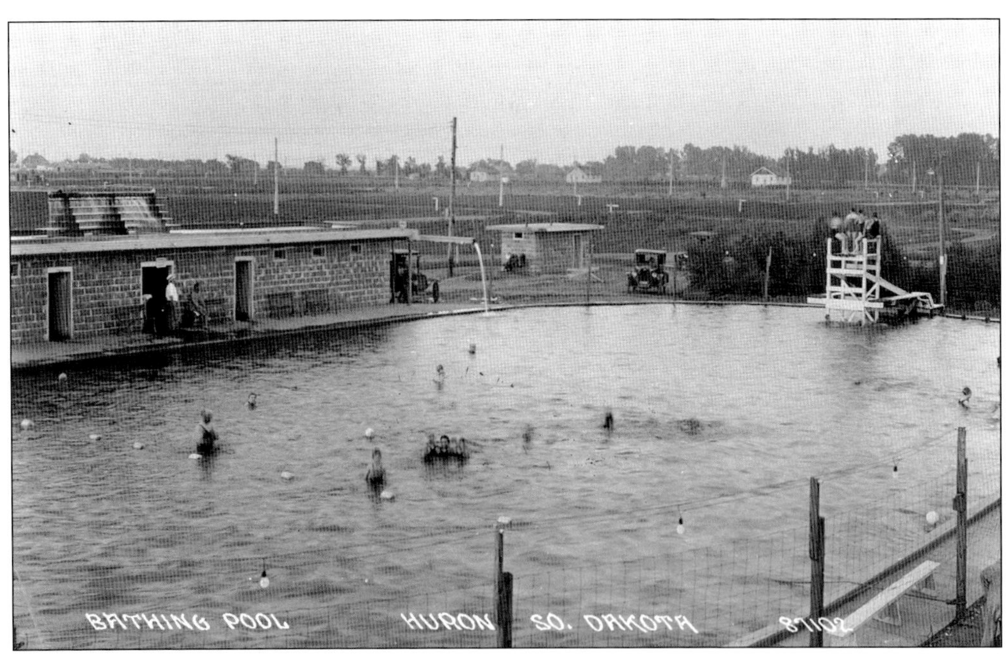

City commissioners discussed building a public swimming pool for several years before the local Altrusa Club stepped in to find a location and raise funds. Jolin's sand pit, west of the fairgrounds, was chosen as the location. The pool was a natural sand pit filled with water from the artesian spring located on the fairgrounds. It opened on July 4, 1926, in conjunction with the city's Fourth of July celebration.

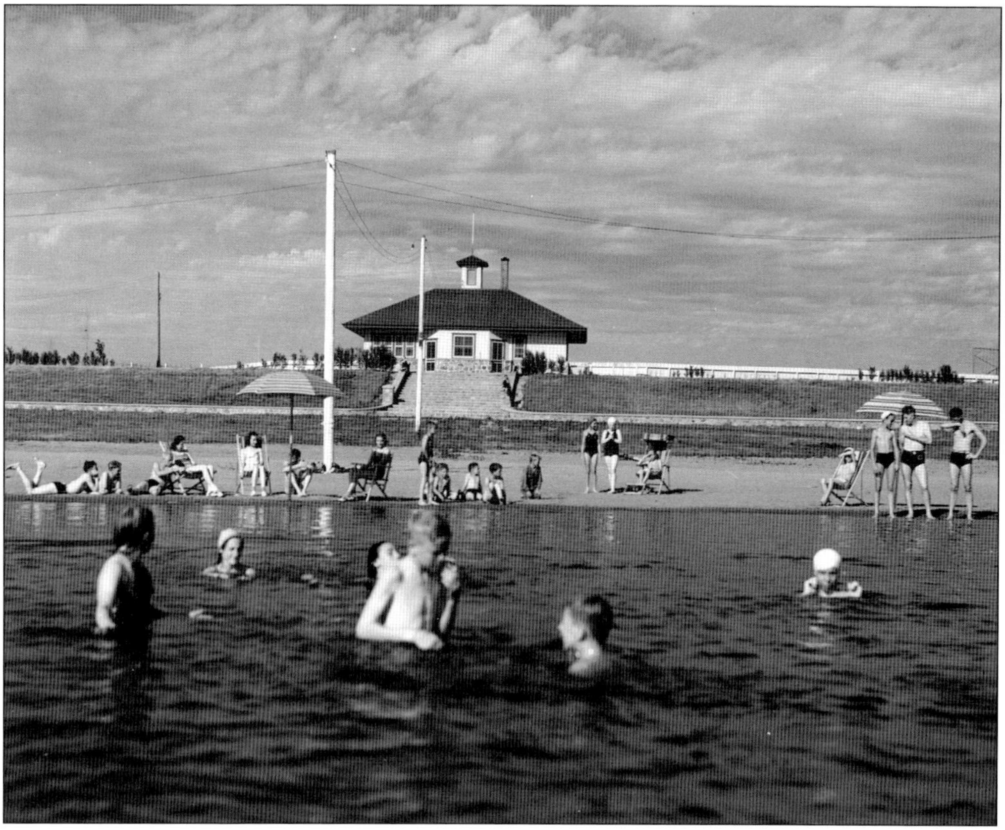

Ravine Lake Park was developed in the 1930s with the help of the Works Progress Administration. One feature of the park was the lake used for swimming. A bathhouse and sand beach were added for the public's convenience. The city's parks department employed lifeguards for the swimmers' safety and offered swimming lessons. (Courtesy of NorthWestern Energy.)

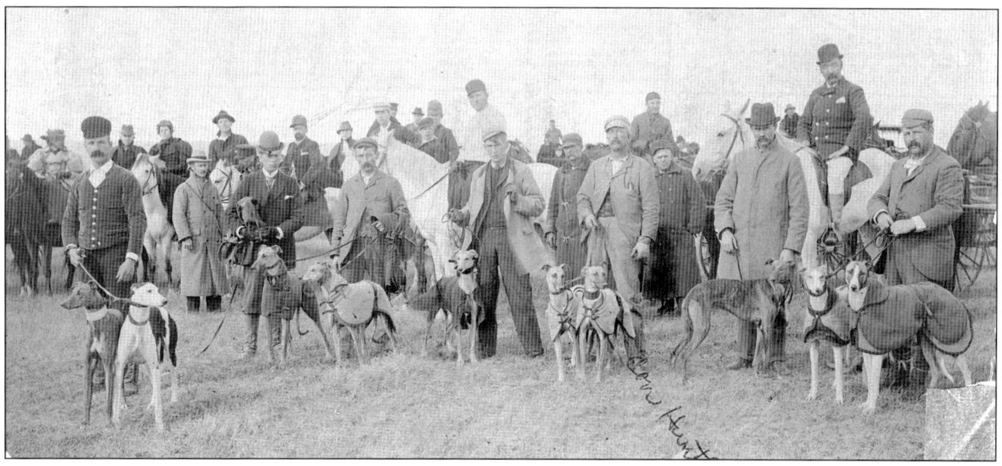

This group of sportsmen gathered in Huron in 1893 for an afternoon of coursing. Greyhounds were released to chase jackrabbits across country fields. The sport drew large crowds who would help scare up the jackrabbits for the dogs to chase. The dog who caught the rabbit received points. The sport faded away as more settlers arrived and started building fences around their property.

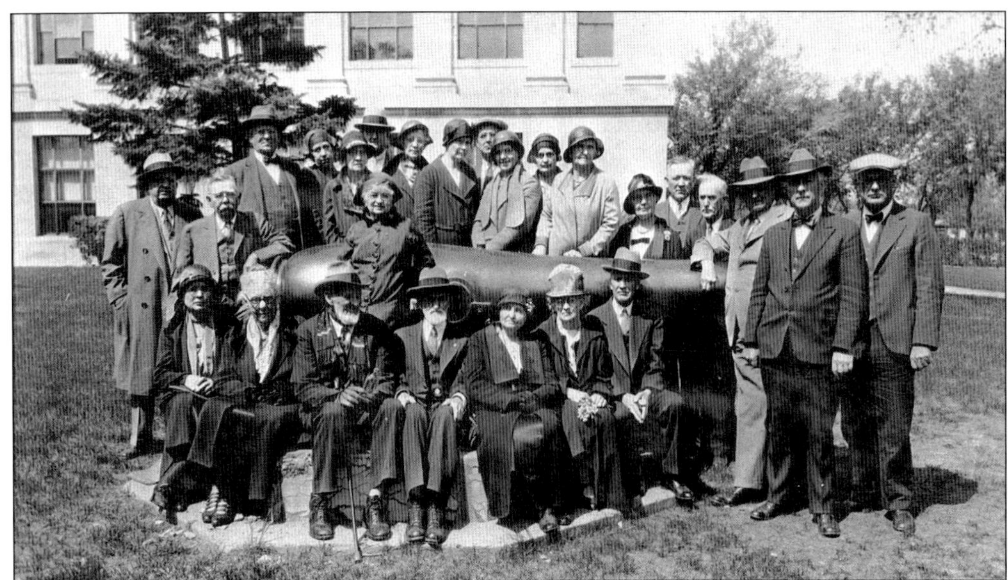

Members of the Beadle County Historical Society gathered on the courthouse lawn for a group photograph. This group included some of Huron's earliest and most influential residents. The woman seated in the center is Eliza Miner. She married Charles Miner in 1880. When they moved to Beadle County and acquired a homestead, she became the first woman homesteader in the county. (Courtesy of Huron Public Library.)

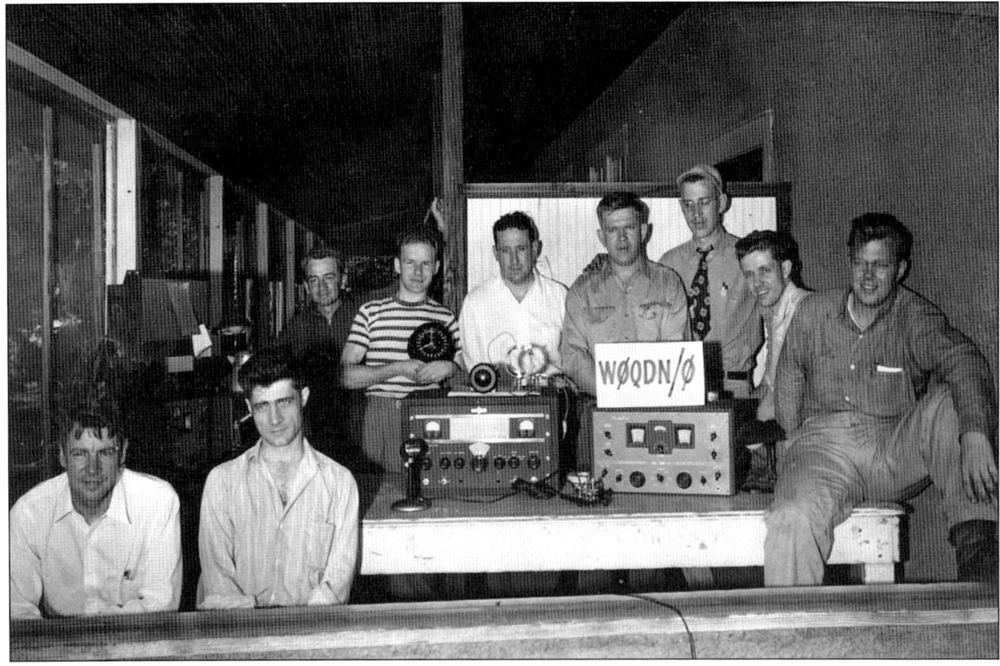

In 1949, members of the Huron Amateur Radio Club joined other radio operators for a 24-hour field day exercise. The club practiced handling emergency messages and demonstrated how its equipment could be used in case of a power failure. Members included, from left to right, Jack Foasberg, Tom Ford, Dick Hart, Ivan Ferguson, Earl Drew, Glen Anderson, Ed Mathews, Don Green, and Chuck Crown. (Courtesy of the Ham Radio Group.)

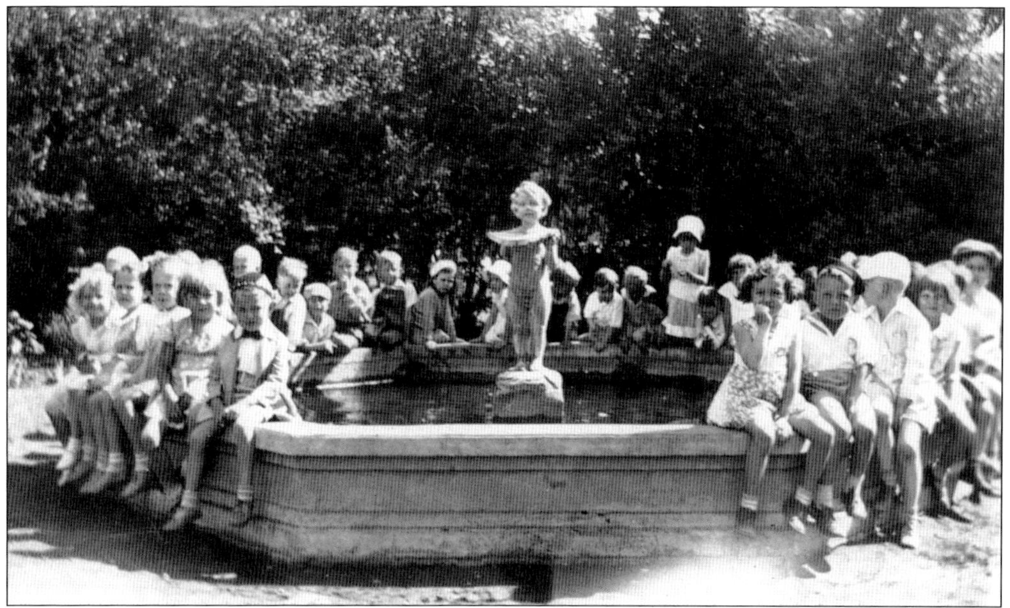

This group of children attended a summer library program in 1934. Due to the small size of the library, many summer activities were held in the park. Children read stories, performed plays, and had tea parties. The water fountain was located near the library in Campbell Park. It was donated to the city by the Fortnightly Club on the city's 50th anniversary. (Courtesy of Huron Public Library.)

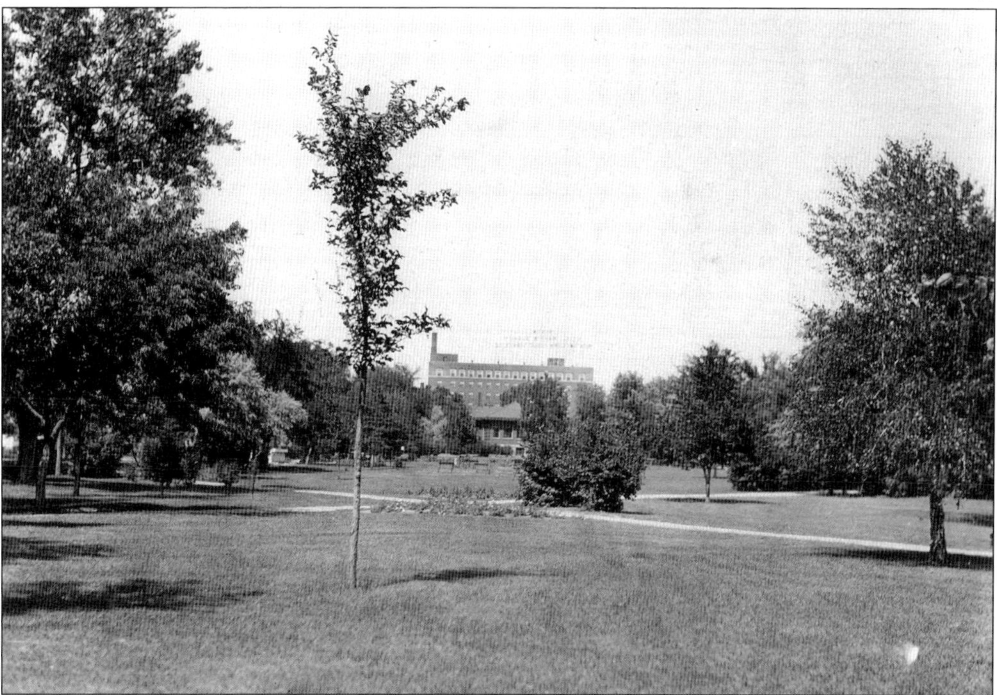

Huron is fortunate to have several public parks. The park seen here is Campbell Park, along Dakota Avenue. The park was the location for many community events like city band concerts and Fourth of July picnics. For Christmas in 1916, a tall pine tree from the Black Hills was brought to the park and decorated with lights while the community gathered to sing carols.

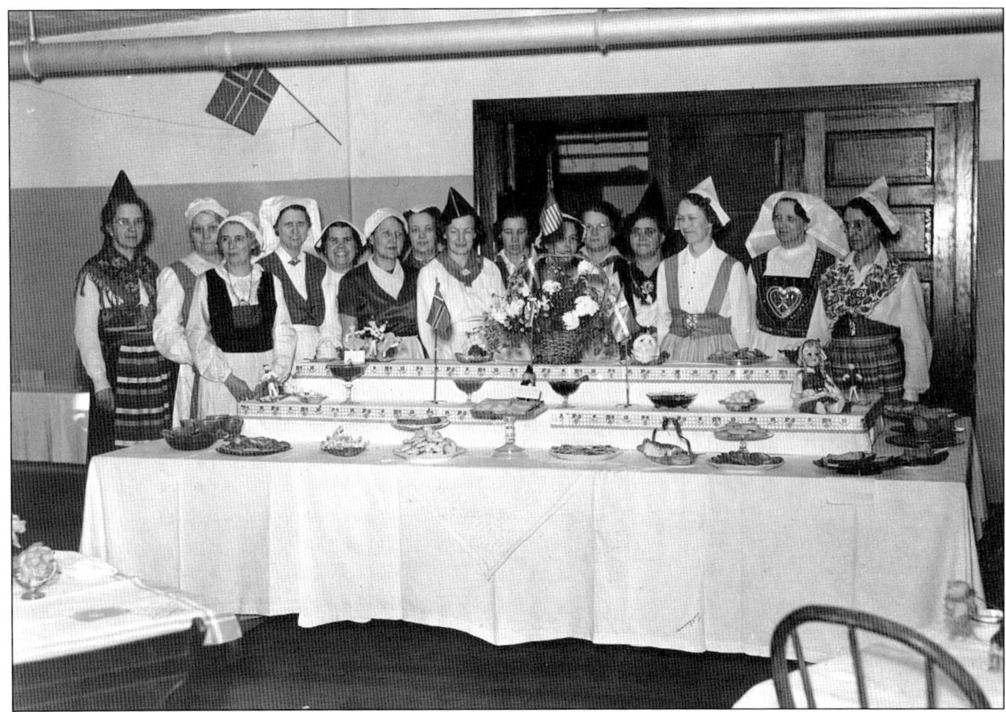

Ladies from the American Lutheran Church served their first smorgasbord dinner in 1938. A smorgasbord is a Swedish buffet-style meal that includes a variety of hot and cold meats, salads, and hors d'oeuvres. The ladies seen here are wearing traditional Swedish, Norwegian, Danish, and German costumes, reflecting the variety of cultures living in Huron. (Courtesy of American Lutheran Church.)

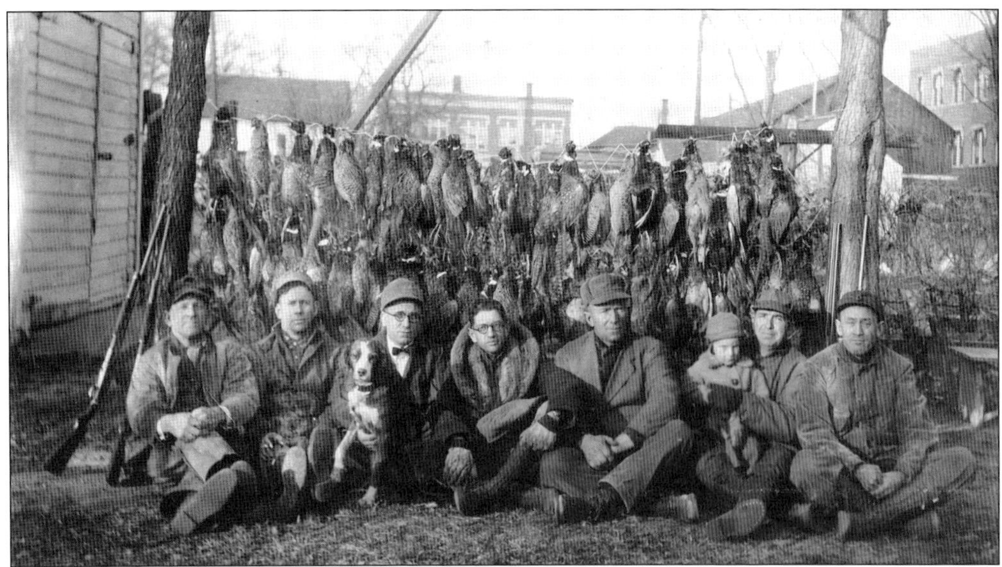

Chinese ring-necked pheasants were first introduced in Spink County in 1908 and then in Beadle County in 1911. This photograph was taken in 1926 of a group of successful hunters. They are, from left to right, Nels Carlson, Lenus Nelson, Clyde Ratelle, J.E. Farrar, John Melum, Rev. Samuel Disrud holding Sheldon Disrud, and John Helseth. (Courtesy of American Lutheran Church.)

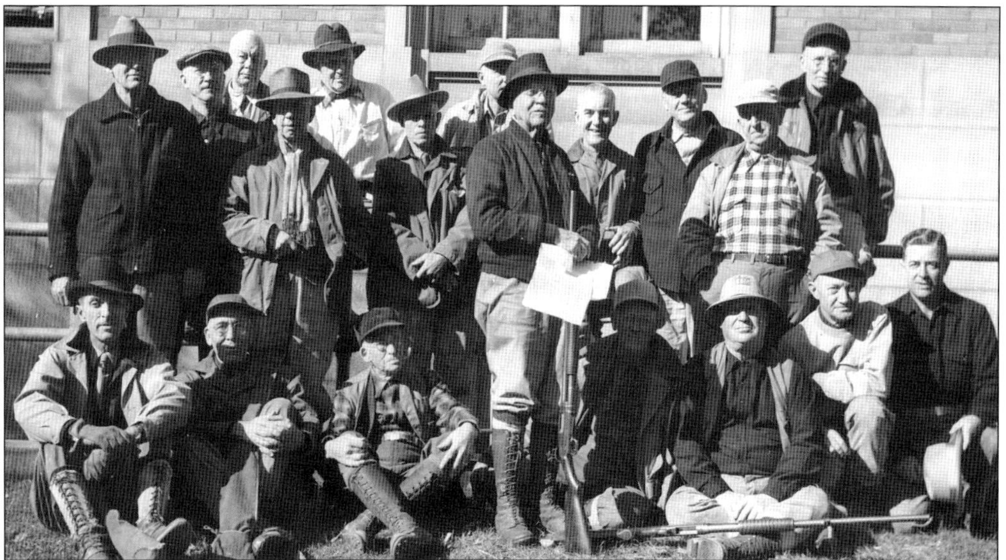

This photograph was taken in 1948 of Judge Archibald K. Gardner and the Gardner's Guerillas. Gardner was a Huron native and senior judge in the federal court system from 1948 to 1959. For several years, he returned to Huron during pheasant-hunting season to hunt with friends who were all prominent local businessmen.

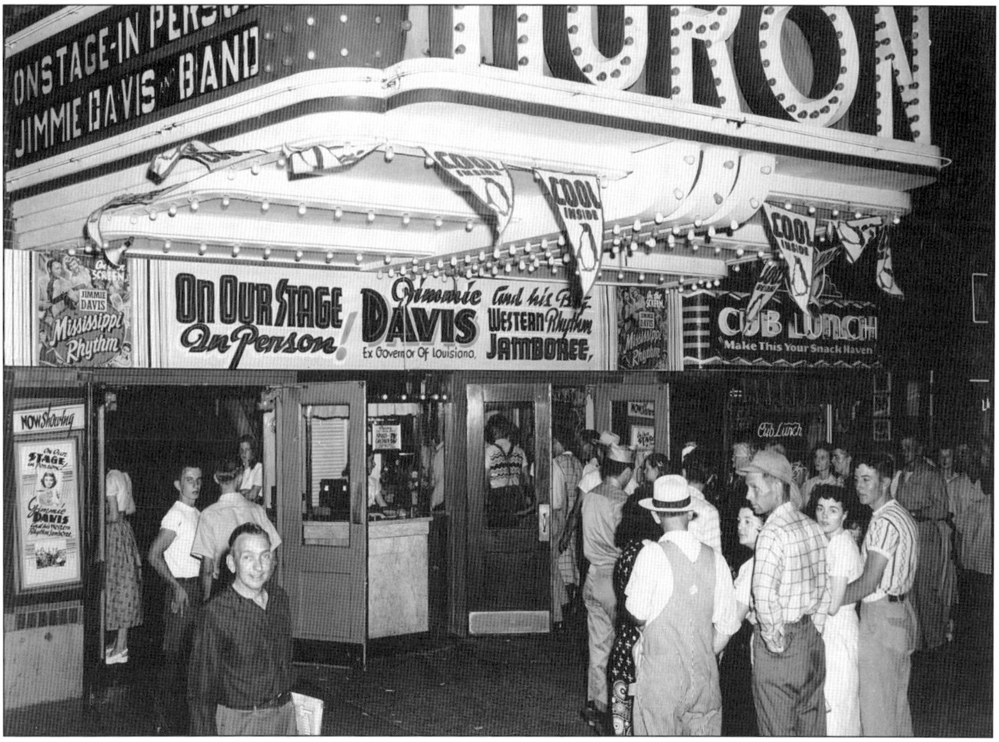

The Huron Theater, on Third Street, was a wildly popular movie venue. The theater also held live performances. The crowd in this photograph is waiting to see the Jimmie Davis Band, a nationally known country and gospel music group. This theater location provided entertainment for close to 50 years. (Courtesy of Jeff Logan.)

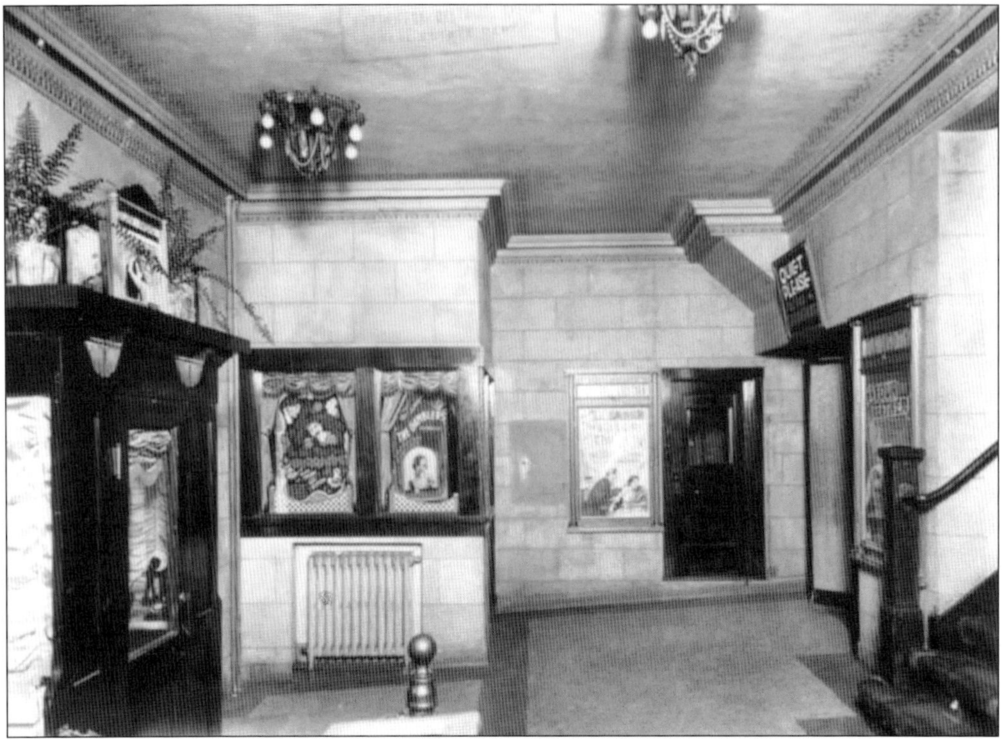

Donald Harris became the owner of the Huron Theater in 1921. He had plans to enlarge the stage in the movie theater auditorium for live performances but decided to construct a new building instead. The new movie theater was spacious, with room for 700 people. The above photograph shows the elaborate lobby light fixtures and carpet on the stairs leading to the auditorium. The photograph below is of the auditorium's interior, which contained a large stage and pipe organ to accompany silent films. The first all-talking picture to play at the Huron Theater was *The Lights of New York* in December 1928. (Both, courtesy of Jeff Logan.)

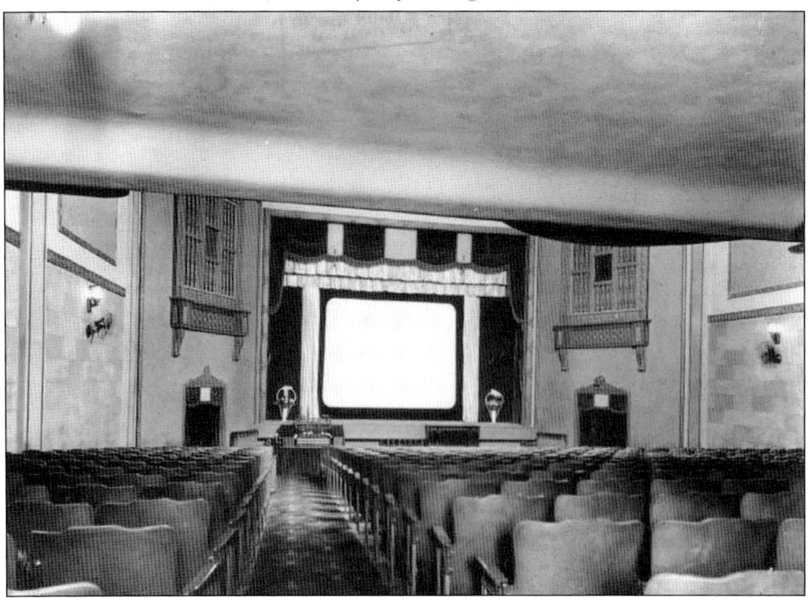

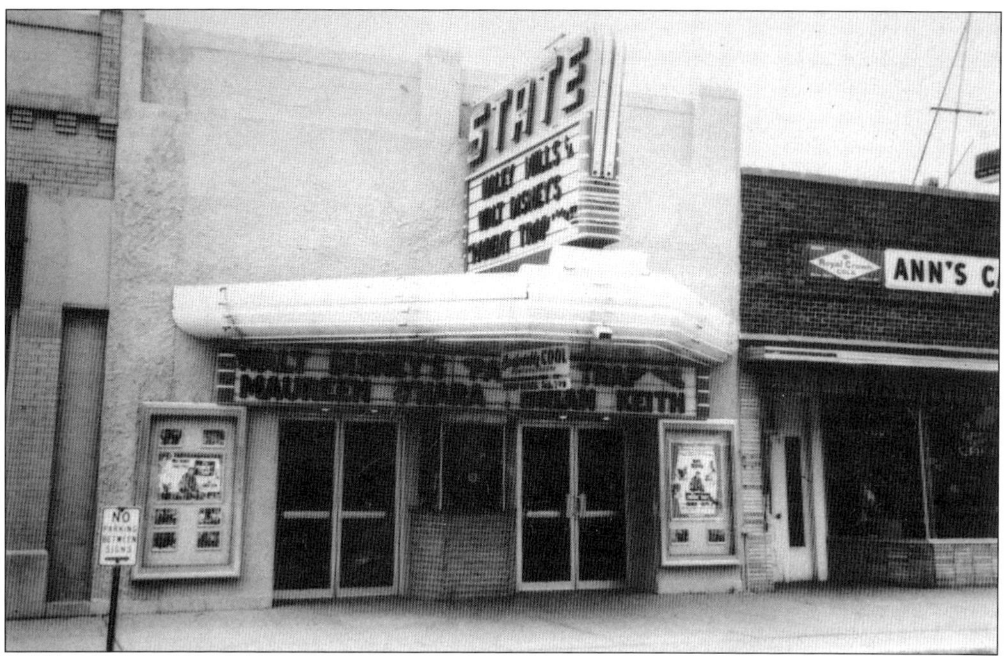

The State Theater opened on Dakota Avenue during the Great Depression. The theater was richly decorated in a Spanish style with stucco, red tile, and Spanish columns. In 1952, the new owners remodeled the building to include a new front canopy trimmed with neon and a reader board for movie titles. This photograph was taken in 1953, after the exterior changes were made. (Courtesy of Jeff Logan.)

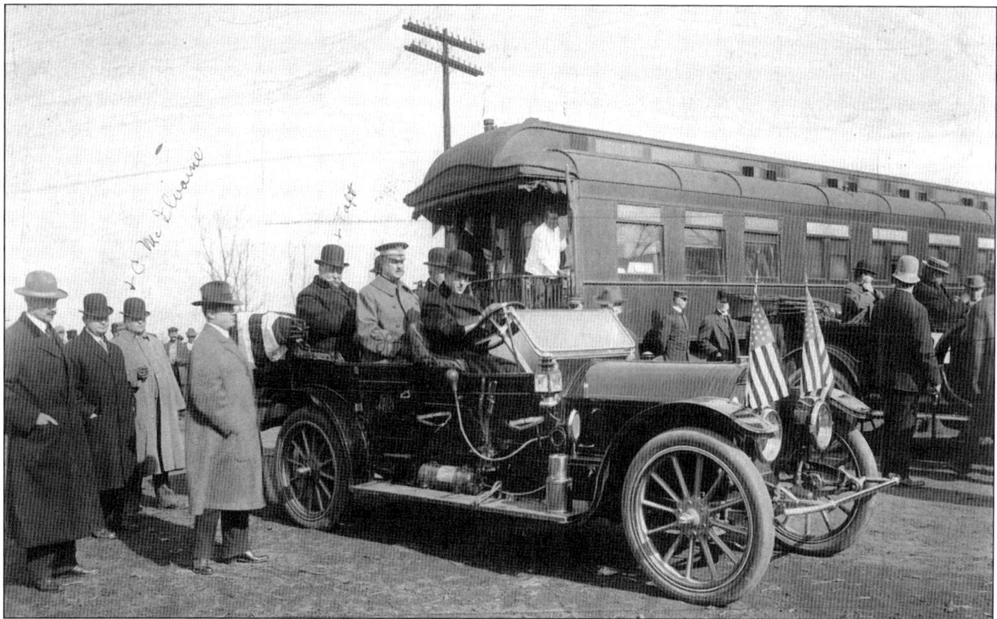

While William Howard Taft was president of the United States, he set off on a train tour of each state. He received a warm welcome when he arrived in Huron in October 1911. Taft can be seen sitting in the back of the car. Other presidents who visited Huron included Theodore Roosevelt and William McKinley.

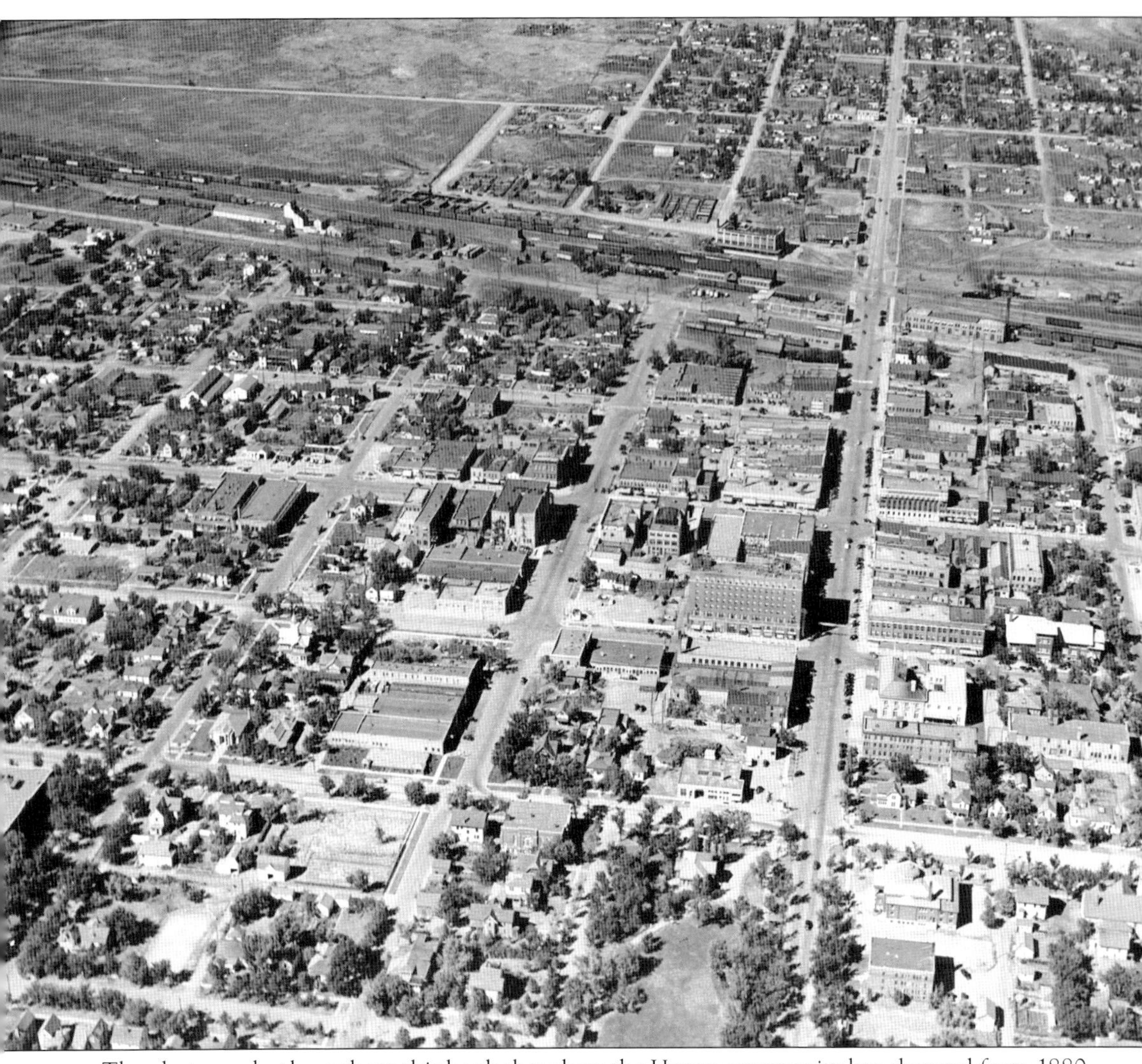

The photographs throughout this book show how the Huron community has changed from 1880 to 1950. Each chapter has shown the variety of activities that took place as the community grew. Businesses have come and gone based on the needs of the community. Buildings have been erected, remodeled, or replaced. The city limits have expanded exponentially. The map in the front of the book showed Huron in 1880. Compare that to this photograph, taken in 1950. Huron had come a long way in those 70 years. The photograph above is of Dakota Avenue looking north. Campbell Park is at the bottom, and the railroad tracks and Swift Company are at the top. (Courtesy of NorthWestern Energy.)

Bibliography

Cahalan, Faith. *History of the South Dakota State Fair.* Huron, SD: The Print Shop, 1989.
History of Beadle County, Dakota. Huron, SD: Beadle County Commissioners, 1889.
Horton, Garner, ed. *Pioneer College: A History of Pierre University and Huron College, 1883–1958.* Huron, SD: Board of Trustees of Huron College, 1958.
Huron Chamber of Commerce. *Huron: The Market of Central South Dakota.* Huron, SD: Huron Publishing Company, 1930.
Huron College. "Huron College: Beginning and Growth." *Huron College Quarterly* 1, no. 4 (1923).
Huron Daily Plainsman: 50th Anniversary Edition, June 1930.
Huron Daily Plainsman: 75th Diamond Jubilee Edition, June 28, 1955.
Huron Daily Plainsman: Bicentennial Edition, February 29, 1976.
Huron Daily Plainsman: Centennial Edition, June 15, 1980.
Huss, Dorothy. *Huron Revisited.* Huron, SD: East Eagle Publishing, 1988.
Jones, Mildred McEwen. *Early Beadle County: 1879–1900.* Huron, SD: F.H. Brown Printing Company, 1961.
———. *Pioneer Residents of the City of Huron.* Vols. 1 and 2. Huron, SD: Huron Public Library, 1975.
Moore, Charles C., ed. *Life in Early Huron, 1880–89.* Vols. 1 and 2. Vermillion, SD: University of South Dakota, 1942.
A People's History of Beadle County, South Dakota. Dallas, TX: Taylor Publishing, 1986.
Polk's Huron City Directory. Kansas City, MO: R.L. Polk & Co., 1883–1950.
South Dakota Historical Society Press. *South Dakota History* 53, no. 1 (2023).
South Dakota State Fair Board. *Dakota State Fair 1910.* Sioux Falls, SD: Mark D. Scott, 1910.